The Isherwood Century

The Isherwood Century

Essays on the Life and Work of Christopher Isherwood

Edited and with an introduction by
James J. Berg and Chris Freeman

Foreword by
Armistead Maupin

THE UNIVERSITY OF WISCONSIN PRESS

The University of Wisconsin Press
2537 Daniels Street
Madison, Wisconsin 53718

3 Henrietta Street
London WC2E 8LU, England

Printed in the United States of America

Publication of this book has been made possible in part by a grant from the Anonymous Fund of the University of Wisconsin–Madison.

Chapter 12, "Pool in Rocks by the Sea: Isherwood and Bachardy," by Edmund White is reprinted from *The Burning Library,* copyright © 1994 by Edmund White, by permission of Alfred A. Knopf, Inc.

Chapter 17, "Documentary Dilemmas: Shifting Fronts in *Journey to a War,*" by Marsha Bryant is reprinted from *Auden and Documentary in the 1930s.* Charlottesville: University Press of Virginia, 1997. Reprinted by permission of the University Press of Virginia.

Library of Congress Cataloging-in-Publication Data

The Isherwood century: essays on the life and work of Christopher Isherwood /
    edited and introduced by James J. Berg and Chris Freeman.
        312 pp.   cm.
    Includes bibliographical references (p.) and index.
    ISBN 0–299–16700–3 (cloth: alk. paper)
        1. Isherwood, Christopher, 1904–1986 2. Authors, English—20th century—Biography.
    I. Berg, James J. II. Freeman, Chris, 1965–
    PR6017.S5 Z74   1999
    823'.912—dc21   99-6742

Contents

Illustrations

Don Bachardy: *Armistead Maupin, April 25, 1979.* Ink on paper. 29″ × 23″. Copyright ©
Don Bachardy. Used by permission.

Foreword

The title of this volume fits its subject to a tee. There was so much about Christopher Isherwood that felt centurial in scope: from his pre-modernist concern for the enjoyment of his readers to his trailblazing commitment to telling the truth, even when it proved unflattering. On a personal level, this union of charm and candor made him a treasure to his friends: a sort of social alchemist whose very presence in a room could bridge the generations. Certainly no other figure in my life made me feel more connected to a past I had never known and a future I had yet to realize. He accomplished this remaining solidly in the present, while never presuming that his celebrated history was a matter of common knowledge. "My friend Wystan was a poet," he once explained to a friend I brought to his house. And he provided this footnote without a trace of condescension.

Chris's comfort around people of all ages was gloriously present at a dinner party he and Don Bachardy threw in the early eighties. An unknown friend of a friend of theirs was performing in a jazz club in the San Fernando Valley—a *cabaret,* if you please—so the couple suggested we retire there for drinks, while warning us that they could promise nothing. The senior member of our gang, Chris, reclined in the back seat of the car, not because he was infirm but because he couldn't bare to watch Don's driving, and the couple had settled upon this peculiar method of travel as the best way to avoid conflict. (Chris once explained it to me this way: "I believe I'm the only person who's fit to be on the road at all; therefore, I prefer to just miss it when other people drive.")

We were all rather giggly by then and speculating wildly about our destination, which, to judge from our suburban surroundings, threatened to be relentlessly hetero. To aid in our deliberations Chris would read aloud from the signs that flickered past his limited low-level vantage point. "Midas Muffler," he would mutter with exaggerated alarm. "That's very bad news indeed." But when we finally arrived at the nightclub, tucked primly into a prosaic mini-mall, he read the last sign he saw with a note of unexpected relief in his voice. "Pioneer Chicken," he crowed. "It *is* a gay place, after all!"

It wasn't—in any sense of the word—but we enjoyed ourselves thoroughly. (It helped that the chanteuse was a touchingly plump Valley Girl version of Sally Bowles.) There were six men at the table that night, each representing a different decade of adult gay life, and it was exhilarating to see the journey laid out before me so attractively. Chris had his arm around a twenty-eight-year-old, whose nipple he would occasionally tweak in a friendly way, much to the honor of the tweakee. I remember catching Don's eye and seeing the twinkle there that I would learn to read so much into in the years to come. "Isn't this wonderful?" he seemed to be saying. "This happy little band of queers in the midst of this ordinariness." Or maybe that's just how I felt at that moment: proud and free and blessedly *special* because of the company I was keeping.

I first met Chris and Don at an Oscar Night party in the home of one of the producers of *Saturday Night Fever*. (There was, I remember a distinct note of protest in the air, since all those catchy Bee Gees songs had been officially excluded from consideration by the Academy.) I established the author's identity by the piercing blue eyes that had recently mesmerized me on a PBS interview. He was very much in his cups that night, but he was gracious when I expressed my fandom and even more so when I told him I was writing a fictional serial for the *San Francisco Chronicle*. "Oh, yes," he said. "That marvelous, funny thing." At which point I lost all sense of proportion and asked if he might consider reviewing *Tales of the City* for the *Los Angeles Times*. Chris countered with an offer to write me a blurb, explaining that he never wrote reviews because they sometimes required one to be critical of other writers. He would rather just celebrate the good, he said. (This policy made so much sense to me that I promptly adopted it as my own—and adhere to it faithfully still.)

Chris's blurb arrived in a letter that likened me to Dickens and declared—even more shockingly—that he had read *Tales* three times and would probably read it again before long. Rereading that letter recently, I was struck by his unfailing graciousness to a young writer. He actually apologized for being late with the blurb, explaining that "writing a blurb sometimes comes as hard to me as writing a sonnet—I mean, there's the same necessity to be brief." The other thing that letter made clear was my impoverished state at the time. "I tried phoning you," Chris wrote, "but the operator told me the number has been disconnected. If there's another, please let me know." When I was able to thank him in person, Chris deflected my gratitude by citing the generosity that Forster and Maugham had shown him as a young writer. He knew full well what effect this would have—linking a callow newspaper serialist to the noble lineage of English literature—and drew great pleasure from it, I think. And his support didn't stop there. When I came to L.A. for my very first out-of-town gig, there were six people who showed up for my autographing at the Unicorn Bookshop in West Hollywood: three friends from back home, the guy I'd picked up the night before at a sex club called Basic Plumbing, and that famous pair from Adelaide Drive.

In the years that followed I cherished a relationship with Chris and Don—then with Don alone—that continued to illuminate my life in ways both personal and professional. Chris was the first writer to tell me that art and entertainment were not mutually exclusive, that I should never apologize for my impulse to keep readers interested. He was also the first to warn me about literary labeling. "Don't let them call it a gay book," he told me emphatically in reference to *Tales of the City.* "You're writing for everyone and *about* everyone." Though Chris has been understandably embraced by the new queer theorists, the man who popularized the Q-word in public interviews had a horror of being restricted to a sub-genre for his honesty. His aim, it seemed to me, was the aim of a true revolutionary: to change literature from the inside and remain squarely under the nose of what he called "the heterosexual dictatorship." I can't help wondering what he would make of the current marketing scheme that keeps gay thought restricted—at least in this country—to a cubbyhole in the back of the bookstore.

Which is not to imply that Chris was in any way cautious about discussing his homosexuality. He spoke out more fearlessly—and more often—than any of his queer contemporaries; certainly more than Truman Capote, who once equated his gayness to his alcoholism, or even Gore Vidal, who wrote brilliantly about our oppression but remained cagey about his own life while he still had a shot at the Senate. Chris was deliciously blunt and remained that way to the end. In 1985, when I talked to him for the *Village Voice* in what proved to be his last interview, he even offered some blasphemous advice to young men who had been ostracized because of AIDS: "They're told by their relatives that it's a sort of punishment, that it's . . . God's will and all that kind of thing. And I think they have to get very tough with themselves and really decide which side they're on. You know, fuck God's will. God's will must be circumvented, if that's what it is."

There were other lessons I learned from Chris: subtler ones that came from observing a successful gay couple in action. The longevity of his partnership with Don was widely celebrated, but it should be noted that they never used it to feel superior to others or to propagandize for some grim replica of conventional marriage. I well remember Don remarking to the *Advocate* that his decades with Chris were no more inherently valid than a lifetime of one-night stands. It wasn't the numbers that counted, he seemed to be saying, but the quality of the love that was shared. And, as Chris's and Don's diaries begin to unfurl before the world, it becomes increasingly clear that the couple achieved a fidelity far deeper and more rewarding than simple monogamy could ever be.

The thirty-year difference in their ages lent a Socratic quality to the union that was fascinating to witness. Chris had early on recognized Don's gift as an artist and supported his education, so that over the years the younger man began to develop an impressive visual counterpoint to his partner's greatest contribution: a sharp but generous eye on the human condition. They were twin lights, separate but together, each feasting off the other's talents and perceptions. And anyone who knew them will tell you how eerie and wonderful it was that a kid from the beaches of Southern California came to adopt the stammer of a well-bred Englishman. Even after years of knowing them, I found it a challenge to guess which of the two was answering the phone at Adelaide Drive.

So I had a reference point already when I met a feisty young man in Atlanta who was fifteen years my junior and reportedly sounded exactly like me on the phone. Terry Anderson worked part-time at a book store called Christopher's Kind and came into my life just as Chris was leaving, so it felt like a pilgrimage of sorts when I took my newfound soul mate to Santa Monica to meet Don. (I remember the guilty thrill I experienced when Don left the room and Terry and I scrambled to take each other's pictures in the straw chairs that Chris and Don had posed in for David Hockney.) Several years later Don would fall in love with Tim Hilton, a young architect as far from him in age as Don had been from Chris, and they would spend their honeymoon with Terry and me on the isle of Lesbos. Both partnerships would flourish for almost a decade, dissolving—or at least reconfiguring themselves—at roughly the same time. And the wisdom that Don had accrued from both sides of the generation gap once again offered me a source of strength and validation.

When Don visited me in San Francisco last month, I told him it didn't seem possible that Chris had been gone for nearly fifteen years. He felt the same way, he said, acknowledging the potency of the words and memories that Chris had left behind. But there was something else that induced that feeling of my mentor's constant presence, something I noticed as we stood on the porch waiting for a cab to arrive. Don bounced on his heels in a way that seemed utterly familiar, and the set of his jaw in profile made me gasp in recognition of the man he was becoming at sixty-five. "Oh, my God, Don," I murmured, and he read my mind on the spot. "I know," he said with an impish smile. "And the haircut doesn't help either."

ARMISTEAD MAUPIN

San Francisco
29 September 1999

Acknowledgments

We would like to thank all of our contributors. Their hard work made this book possible, and their enthusiasm for Isherwood and for *The Isherwood Century* was tremendous. For their assistance in putting this collection together, we thank especially Don Bachardy, Dan Luckenbill, Stathis Orphanos, James White, Robert Peters, Edmund White, David Bergman, Peter Shneidre, and Carola M. Kaplan.

For permission to reprint some of the contributions to our book, we would like to thank Knopf and the University Press of Virginia.

Armistead Maupin told us about his relationship with Isherwood, and our conversations with him helped us understand how writers help each other.

With astonishing ease, Karen Kuhlman quickly orchestrated permission from David Hockney for us to use his collage for our cover. We are especially grateful to Mr. Hockney for providing us with the perfect visual introduction to our book.

During our trip to Los Angeles, Monte Bramer was the consummate host, taking us out on the town and sharing his stories of L.A. with us. We especially enjoyed attending a performance of *Cabaret* with him. Jack Larson opened his beautiful home to us and shared lots of memories of Isherwood and of Hollywood. We appreciate his hospitality and warmth. Jim Weatherford and Dan Luckenbill arranged a wonderful dinner party where we talked about Isherwood over Greek food. Robert Peters and Paul Trachtenberg spent a day with us in Huntington Beach, discussing Isherwood and enjoying the surfers.

We spent a day at UCLA Special Collections reading some of Isherwood's papers, and the staff there were very helpful. The Vedanta Society of Southern California and Brother Eddie at the Ramakrishna Monastery in Trabuco Canyon helped us understand Isherwood's spiritual life.

St. John's University helped fund the research trip to California through its Faculty Development program. Ozzie Mayers, Clark Hendley, Beverly Radaich, Krisann Kleibacker, Anne McCarney, Matthew Blaisdell, and Michael Sersch offered help along the way.

At the University of Wisconsin Press, Raphael Kadushin was a terrific editor. His excitement and enthusiasm about this project from the outset helped keep our spirits up, and Jenny Ebert, Juliet Skuldt, and Margaret Walsh helped expedite the production process.

We would also like to thank the following for their help and encouragement along the way: Robert Caserio, Dennis Denisoff, Peter Parker, Joseph Allen Boone.

Kevin Kopelson offered us counsel. Charisse Gendron and John Knapp read the entire manuscript and offered much helpful editorial advice.

Gary Schiff and Jason Howard endured busy weekends and didn't complain too much about all the time we spent working on this project. They also provided encouragement, ideas, and support to us at home.

The Isherwood Century

James J. Berg and *Chris Freeman*

Introduction
The Isherwood Century

In January 1941, the writer Christopher Isherwood was living in Los Angeles, but his mind was in Europe. Feeling distant from the war on the Continent and ambivalent about himself as a pacifist and a writer, he wrote in his diary: "I must really try to keep this journal more regularly. It will be invaluable to me if I do. Because this year is going to be one of the most decisive periods of the twentieth century—and even the doings and thoughts of the most remote and obscure people will reflect the image of its events. That's a hell of a paragraph to start off with. Why are we all so pompous on New Year's Day? Come off it—you're not Hitler or Churchill. Nobody called on you to make a statement. As a matter of fact, what did you actually do?" (*Diaries 1*:132). Isherwood's instinct as a writer and his awareness of the events around him are clear from this passage, as they are from the voluminous diaries. What's remarkable about this passage is his inscription of himself into history. Part of what he did was *write*—he is aware that what he records will be important and useful for himself, and he knows that if he writes clearly and sharply enough, it will be useful to others. There is no pomposity in this claim. Instead Isherwood declares his commitment to recording the events in his world, and he can only do so from his place in that world. As the diary entry shows, Isherwood had a wry, self-deprecating sense of humor and an unassuming recognition that he was a part of history but not a maker of history.

3

Feeling himself to be both remote and obscure in 1941, Isherwood nevertheless continued to write in his diary and to work on his craft. Paradoxically, at the end of the twentieth century, Isherwood remains remote and obscure, but at the same time he is one of the most celebrated writers of his time and ours. While he is lesser known than many of his contemporaries—for example, W. H. Auden or Truman Capote—Isherwood's influence is strong among his readers and extends to many of the writers who came after him. For what Isherwood actually did was document the twentieth century, contribute to the development of memoir and autobiographical fiction, and pioneer gay writing in America and abroad.

Documenting a Century

The American Isherwood is a primary focus of this collection. Naturalized in 1946, Isherwood wrote most of his work—and some of his best—as a citizen of the United States and a resident of California. He published his first novel at twenty-four and in the next ten years published two more novels, an autobiography, and two plays and a travel book in collaboration with Auden. Such early success helped to solidify his reputation as the brilliant young English novelist of his day. As Somerset Maugham said to Virginia Woolf, "That young man holds the future of the English novel in his hands" (*Christopher and His Kind,* 325). Unfortunately, such acclaim almost inevitably meant that he would forever be thought of as falling short of his potential.

Sometimes considered lightweight and simplistic, or as merely documenting his life with little analysis, Isherwood's writing can now be seen as fulfilling its early promise in new ways. As Auden recognized, Isherwood's challenge in fiction was to "solve the 'I' problem in narration" (*Diaries* 1:469). He met that challenge by developing a new form of documentary fiction, one that mixes autobiographical recording and introspection. Isherwood wanted to continue to tell stories that mattered to him, and his development as a writer led him away from the modernist concern with form and toward what might be called parable. Isherwood's fiction attempts to teach by example, to show modern men and women living their lives with integrity and intention.

Literary criticism in the middle part of this century was ill-equipped to appreciate Isherwood's work, as it was primarily interested in impersonal narrative technique and formal innovation. As Isherwood explained in a 1965 lecture at the University of California, Los Angeles: "I'm not finally concerned with this question of form. I'm very much concerned with it up to a point, but in the end, if I find that there's something I want to say, then that comes first." The nature of criticism has changed in the last twenty-five years as New Criticism has been seen more as a tool and not as the raison d'être of literary scholarship. Contemporary scholars have developed new methods through queer theory, new historicism, and feminist theory to deal with memoir and autobiography as viable literary forms. Hence literary scholars are more able to approach Isherwood's work and to understand and value his contributions, as shown here by the essays in Part 3, "The Writer in Context."

Because literary critics have not necessarily been Isherwood's best readers, we have chosen to arrange this volume in a way that does not privilege their point of view. Instead we take scholarship as simply one part of the legacy of Isherwood's life and work. Parts 1 and 2 of this book address Isherwood's life in a more personal way. We want the reader to become acquainted with Isherwood the man: the way he lived, the way he worked, and the way he and Don Bachardy made their lives together. Meeting Isherwood this way will give the reader a more complete understanding of his complex personality and the multitude of concerns that affected his work and that have affected his reputation. Part 4 is devoted to the spiritual aspects of Isherwood's life and work from the point of view of people who share his values or who recognize the influence of Vedantic philosophy in his life.

Why do we call our book *The Isherwood Century*? In chronological terms, the Isherwood Century extends beyond his own lifetime, from 1904 to 1986. Isherwood's close relationship with E. M. Forster, as well as his ties to his parents, whose lives he investigated and wrote about in *Kathleen and Frank,* links him to the late Victorian and the Edwardian periods in England. As Forster's letters indicate and as Isherwood discusses in *Christopher and His Kind,* the two writers valued each other as friends and colleagues, their deepest connection coming perhaps through Forster's posthumously published gay novel *Maurice.* Forster relied on younger writers' opinions of *Maurice* and showed Isherwood the manuscript soon after they met. Isherwood saw Forster as the "Master" and cultivated that relationship in their early associations. However, because Isherwood began to incorporate gay issues into his published fiction, notably in *The World in the Evening* (1954), their relationship began to shift as Isherwood became a mentor figure, with Forster admiring and envying his candor and courage.

The Isherwood that is perhaps most familiar is the politically active writer of the 1930s. After the 1972 publication of Samuel Hynes's seminal study, *The Auden Generation,* this period of Isherwood's career became inextricably associated the English writers who came of age between the wars: Auden, Edward Upward, Stephen Spender, Cecil Day Lewis, Louis MacNeice, and others. We believe, however, considering this coterie of writers a quarter of a century after Hynes, that Isherwood emerges as the pivotal figure of his generation. We say this not to detract from the importance of Auden as a literary figure, but rather to highlight the fact that Isherwood was able to develop his identity and his vocation as a writer even as his involvement with the world continued to expand. Although he left some of his convictions and activities of the thirties behind, he explored new beliefs and incorporated them into his work, which encompassed not only fiction and autobiography but also television, film, and religious writing. His influence, we would argue, grew as the century progressed, and his role as a "leader" of the so-called Auden generation broadened to include younger generations of writers and artists. In particular, Isherwood's emergence in the 1970s as a voice for the gay community and his influence on gay writers through the end of the century have become increasingly recognized and are explored further in this book.

Isherwood became a "gay writer" gradually in the sense that his fiction from the mid-1950s on included gay characters and issues. In *The World in the Evening,* for example, he gives us a gay couple, an early definition of camp, and an impassioned discussion of gays in the military. His masterpiece, *A Single Man* (1964), presents a day in the life of a middle-aged gay man that resonates with gay readers more than thirty years later, as David Garnes's poignant essay in this collection testifies. Isherwood followed his fictional "coming out" with an autobiographical one in *Kathleen and Frank,* purportedly a biography of his parents but actually, as he said, "chiefly about Christopher" (510). His coming out in that book was rather matter-of-fact: "Despite the humiliations of living under a heterosexual dictatorship and the fury he often felt against it, Christopher has never regretted being as he is. He is now quite certain that heterosexuality wouldn't have suited him; it would have fatally cramped his style" (380). By the time these books were published, Isherwood and Bachardy had become a model of a long-term gay relationship, and the essays in this volume by Dan Luckenbill and Stathis Orphanos, in particular, document the significance of this couple to gay men of their generation.

Chris and Don Alive

This book began as a panel discussion at the Modern Language Association convention in December 1996. Titled "Christopher Isherwood: Ten Years Gone," the panel was designed to address the question of Isherwood's legacy. The liveliness of the discussion following the panel convinced us that there was a lot of interest among scholars and fans alike in a book on Isherwood's life and work. During the three years that we have been working on this project, we have been impressed by the breadth of interest, the quality of ideas, and the deep respect for Isherwood among people who knew him either personally or through his work. Most of the work collected here was written especially for this book, including new work by some of Isherwood's friends who saw *The Isherwood Century* as an opportunity for them to write about his impact on their lives.

For a long time the two of us have felt close to Christopher Isherwood as readers, as scholars, and as gay men. The week we spent in July 1998 in Los Angeles, however, took our involvement with him to a new level. We went not knowing exactly what we wanted to accomplish. We knew we wanted to meet Don Bachardy, to see Isherwood's environs, and to do some research. What we experienced was a series of "Isherwood moments" in which things went better for us than we imagined, doors were opened, and many people wanted to talk to us and tell us of Isherwood's importance to them.

Our first stop was the temple of the Vedanta Society of Southern California, near Hollywood and Vine. Isherwood writes in his diaries of attending Wednesday night talks by Swami Prabhavananda, and we were able to attend a Wednesday night talk by the current leader of the society, Swami Swahananda. We had notified them of our visit via e-mail, and one of the monks arranged for us to have dinner with Peter Shneidre. Peter told us of his friendship with Isherwood, and we convinced him to write an essay about Isherwood's Vedantism. Peter would be the first of many people during this week to take us directly to Isherwood; what came through in all of our conversations was fondness and a lasting connection to Isherwood. Peter also encouraged us to visit the Ramakrishna Monastery in Trabuco Canyon, where we happened upon a monk named Eddie who had known Isherwood well in the 1960s. He gave us a tour of the grounds and shared with us his view that Isherwood's writings provide the best introduction to Vedanta for a Western audience.

Though we were nervous about meeting Don Bachardy, with whom we had corresponded since April 1997, he immediately put us at ease and talked freely about his relationship with Isherwood, their work together, and his life after Isherwood. It is clear that he takes his role as Isherwood's executor seriously and that he has a loving interest in promoting Isherwood's work among scholars and readers. He helped us contact other friends and associates who proved supportive even if their contributions do not appear in the final volume. Sitting in the living room of Don and Christopher's house, and later being painted by Don in his studio, gave us a kind of immediate connection experienced by few scholars.

Visitors often comment on the abundance and variety of art in Chris and Don's house, which includes drawings, paintings, photographs, and sculpture. We were especially delighted to see David Hockney's *Christo-*

pher Isherwood Talking to Bob Holman, Santa Monica, March 14, 1983.
Depicting Chris and Don in animated conversation with a visitor in their
living room, this photographic collage captures for us what we hope *The
Isherwood Century* will provide our readers—the sense of Isherwood and
Bachardy actively constructing their lives and their work together. Rather
than fragmenting or freezing his subjects, Hockney's cubist technique adds
layers of complexity and meaning to the scene by multiplying the visual
image of the two men, making a dynamic portrait, one that shows Chris
and Don *alive.*

Later in the week one of our contributors, Dan Luckenbill, arranged a
dinner party for us, and we felt Isherwood's spirit with us. At this party
we were able to meet another of our contributors, Stathis Orphanos, and
one of Isherwood's friends from the 1950s, actor and writer Jack Larson.
The people in Isherwood's diaries were suddenly real for us, as we were
entertained by stories about Marilyn Monroe, Montgomery Clift, and
Marlene Dietrich. We felt as though we were gaining a better sense of
what Isherwood's life was like.

Returning from Los Angeles to put the finishing touches on this book,
we felt closer to Isherwood as a person. This intimacy is akin to the feeling
we get from reading his work, especially his diaries and *A Single Man*—a
feeling we believe many of his readers share, despite the feelings of remote-
ness and obscurity he sometimes felt in his life.

PART I
MEETING ISHERWOOD

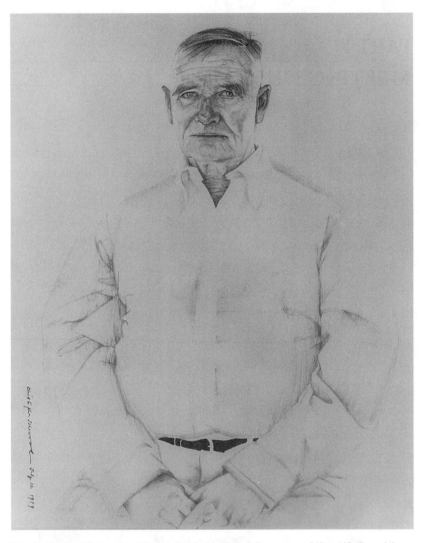

Don Bachardy: *Christopher Isherwood, July 12, 1979.* Ink on paper. 24″ × 19″. Copyright © Don Bachardy. Used by permission.

> Christopher's genius is to be entirely Christopher, and yet, at the same time to act out roles, as Chris, Mr. Issyvoo, and someone who calls himself "I," and this juggling of masks and personae has fascinated thousands of readers.
> Stephen Spender, *Letters to Christopher*, 11

This section serves as an introduction to Christopher Isherwood primarily through the words of people who knew him. Given the highly personal nature of Isherwood's writing, we believe that attempting to understand him as a person provides insight into knowing him as a writer. The essays in this section give an impression of Isherwood as a kind, thoughtful, complex man who is a good and trusted friend. He also appears here as a writer who encourages other writers in their work and as a role model to younger gay men. Although often treated as a touchstone by people seeking spiritual guidance, Isherwood usually refused to give advice, preferring to listen rather than to preach. Because of the intimacy of some of these relationships, we get a familiar perspective on Isherwood's life and death.

Katherine Bucknell, the editor of Isherwood's diaries, offers an overview of his life and writing career in her essay, "Who Is Christopher Isherwood?" She considers the genre of semiautobiographical fiction that Isherwood pioneered and traces the two halves of Isherwood's literary life: the British and the American. Bucknell examines Isherwood's dedication to the historical and calls him "one of the century's most acute observers" and "a magnificent resource for understanding the culture we live in now."

Dan Luckenbill, Stathis Orphanos, and Michael S. Harper knew Isherwood in Los Angeles in the 1950s and 1960s. Their personal reminiscences offer a picture of Isherwood as a teacher and writer in this period. Luckenbill and Harper knew Isherwood first as a teacher and later developed friendships with him and Don Bachardy. Luckenbill's memoir depicts Isherwood and Bachardy in their role as a domestic couple, each with his own artistic pursuits, a theme that will be developed further in Part 2, "Artist and Companion."

Harper's memoir traces the significant effect knowing Isherwood had on him as a young black man and as a developing writer. Isherwood was the first teacher who took Harper seriously and encouraged his literary and educational pursuits. Harper's poem, which he describes as a "riff" in remembrance of Isherwood and the intersection of their lives, points to the contradictions inherent in Isherwood as a man of his time: he is seen as a foreigner and a liberal, who nevertheless reflects attitudes pervasive in pre–civil rights America. Orphanos, a photographer and writer, was, like Harper, a student at California State University, Los Angeles, but Orphanos never took a course from Isherwood. However, he was an admirer of Isherwood's writing and, with a little encouragement from a fellow student, called him one day to ask for a meeting. The evolution of their relationship shows how accessible Isherwood was to younger artists and how willing he was to offer friendship and encouragement to them. Harper and Orphanos depict an aspect of Isherwood's life that is familiar to readers of A Single Man; they could, in fact, be seen as some of George's students in that novel.

Two scholars, Robert Peters and Carolyn Heilbrun, write about the different personal effects meeting Isherwood had on their lives. In Peters's case, Isherwood appeared at a time when Peters was struggling with his sexuality in a community that did not provide support for such a struggle. Isherwood showed him, by example, that it was possible to live a productive and happy life as a gay man in the 1960s. Heilbrun's experience of Isherwood was somewhat different. However, she found Isherwood and Bachardy to be compassionate and willing to listen to her spiritual dilemma. Facing a significant challenge in her life after writing her monograph on Isherwood, she experienced from them "a memorable act of goodness which remains with me now long after my spiritual angst has melted away."

James White, a novelist and teacher, met Isherwood upon the publication of White's first novel, Birdsong, in 1977. What began as a professional mentorship turned into a deep and lasting friendship that continued even after White left Los Angeles to become "immobile in Mobile." As a tribute to his friend, White catalogued Isherwood's papers. He describes in his essay how he continued to learn from Isherwood—and even to grow closer to him—after his death.

1 *Katherine Bucknell*

Who Is Christopher Isherwood?

The Anglo-American novelist Christopher Isherwood (1904–1986) is popularly known through the musical *Cabaret,* which was revived in London a few years ago and recently reopened in New York to great acclaim. *Cabaret* was inspired by *Goodbye to Berlin* (1939), a group of loosely associated pieces of semiautobiographical short fiction, based on Isherwood's life in Berlin during 1930 and 1931, as the Nazis were rising to power. The Berlin stories have been a chief source of Isherwood's fame partly because they describe a period and place in modern history that has proven to be of incalculable and horrible significance. Isherwood's portrait of the Berlin demimonde and of the morally bankrupt middle classes has generally been taken to reveal a cultural condition, or let us say a widespread state of mind, which somehow explains—and perhaps even foretold—what was to happen in Europe and the world at large during the next fifteen years.

How was he able to achieve this? If it was partly chance that Isherwood happened to be in Berlin when he was, it certainly was not chance that he wrote about it in the way that he did. And by the time his prologue to Europe's coming catastrophe was published, he was already on his way to southern California, seeking a new life at the epicenter of a very different series of cultural upheavals which were to shape the second half of the century and about which he would also write. In California his first novel, *Prater Violet* (1945), was about moviemaking, the distinguishing cultural

13

activity of our time. A later California novel, *A Single Man* (1964), takes up the topic of sexuality—*the* topic of this half, or at least third, of the century. And his last book, *My Guru and His Disciple* (1980), charts an at first sight eccentric path into Eastern religion pioneered by Isherwood but later followed by countless other disillusioned Westerners. Thus in the second part of his career, Isherwood did for southern California what he had previously done for Berlin in the 1930s, and his later work has a similar importance insofar as postwar California was a seedbed for the culture we live in now.

What is semiautobiographical fiction? Isherwood wrote a lot of it. Common sense says it is writing that is based at least partly on something that actually happened to the author, but in which the author makes changes for one or more of various reasons, such as: a wish to *improve* the truth; a *reluctance to reveal* the truth; or a conviction that *in order to convey* the truth of "real life," the author *has* to change it, has to get at a particular essential quality which might not be expressed by a simple reporting of facts. These impulses might seem mutually exclusive, but in Isherwood's various works, he changed his material at different times for each of these reasons, depending on what he was writing about. He never worked exactly the same way twice.

Consider these well-known lines from the opening chapter of *Goodbye to Berlin:* "I am a camera with its shutter open, quite passive, recording, not thinking. Recording the man shaving at the window opposite and the woman in the kimono washing her hair. Some day, all this will have to be developed, carefully printed, fixed" (13). Isherwood came to rue this metaphor of the camera as being misleading (it has been rather relentlessly used to explain much of his work). The modern and mechanical process of "recording" accurately evokes a new impulse in his work during the 1930s toward historical realism, but it has been wrongly construed to omit the shaping imagination of the artist. Nowadays we are accustomed to recognizing that even photography is interpretative. Isherwood as a writer was incapable of being "passive," of "not thinking," and he knew full well that the mere act of recording his experience, of writing it down, changed it. This is why he so often appears in his stories as a character and narrator. Such a literary device makes an implied philosophical statement: that it is not possible for a writer to be entirely objective. But Isherwood does not offer readers an "unreliable" narrator; he simply offers the opportunity for readers to form their own opinion of the precise way in which the narrator's point of view may be intervening between reader and "reality." He puts himself at the edge of the picture in order to remind us that he is filtering reality, not just recording it.

Writing a book, for Isherwood, always begins with observation, with collecting information; but he might then go on, with the information, to produce novels or autobiography, works ranging the spectrum from fiction to fact. He recorded his first observations in his diaries, which he returned to again and again as source material. During the second half of his career, in the mid-1970s, he wrote an autobiography, *Christopher and His Kind* (1976), in which he retells the story of his life in Berlin in the 1930s, revealing how he lived as a homosexual and explaining exactly how he worked up his early novels from his real-life experiences. Later he commented that even *Christopher and His Kind* couldn't get at the truth of those years. Clearly, for Isherwood, his diaries were of utmost importance.

Isherwood wrote in his diary several times a week almost continuously for about sixty years—from the early 1920s until July 1983, a month before his seventy-ninth birthday. He may have been introduced to diary keeping by his mother, who first began a diary of her own at the start of 1883, a magical one hundred years before Isherwood was to write in his for the last time. And he was to incorporate long passages from his mother's diaries and from his mother's and father's letters into his late book about his parents, *Kathleen and Frank* (1971).

Diary keeping attests both to Isherwood's obsession with the passage of time and to a puritanical need to account for himself. In the late 1950s he wrote in his diary: "Who are you—who writes all this? Why do you write? Is it compulsion? Or an alibi—to disprove the charge of what crime?" (*Diaries* 1:756, June 5, 1958). The diaries served as evidence, accumulated week by week, that he was not wasting his life: he was paying attention, he was doing something of value, he was keeping a record.

He used his diary to discipline himself in periods of laziness or dissipation, to organize his thoughts, and to right himself in moments of spiritual uncertainty. Page upon page reflects the clarity of his mind, his absolute mastery of syntax, his easily ranging, precise diction, his effortless power of description, his gaiety, his delight in the ridiculous. But the diaries go well beyond simply recording what happens, for Isherwood tries persistently to understand what he is recording. He continually examined his impressions, and this practice—the Socratic prerequisite for a worthy life—carried over from the diaries into the fiction.

For his novels, he analyzed and dissected the diaries, lifting out an episode here, a character there, combining them with others perhaps originally unrelated, and inventing whatever additional circumstances and atmosphere were necessary to convey the essence of his experience and of the fabric of society around him. Because his style is understated, Isherwood achieves with the slightest colorations of tone entirely various literary effects, even when drawing closely on real events. And like the modernist forebears he admired—Henry James, E. M. Forster, Virginia

Woolf, Katherine Mansfield, for instance—he makes his fictional points by showing rather than by telling. Isherwood was a master of compression and of the select detail, and he tended to constrain his imagination, so that in his best fiction he never invents more than necessary. His novels are works of the imagination, but they are not works of fantasy.

In this respect, his writing shares an important historical impulse with the mature work of his school and university friend Edward Upward. Upward nurtured himself on an idiosyncratic tradition of plain stylists and autobiographers—from John Bunyan, Daniel Defoe, and William Cowper to Hale White, Robert Tressall, and George Gissing. He became a doctrinaire Marxist during the early 1930s and eventually went on to write social-realist fiction. In a 1937 essay, "A Marxist Interpretation of Literature," Upward rejected fantasy—the genre in which he personally excelled in youth (his early work won him comparisons with Kafka). The Marxist essay, heavily influenced by Lenin, argued that imaginative writing reflects the material world and must, in order to be *socially valuable,* accurately represent not only the existing and past conditions of the society in which it is written but also the forces beneath the surface of material reality which will shape the future of society.

Upward's conversion to Marxism made a big impression on Isherwood, and Isherwood's regret at not being able to commit himself, like Upward, to the cause of the workers is made obvious in several of his novels. Moreover, in his later diaries Isherwood records how much he admires Upward's novels of the 1960s and 1970s for their strict political commitment. In Isherwood's work, we see his own subtle rendering of what Upward, the Marxist, might have called the condition of society and the hidden forces which will shape the future.

Both Isherwood and Upward were trained as historians: they were top history students together at their public school, Repton, and both went up to Cambridge University with prestigious financial awards in history. Neither could bear the lifeless way he found history being taught at Cambridge. Upward changed subjects to English, but Isherwood, a year younger, was not allowed to do the same. He worked less and less, grew cynical and defiant, and soon found himself spoofing the questions in his second-year tripos exams. He was asked to leave and did.

And yet Isherwood had read an awful lot of history books by then and assimilated what we might call an historical point of view. It is not surprising that he went on in his fiction to write a new kind of history: subjective, intuitive, vivid, entertaining, widely accessible, and also informed by the then new psychological understanding associated with the contemporary influence of Freud as well as by Upward's Marxist-Leninist determinism.

In the end, Isherwood—with his output of autobiography, family history, and travel writing as well as fiction and drama—is among the founders of a new documentary fiction, now widely practiced in various forms by American writers in particular. He had, for instance, an obvious influence on Truman Capote. Several critics have observed that Capote's fictional heroine Holly Golightly in *Breakfast at Tiffany's* (1958) is simply an American version of Isherwood's Sally Bowles,[1] and Capote's tale is not diminished by this observation. But Capote's Manhattan gangsters are not the equal in evil to the Nazis of Isherwood's Berlin, and it is the sinister Nazi presence which gives Isherwood's tale its tremendous moral and historical importance. This perhaps helps to explain why after *Breakfast at Tiffany's* the ambitious Capote turned away from fiction and, for his next big work, *In Cold Blood* (1966), decided to write—in the new journalistic style he and Lillian Ross before him had been turning out for the *New Yorker*—about a heinous and real crime he had discovered in the newspapers, the murder of four members of an innocent farming family in Kansas. Capote had recognized that to achieve widespread importance in the twentieth century, he needed to address himself to the truth of historical events and to the problem of man's inhumanity to man.

The new documentary fiction has become a North American and perhaps Anglo-Saxon or Puritan counterpart to the magic realism of South American and Latin culture—a stylistic relationship that in a sense corresponds to the one in Renaissance painting between northern, Dutch realism and Italian realism. Magic realism, so rich in meaningful transformations, tends to empty symbols of their power as it reaches for ever more amazing effects; Isherwood's historically based semiautobiographical fiction and his more pure autobiography are restrained and less obviously exciting at first, but they have a latent power and a gripping relevance to ordinary life.

Isherwood emigrated to New York in January 1939, eight months before World War II began, with W. H. Auden, his close friend and theatrical collaborator. Both were homosexual, and they had been sexual partners, but they traveled together as friends and as fellow writers. Neither saw any future for his artistic development in Europe, nor any real possibility of happiness. At home they had become famous too young and too easily; they were celebrated, copied, continually observed. They had neither the privacy nor the freedom to risk real growth. The diaries which I have been editing begin in January 1939 with their sea voyage to New York. Almost all of Isherwood's earlier diaries, from the 1920s and 1930s, do not survive.

At thirty-four years of age, Isherwood was already the well-known author of five works of semiautobiographical fiction (the fifth, *Goodbye to Berlin,* just about to be published) and, with Auden, of three plays. In London, he had worked as a writer on two film scripts, and during the preceding year he had been preparing a travel book with Auden, *Journey to a War,* about their trip to China to observe the Sino-Japanese conflict. Isherwood had spent most of the 1930s away from England, in various countries in Europe and around the Mediterranean, and he planned to stay in America for good.

Auden achieved startling success and celebrity almost instantly in New York, but Isherwood found he could not work, and he was increasingly anxious about the possibility of war. So he set off for California in May 1939, hoping for guidance from his pacifist friends, Gerald Heard and Aldous Huxley, who were already settled there. He had every reason to believe he might be able to find work in the Hollywood studios.

On the Atlantic crossing, Isherwood had realized that he was a pacifist. His father had been killed at Ypres, in Flanders, in May 1915. The body was never found, and only the passage of time eventually seemed to confirm the death. At the time, Isherwood was ten years old. In adulthood he felt unwilling to fight against an army which might number among its force the German boy he had loved and lived with through most of the 1930s, Heinz Neddermeyer. Isherwood was publicly criticized for failing to return to England during the war, even though in 1940 he wrote to the British embassy in Washington offering to return home. In July 1939, he had already begun the lengthy procedure to obtain U.S. citizenship. And in mid-1940, when his childless uncle died and Isherwood inherited Marple, the family estate in Cheshire (near Manchester), he passed on both money and property to his younger brother in England, which emphasizes how entirely committed he was to his new life in America.

Perhaps giving up his inheritance also emphasizes his commitment to his new vocation as a Hindu. Gerald Heard introduced Isherwood to the Indian monk Swami Prabhavananda in the summer of 1939. Prabhavananda was a follower of Ramakrishna, the nineteenth-century Hindu holy man whose life inspired the modern renaissance of Vedanta. Prabhavananda was then teaching both Heard and Huxley. Isherwood loved Swami Prabhavananda almost from the moment of meeting him. Despite a natural and persistent skepticism, he came to believe more and more as the years passed in the swami's personal sanctity and above all in the swami's belief in God. In a 1957 diary entry, he expressed it like this: "I believe that there is something called (for convenience) God, and that this something can be experienced (don't ask me how), and that a man I know (Swami) has had this experience, partially, at any rate. All this I believe because my instinct, as a novelist and a connoisseur of people, assures me, after long, long observation, that this is true in Swami's case" (*Diaries* 1:728–29, September 29, 1957). The guru-disciple relationship of Vedanta was attractive to Isherwood partly because, like other mentors Isherwood had, the swami was a father figure, a replacement for Isherwood's real father. But also "belief in another's belief," as Isherwood once put it, was the only way in which Isherwood could achieve faith in God (*Diaries* 1:749, April 28, 1958).

Swami Prabhavananda instructed Isherwood in meditation and in Hindu ritual and belief. For nearly four decades—until Prabhavananda's death in 1976—the pair talked, worshiped, prayed, and meditated together, and they also translated a number of Hindu religious and philosophical texts. For Isherwood, Vedanta was a process of gradually overcoming worldly attachments and habits of thought and behavior in order to free the spirit so that it could recognize and achieve oneness with God. In a sense, Vedanta proved to be a natural elaboration upon the training Isherwood had already begun as a novelist. In 1940 he set down in his diary a "prayer for writers," which asks that he grow to feel the same detached love for his fellow man as the artist feels for his work: "Oh source of my inspiration, teach me to extend toward all living beings that fascinated, unsentimental, loving and all-pardoning interest which I feel for the characters I create. May I become identified with all humanity, as I identify myself with these imaginary persons. May my art become my life, and my life my art" (*Diaries* 1:106, July 14, 1940).

On a worldlier note, as soon as he arrived in California, Isherwood was welcomed into the brilliant emigré community—Hollywood's intelligentsia—and through both previous and new acquaintances, he got his first real movie-writing job there, at MGM. Europeans had been coming to work in Hollywood films for several decades, but as the war approached the numbers grew. Geniuses took refuge along with ordinary professionals; many were employed by the studios, others became domestic servants, some found no work at all. Isherwood's friendships ranged widely among this charismatic and increasingly influential group: Aldous and Maria Huxley, Greta Garbo, Charlie Chaplin, Bertolt Brecht, Thomas Mann, Igor and Vera Stravinsky, later Charles Laughton, Tony Richardson, and many others. Over the years, as Isherwood's screenwriting jobs moved him around the studios, he came to know what a gossip columnist might call "everyone" in Hollywood.

During the war, Isherwood registered as a conscientious objector and planned to do Civilian Public Service, but even after Pearl Harbor, when the draft age was raised to forty-four, he was never called up. He went east to Haverford, Pennsylvania, and worked in a Quaker refugee hostel helping to receive and resettle uprooted Europeans, mostly German Jews.

When the hostel closed, he returned to California and movie work, but could not settle down. So, early in 1943, he moved into the Vedanta Center in Hollywood, and for a little over a year, he tried to become a Hindu monk, with all the discipline and sacrifice such a way of life entails. He continued his writing and his film work while observing the daily rituals, and he was celibate for about six months. Gradually he became involved with a young man he met through a friend, and he began to realize he could never be a monk. Still, he remained in the monastery until some months after the affair ended, and the conclusion to the novel he was then writing, *Prater Violet,* expresses Isherwood's recognition that the primary obstacle to his becoming a monk was not the vow of celibacy but the annihilation of personal identity: "And, at this moment, but how infinitely faint, how distant, like the high far glimpse of a goat track through the mountains between clouds, I see something else: the way that leads to safety. To where there is no fear, no loneliness . . . 'No,' I think, 'I could never do it. Rather the fear I know, the loneliness I know . . . for to take that other way would mean that I should lose myself. I should no longer be a person. I should no longer be Christopher Isherwood. No, no. That's more terrible than the bombs. More terrible than having no lover. That I can never face'" (126).

Prater Violet is set in England during the 1930s, but the main character, an uprooted and guilt-ridden Viennese poet and filmmaker, Friedrich Bergmann (based on Isherwood's friend and screenwriting mentor, Berthold Viertel), stands for the many European intellectuals arriving in Hollywood in the years leading up to the war. These moral refugees were to play a major role in shaping the movie culture which defined America to itself during the 1940s and 1950s and which became a source of both fantasy and self-understanding for much of Western society in the second half of the century. The narrator of *Prater Violet,* "Christopher Isherwood," recognizes Bergmann's face on meeting as "the face of a political situation, an epoch. The face of Central Europe" (17). Bergmann's genius as an artist and a film director epitomizes the highest aspirations of European culture, but—as if by some Nietzschean principle—his neurotic artistic perfectionism and appealing sensuality make him the willing lackey of his British studio bosses. He is easily manipulated, permits commercial interests to corrupt his aesthetic ideals, fails to impress upon his English employers the importance of the socialist uprising in Austria in February 1934, fails to make them attend to his insistent prophecy of war. Isherwood shapes the story to chart also, by implication, the relationship between the English and Central European powers through the 1930s. Thus, Bergmann's gifted and anguished personality serves as a partial explanation for the way in which fascism was able to take hold in the homelands of so many who clearly saw its evil.

Both Bergmann and the Isherwood character are paralyzed by "the dilemma of the would-be revolutionary writer or artist, all over Europe" (49), and they make this dilemma the subject of the screenplay they are writing. Each becomes absorbed entirely in completing the film, despite doubting its artistic value, and in pursuing bourgeois success and comfort; neither remains committed to the cause of the workers. When Bergmann says to Isherwood during the 1934 socialist uprising, "I am bitterly ashamed that I am here, in safety" (96), he refers not only to his wife and child in Vienna, but also to those fighting in Vienna for what he himself purports to believe in. The remark reverberates, as indeed does the whole novel, within the circumstances of the Second World War during which Isherwood was writing it. Viertel's own wife and three sons had been safely in Santa Monica since 1928, but Isherwood describes in his diaries other refugees, who arrived in America while their wives and children or other relatives were left behind in Europe; one man received news that his wife, a Jew, had died in a concentration camp in Austria. The sense of guilt expressed by some of these refugees evokes unavoidably the guilt borne silently by all those who were safe during the war, and in particular by the figure of the artist and intellectual upon whom Isherwood self-accusingly focuses in the novel.

During the summer of 1945 Isherwood fell in love for real with a young man from Kentucky who had recently been discharged from the navy, William Caskey. In August, when the war finally ended, Isherwood left the Vedanta Center for good, and soon he and Caskey moved in together. They had their happiest and most productive months together during the following year when Caskey studied photography and Isherwood revised his wartime diaries. In the summer of 1947, they lived in New York, and from there they began a seven-month journey through South America, described by Isherwood in his second travel book, *The Condor and the Cows,* for which Caskey took the haunting photographs.

Apart from the travel book, the years with Caskey went largely unrecorded. Isherwood made almost no diary entries for the second half of the 1940s, and while he was living with Caskey, his career as a writer foundered. By October 1948, when they settled down together again in California, their relationship was troubled and far from monogamous. Isherwood had writing jobs at the movie studios, and he was also writing scripts with friends such as Aldous Huxley and Lesser Samuels. But in his own fiction, he was laboring against writer's block. His domestic life was turbulent and drunken; he started and restarted his novel, producing after seven long years his least impressive book, *The World in the Evening.* It marked the culmination of artistic difficulties long in the making.

When he was seventeen, Isherwood had told his mother in one of his many letters from boarding school, "I have got an essay on 'omission is the beginning of all Art' which it may amuse you to see. I will send it on Wednesday" (Ramsden, 14, February 13, 1921). How does the artist know what to omit? Isherwood always aspired to work on an epic canvas, but he usually produced individual portraits or small groups of interrelated figures. He said in *Christopher and His Kind* that he had decided to publish his stories about Berlin as disconnected fragments only because a friend, John Lehmann, needed short pieces of material for his magazine, *New Writing.* Freed from conventional obligations of plot, Isherwood had produced the impressionistic, open-ended novel *Goodbye to Berlin,* the form of which implies that the stories and characters contained within the book are each part of and even stand for the many similar and not so similar people living outside the book, in real life. But the nonchalant statement about writing for the magazine is misleading—for in fact Isherwood's whole artistic method depends upon omission.

One of the main ways he organized and compressed material in his fiction was to focus on his own relation to a single character: himself and Mr. Norris, himself and Sally Bowles, himself and Berthold Viertel, and even in *Lions and Shadows*—which includes many friends—himself and one friend or mentor at a time, chapter by chapter. This practice corresponds to some of his real-life relationships and is epitomized in his friendship with the swami. Isherwood's narrative persona in his early works tends to be a bit like the narrator in a Henry James short story: bland, obtuse, without sexual identity, and intensely focused on the other figure in the tale. As Isherwood matured as an artist, his narrative persona became more vivid, more complicated, more dynamic, and in most respects truer to Isherwood's real-life personality; in *A Single Man* the persona finally emerged as a character in its own right, and the Jamesian narrator disappeared altogether. But this was only in 1964. As Isherwood points out in *Christopher and His Kind,* early in his career, he could not without scandal and without possible legal difficulties write about homosexuality in the way that he might have liked. When he introduced two explicitly homosexual episodes into *The World in the Evening,* written during the early 1950s, his publishers in both London and New York asked for changes. Thus the book is marred both by repressed anger about the difficulties of trying to write as a homosexual and by psychological inaccuracies.

At the beginning of the 1950s, Isherwood's friend John Van Druten adapted some of his Berlin stories for the stage. This changed Isherwood's life. *I Am a Camera* became a hit, and Isherwood was famous. He had a modest share of the earnings from the play, from the subsequent films, and from the musical *Cabaret,* even though, as he himself said of *I Am a Camera,* "This isn't my own child" (*Diaries* 1:441, November 8, 1951).

And soon, his life was to change again. In February 1953, Isherwood became involved with an eighteen-year-old college student, Don Bachardy, and it rapidly became clear that Bachardy was to be the most important person in Isherwood's life. From the outset, his feelings toward Bachardy were fatherly as well as romantic. Bachardy was young and still only half-educated when they met, and he modeled himself on Isherwood to such a degree that he even acquired Isherwood's half-British and half-American accent when speaking. But Bachardy was also fiercely independent and rebellious—traits always attractive to Isherwood—and he was intelligent, sensitive, and tenacious. In 1960 Isherwood recorded in his diary that Bachardy "has mattered and does matter more than any of the others. Because he imposes himself more, demands more, cares more—about everything he does and encounters. He is so desperately alive" (*Diaries* 1:845, February 14, 1960). They shared one another's projects and concerns intimately, with a continuing emphasis upon self-reflection, so that living and working *together* became in itself an artistic undertaking.

Falling in love with Bachardy triggered a powerful sensation in Isherwood of the numinous richness of life, and he was at first overawed by his emotions. One passage in his diary suggests that this experience of love was to move him, over the longer term, away from fiction toward a new, much closer connection in his work with real life:

... the nice smell of redwood as I lifted the garage door. And the feeling of impotence—or, what it really amounts to, lack of inclination to cope with a constructed, invented plot—the feeling, why not write what one experiences, from day to day? And then, as I slid my door back, this sinking-sick feeling of love for Don ... and the reality of that—so far more than all this tiresome fiction. Why invent—when Life is so prodigious?

Perhaps I'll never write another novel, or anything invented—except, of course, for money. (*Diaries* 1:455–56, April 20, 1953)

As he grew older, Isherwood's writing was to become increasingly autobiographical. At the conclusion to *Christopher and His Kind* he referred to Bachardy, without naming him, as "the ideal companion to whom you can reveal yourself totally and yet be loved for what you are" (339). Being able at last to reveal himself fully to the right companion in life seems to have made it possible for Isherwood to reveal himself more fully in his writing. In the years he spent with Bachardy, he was to produce three more novels before turning entirely to family and personal history.

This trend could be understood as creeping narcissism, but it might also be understood as something altogether different. Despite Isherwood's certainty that he could not give up his identity, take a Sanskrit name, and become a monk, his Hinduism had nonetheless over the years greatly enhanced his sense of self-detachment. He made japam every day for decades—i.e., repeated his mantra, one of God's names, chosen for him by the swami, while counting the repetitions on a rosary—as a means of achieving spiritual focus. Making japam was a kind of spiritual parallel to writing in his diary—a technique of reflection and self-mastery. When Isherwood first began making japam, in 1939 and 1940, he sometimes reported in his diary dreams and semimystical or psychic experiences in which he seemed to be observing himself as if he were another person. The swami explained that such out-of-body experiences resulted from his practice of yogic disciplines and warned Isherwood not to meditate too much at first. A 1955 diary entry makes clear that despite a deep sense of engagement with the various aspects of his life—his relationship with Don Bachardy, his spiritual life, his art, the shared project of living in the right way—Isherwood's commitments had become somehow impersonal. He calls them symbolic: "In the night, quite often now, I wake—not with the horrors, but calmly and lucidly. Then I know certain things clearly—it's almost as if they belonged to another order of reality: that I shall die one day—that much of my life has been wasted—that the life of the spirit is the only valid occupation—that I really care for Don and that I have, as it were, adopted him, much as I adopted Heinz, but more completely. In the daytime, these facts are obscured, by studio noise and as-if behavior, and insane resentments and mental and physical slumping. Also I know that all occupations, even Art, are symbolic, and all are valid, so long as they represent right-livelihood" (*Diaries* 1:519, August 8, 1955). Finally, many years later, in the mid-1980s when Isherwood was mortally ill with cancer and Bachardy, by then an accomplished painter, was drawing him on his deathbed, Isherwood commented on his own likenesses in the third person, "I like the ones of him dying" (Bachardy's diary, December 2, 1985, *Last Drawings,* xiv).

This sense of detachment from self permeates Isherwood's later writing. In the novels of the 1930s, the narrator who appears in the text paradoxically conceals Isherwood's true personality, including his sexuality, which is inseparable from it. The early narrator figure thus serves as a barrier between author and reader and does not reveal or express the author's true self. This is partly because the young Isherwood was still attached to his personality, wanted to control it, protect it, hide it. In later years, Isherwood's detachment had advanced to such a degree that he could write about himself as if he were another person. In *A Single Man,* still a novel rather than autobiography, the main character, George, draws profoundly on the psychological and emotional being of the real Christopher Isherwood—including the homosexuality until then hidden from his public—but Isherwood handles this character, George, with great freedom. Intimate details are revealed, some as true to the real Christopher Isherwood as they are to his fictional creation. And yet the character is like a ghost. We are made *most* aware of his spectral otherness:

Staring and staring into the mirror, it sees many faces within its face—the face of the child, the boy, the young man, the not-so-young man—all present still, preserved like fossils on superimposed layers, and like fossils, dead. Their message to this live dying creature is: Look at us—we have died—what is there to be afraid of?

It answers them: But that happened so gradually, so easily. *I'm afraid of being rushed.*

It stares and stares. Its lips part. It starts to breathe through its mouth. Until the cortex orders it impatiently to wash, to shave, to brush its hair. Its nakedness has to be covered. It must be dressed up in clothes because it is going outside, into the world of the other people; and these others must be able to identify it. Its behavior must be acceptable to them.

Obediently, it washes, shaves, brushes its hair, for it accepts its responsibilities to the others. It is even glad that it has its place among them. It knows what is expected of it.

It knows its name. It is called George. (10–11)

Isherwood's impulse as he grew older to write increasingly openly about himself and about his family is the result of a kind of liberation from his personal identity. Christopher Isherwood, like George, became symbolic, a useful vehicle for portraying human nature.

In 1959, Isherwood and Bachardy bought a house overlooking the ocean in Santa Monica; they were to live there together for the rest of Isherwood's life. The same year, Isherwood took up teaching. For a man who had deliberately ruined his promising career at Cambridge in order to free himself from his mother's ambition that he become a university don, this was a remarkable development, the final conclusion to his rebellious youth. He now accepted a place in the Establishment, and he undertook a conventional relationship to the young that was entirely different from the romantic and fatherly bond he had shared outside society and in defiance of society with the various boys who had, in a sense, culminated in Don Bachardy. Isherwood was a success as a teacher, and although he still found aspects of institutional life tedious and frustrating, he found acceptance and formal recognition gratifying. Teaching provided a source of steady income that, unlike film work, did not interfere with his writing.

The early 1960s brought conflict in Isherwood's relationship with Bachardy, who was struggling to establish himself independently, as an artist and as a man. Ultimately the conflict was to be resolved, but not without pain and a tremendous effort of love. *A Single Man* reflects Isherwood's fear of being abandoned by Bachardy and his fear of aging and death, but it also evokes the challenge of sustaining his mature identity—no longer a renegade English writer, but now a permanent member of a community in which he wished openly to coexist with others like and unlike himself. The persona of the college professor proved to be one Isherwood could write about with exquisite comedy. In the 1930s in *Lions and Shadows* he had deftly mocked the subtle, hypnotic power "Mr. Holmes" exercised over himself and his classmates at Repton; now he was able to draw upon his own personality as a teacher to create a new classroom magician for *A Single Man*. In a sense he was portraying himself as having grown into the role of one of his adolescent heroes, G. B. Shaw.

A Single Man is modeled on Virginia Woolf's *Mrs. Dalloway,* but instead of one day in the life of a Mayfair hostess, it presents one day in the life of a southern Californian literature professor: George is a middle-aged Englishman, a foreigner, and a homosexual. He is lonely because his companion has recently been killed in a car crash, and, like any aging person, George fears his own death; but otherwise he is not unhappy—not with himself. George is unhappy with *society* because society cannot understand or accept him as he really is. He keeps his true nature hidden, not least because when he does allow it to emerge, he risks having it explained away by psychology. As a homosexual, his plight is not psychological but social and political—a radical notion at the time the novel was written, although Isherwood knew by then that such a view was supported not only by his own experience and impressions but also by the work, for instance, of his longtime friend the psychologist and psychotherapist Evelyn Hooker. Hooker studied Los Angeles homosexuals for many years; in 1956, she had presented the first-ever research demonstrating that as high a percentage of homosexuals was psychologically well adjusted as heterosexuals.[2]

Outwardly George is cultivated and presentable; but secretly he is a ferocious, angry monster. He is a raging misogynist, dislikes children, has breathtakingly sadistic fantasies. Isherwood deliberately emphasizes these characteristics. From the point of view of the conventional heterosexual community which Isherwood clearly meant *A Single Man* to shock, George is a monster because he is a homosexual; he is "unspeakable" (27,

29). But from Isherwood's point of view, George is a monster simply because he has long been persecuted and, at the moment, is unloved. Indeed, George's condition is emblematic of the hidden monstrousness of human beings generally. And the novel's widest importance lies not in its candid depiction of homosexual anger but in its foretelling of the way in which any number of sexual, ethnic, and religious groups, living side by side in a culture then prosperously at peace, were all about to come out of hiding during the 1960s and 1970s.

The students in George's class include a nun, a recent emigré from Germany who barely speaks English, a divorcée of implied Spanish or Mexican background, a Chinese boy, a Japanese girl who was interned with her family during the war (all their property confiscated), a Swedish boy, a black girl, a "crazy" beatnik boy curious about drugs and sex, a Jewish boy, a homosexual boy. In other words, Isherwood depicts a class in which every student is a member of a group which may be called a minority. And one subject of their morning discussion is the relation of the minority—any minority—to the majority. In his role as a college professor, George leaves his own affinities unmentioned; his minority is still a secret tribe for whom he may not speak out loud. As a result, his classroom polemic works as a long double entendre which makes an implied claim for the right of the homosexual minority to be recognized along with the rest, and which, more important, also highlights the ways in which the other minorities are like George's own.

On the surface, the characters in *A Single Man* share a loose consensus about freedom and tolerance—a modern American dream—but underneath lie suspicion and unrealized conflicts. Each character has hidden needs and resentments; each character in his or her fundamental nature is at odds with the group. Near the end of the novel, Isherwood describes a bit of Californian landscape which symbolizes this:

Up the coast a few miles north, in a lava reef under the cliffs, there are a lot of rock pools. You can visit them when the tide is out. Each pool is separate and different, and you can, if you are fanciful, give them names, such as George, Charlotte, Kenny, Mrs. Strunk. Just as George and the others are thought of, for convenience, as individual entities, so you may think of a rock pool as an entity; though, of course, it is not. The waters of its consciousness—so to speak—are swarming with hunted anxieties, grim-jawed greeds, dartingly vivid intuitions, old crusty-shelled rock-gripping obstinacies, deep-down sparkling undiscovered secrets, ominous protean organisms motioning mysteriously, perhaps warningly, toward the surface light. How can such a variety of creatures coexist at all? Because they have to. The rocks of the pool hold their world together. And, throughout the day of the ebb tide, they know no other.

But that long day ends at last; yields to the nighttime of the flood. And, just as the waters of the ocean come flooding, darkening over the pools, so over George and the others in sleep come the waters of that other ocean—that consciousness which is no one in particular but which contains everyone and everything, past, present and future, and extends unbroken beyond the uttermost stars. (183–84)

The landscape of the rock pool is, relatively, unchanging. By contrast, *A Single Man* portrays a society about to break up; it will be fragmented by sexual liberation, gay liberation, women's liberation, the civil rights movement, black power, the drug culture, the peace movement, the generation gap. Each of these movements is represented or implied by the individual members of George's class. A decade after the novel appeared, Isherwood wrote in his diary about George's bout of hatred on the freeway in the book's opening passages, "I wrote that hate passage as a parable for all the members of all the other minorities as well as mine. Because we are all so unwilling to admit that our own dear little injured minority can ever feel hate—except of course when it is 100% *justified*. . . . The vast majority of all minority members sometimes give way to a paranoia which makes them temporarily insane" (unpublished diary, September 14, 1973). In recent decades, the final emergence of such minority-group interests has revealed the extent to which Isherwood, as in his writings about Berlin in the early thirties, again revealed a cultural condition—a widespread state of mind—which indeed foretold something of what was to happen in Californian culture, and in American culture, over the following years. As Upward's Marxist rubric might have it, he succeeded in portraying the forces at work beneath the surface of material reality which were to shape the future. The old double-edged controls of politeness and repression are now gone, leaving Americans with the enervating dichotomy of political correctness and incessant litigation. And the liberal excess of understanding and tolerance of which Isherwood also forewarned—a phrase he uses in *A Single Man* is "annihilation by blandness" (27)—is accompanied nowadays by the need to legislate personal relationships and to advertise individual eccentricities on confessional talk shows.

The passage about the rock pools makes clear that Isherwood's own idea of liberation had a higher, spiritual dimension which would render such worldly concerns irrelevant. In *A Single Man* his religious beliefs are only implied—for instance, when he refers in the rock-pools passage to a universal consciousness symbolized by the ocean. His next novel, *A Meeting by the River*, describes Vedanta beliefs explicitly and takes as a theme the difficulty of the monastic vow. And his last book, *My Guru and His Disciple*, traces his own spiritual development, which grew from the principle of religious and personal love and offers a counterpoise to the hatred essential in *A Single Man*.

Still, in *A Single Man,* Isherwood also portrays—in the friendship between the "crazy" youth, Kenny, and middle-aged George—a symbolic meeting of youth and age which reflects the need of human society to cohere outside of the family bond. Numerous allusions—to Huxley, Tennyson, Greek mythology, the Platonic tradition, Stephen Dedalus and Bloom in Joyce's *Ulysses,* Lily Briscoe and Mrs. Ramsey in Virginia Woolf's *To the Lighthouse*—make clear their relationship is meant to carry all the significance that any such relationship in literature or mythology has ever carried, and the relationship is complex and changeable. It is that of teacher and student, father and son; it is both personal and impersonal, incorporating a Socratic dialogue and a near seduction; it is erotically charged, as such relationships often are; and toward the end of the novel, the natural precedence of age over youth is reversed, as with Lear and his fool, so that George becomes a child and Kenny his nanny.

It is above all a guru-disciple relationship: Kenny seeks to obtain esoteric knowledge from George. He prefers to address George as "Sir," expressing his respect for George's age and presumed wisdom, and for George's difference, which he recognizes but is not obliged to celebrate. The guru-disciple relationship is one in which Isherwood thrived in his own spiritual and personal life—with the swami (where it did not depend upon a homosexual affinity: the swami was celibate but straight) and in an entirely different way with Don Bachardy. It certainly offers a way of bridging the generation gap which was to wrack Western culture during the decades following the publication of *A Single Man.* And it is an ideal which can be of use to us all.

Christopher Isherwood, as a novelist, offered some of his best works of fiction during the 1930s, though clearly a few came later. Over the course of his career he turned increasingly to autobiography, recognizing it as a form which had special relevance for him and for which he possessed special gifts. At his death his diaries were still unpublished, although some of them had been read by friends. There can now be little question that in their sheer bulk they comprise a major part of his life's work. More important, in their technical brilliance, their personal and historical interest, their insight, their comedy, their sometimes stunning beauty, they also comprise a major part of his artistic achievement. The diaries offer a unique and detailed portrait of Isherwood's life in southern California from 1939 to 1983, and they are a magnificent resource for understanding the culture we live in now.

Notes

Adapted from a lecture, Nantucket Atheneum, August 1998. Christopher Isherwood's *Diaries, Volume One, 1939–1960* was published in England in 1996 and in the United States in 1997. A reconstructed diary of the postwar period and *Diaries, Volume Two, 1960–1983* are in preparation.

1. For instance, the writer Lucy Bucknell in conversation with me, 1997; Edmund White in "The Mérimée of Monroeville," *Times Literary Supplement,* February 20, 1998, 14.

2. Her paper, "The Adjustment of the Male Overt Homosexual," was later published in *Projective Techniques,* the journal of the Society for Projective Techniques and the Rorschach Institute, since retitled *Journal of Projective Techniques and Personality Assessment.*

Isherwood in Los Angeles

Writing about oneself destroys the past.
Christopher Isherwood

I first encountered Christopher Isherwood in the late 1950s in central Illinois.[1] I was about fifteen when I read the play *I Am a Camera,* adapted by John Van Druten from Isherwood's *The Berlin Stories,* in one of John Gassner's *Best American Plays* anthologies. These books had no illustrations of the productions. The introduction said nothing about the Isherwood whose stories formed the play and who was a character in it. There was mention of "expatriates" and the characters' "dissipation," and somehow I knew that to mean homosexual. I first heard Isherwood's voice during the hot Midwest summer of 1962. On a Columbia Records series he read from the last pages of *Prater Violet.*[2] I was stirred to hear of the lovemaking with "J" and the probable "K" and "L" and "M," and somehow I knew that this referred to love between men. Isherwood's name, then, was mixed with my coming to know myself as homosexual. I could have had no idea our lives would cross or that he would be a part of so many stages of my friends' and my education.

I moved to Los Angeles to attend college, finishing at UCLA as an English major. In February 1965, the student newspaper printed an article with the headline "Playwright Isherwood Conducts Writing Course." The article noted that Isherwood was a Regents' Professor in the philosophy department. He would give lectures and conduct a "special course, open to both students and faculty, on the practical problems of writing. He will also allow free time for criticism of student and faculty manuscripts."[3] Although my schedule for the semester was set, I managed to get into this class; it was one that would change my life.

I bought Isherwood's latest book, *A Single Man,* paying what was then a high price for the hardcover edition. On the front of the dust jacket were just the title and the author's name. But on the back was a drawing of Isherwood, signed "Bachardy." The drawing resembled a portrait bust, an image of a handsome man in middle age, his eyes strong and far-seeing. There was a statement that the drawing was by Don Bachardy. Copy inside the book gave some biographical details about Isherwood, perhaps the first time I had seen them put together. There was an odd conclusion: "He is unmarried and lives in Santa Monica, California."

Also announced in the student newspaper was a public lecture by Isherwood, "Writing as a Way of Life." That seemed to promise the answers I needed then—some key to becoming a fellow writer. This lecture provided an opportunity for me to connect the Bachardy drawing to a live person. I was startled that I found Isherwood so attractive and was unable to fit his image with those of persons who shared his age. He didn't dress like a professor. Although he wore a jacket and tie of some sort, he wore loafers with white socks, not the usual dress dark socks.

I'm not sure if the lecture gave me the key I sought, but it was the first of several fortunate encounters I would have with writers and artists. William Faulkner was then perhaps the most studied author in American academies, so it was refreshing that Isherwood, when asked about him, replied merely, "Oh, I respect him." He called Joyce his least favorite of the "great writers"—Joyce was not silly enough for him.[4]

The class lectures were recorded and transcribed under the direction of Richard Montague, a professor in the philosophy department.[5] Isherwood did not lecture in the strict sense, and there were no examinations or papers. It would take me some years to realize that these sessions stemmed from fertile "table talk" and interview talk. The range of topics was probably staggering for almost anyone attending, let alone those of us who were young students.

Isherwood made asides, noting, for example, "that infamous sentence," by which he meant "I am a camera," or saying of Sally Bowles, "I could have got more out of her." He might surprise himself even while lecturing. He realized that characters from the play *The Ascent of F6* were distant relatives of those in the book he told us he was then writing, *A Meeting by the River.* He'd talk about one of his screenplays; he'd introduce Eastern religion by talking about the Ramakrishna biography he was working on. There were corrective remarks on world culture: "Nobody really elected us to be the standard bearers of the arts, and it may be entirely new things will evolve in Asia."[6]

Isherwood mentioned homosexuality, a word seldom heard in classes in those days, and I have a note that, in introducing some idea, he said, "Now that we're coming out more and more . . ." and then laughed at his double entendre. I can't tell from my scribbled notes what he was discussing at the moment. He did mention homosexuality when discussing the bisexuality of characters in *The World in the Evening*. There was no mention of homosexuality when the class talked about *A Single Man*. Isherwood did not reveal facts about his past love life, so when someone asked if Waldemar were the same character as Otto, his reply was brief: "He's a combination of a certain type of Berlin street boy."[7]

I wanted to know how things got done with writing. I had never known the inside workings of the New York publishing world, so I asked how to find people with whom to share my first ventures. He answered that it was a good idea to show your work to a few people, but not to many, because each reader would come up with ideas. He said that he showed his work to his friend Don Bachardy.[8] I don't think I was able to put it together that Bachardy was his lover, and I had no image of "Bachardy," as far as I can remember. It was tempting to project pieces of George in *A Single Man* onto Isherwood, but none of them fit precisely. George's lover Jim was dead. Isherwood's was not, but it was not to be spoken of in public in that class at UCLA in the spring of 1965.

The class announcement had indicated we could turn in work to him, and I did. I still hold a memory of him at a desk in a UCLA office, a large window and light behind him as he talked about my story. I had the nerve to turn in a "gay" story. It was a wholly imaginary homosexual encounter in New Orleans in which the protagonist viewed a sexual encounter between two loving men, but then paid a sailor for sex. Isherwood inquired, "Just what occurred in this story?" Well he should have asked. I replied that the character was disillusioned. Isherwood continued, "What was the nature of the disillusionment? What did the sailor feel?" He went on to tell me there were enormous possibilities in writing about everyday things, like being a mother. He mentioned "Paul's Case," by Willa Cather, a story that I didn't know. He spoke of the books of J. R. Ackerley. I think he mentioned these two writers to see if we could come out to each other, but since they were unknown to me at that time, I couldn't really fit things together until years later. Since I had observed little, there was little I could write about. Since I knew no sailors, I would have to wait for more experience.

Book reviewers were often not kind to Isherwood. I'm not sure when I first read a 1962 review that trashed *Down There on a Visit*, but I've often looked it up just to confirm how negative and nasty it is. It dismissed all of the major themes of Isherwood. His depiction of Los Angeles is reduced to a mention of palm trees. Vedanta is reduced to "yoga." Homosexual life is reduced to mentions of Sodom and assertions that homosexuals are effeminate bores and not amusing even to each other, let alone to such reviewers as William P. Smith in *Commonweal.*[9]

Academics ignored Isherwood's works. They were not anthologized in textbooks and not studied in classes. In the fall of 1965, I was accepted into UCLA's undergraduate English honors program. When I asked my professor and adviser whether for my honors thesis I could write about Isherwood, he replied that Isherwood had not written enough work that was important. I doubt that this response came from what we now call homophobia, but it came from a set of assumptions in which urban New York writers, Southern writers, and English writers living in England were placed above those who might happen to live in and work in and write about Los Angeles. It was as if this adviser apparently concurred with the reviewer of *Down There on a Visit.* If a writer's themes were Los Angeles, gay life, and alternative religion, then his books were not significant. They were not to be studied in departments of English. But how could one have written about Isherwood in the critical context of those times? Although Isherwood in his class discussed his sources and themes, these still did not fit into that period's academic criticism, derived from the theories of the New Critics. There was close attention paid to the text, with detailed analysis of symbols and imagery. There was little attention paid to authors' biographies and almost none to social issues, certainly little to homosexuality. I probably wouldn't have known what to write or how to write about the homosexuality that interested me and defined me. Several things conspired to keep me from graduate school, but this answer, denying me time to explore works and themes that meant everything to me personally, was one of the conspirators.

Thanks to the University of California Education Abroad program, I became an "expatriate." I spent 1966 traveling in Mediterranean countries and going to school in Greece. I wasn't exactly "dissipated," but I did meet Greek sailors. I also met writers and artists, particularly the great Greek painter Yannis Tsarouchis. Since the 1940s, he had used the traditions of Greek art to draw and paint male nudes. Few artists did so at that time, and his works were astonishing in their immediacy. After Europe, life was dull back in Los Angeles. Unlike in Athens, there was almost no neighborhood feeling, there were no sidewalk cafés. Unlike the mix of Mediterranean cultures I'd just experienced, Los Angeles offered little artistic or literary tradition. There were the Beat writers of Venice West. There was Isherwood. There was his friend Aldous Huxley, there was Henry Miller.

None of these was thought of as a Los Angeles writer, and none was studied at UCLA. In the mid-1960s in Los Angeles, one could be proud of the theaters and the Music Center. These emulated New York, of course, and it would take some years for them to assert themselves as homes for Los Angeles culture and not just places other artists visited on tour. At the new Los Angeles County Museum of Art, local artists were shown only in the rental gallery in the basement.

One area in Los Angeles with a neighborhood flavor had art galleries and shops. It was located around La Cienega Boulevard, south of Santa Monica Boulevard. The galleries opened on Monday nights, and, in those innocent times, one could wander in and out of them for openings. On a visit back to Los Angeles from the Army Artillery Officer Candidate School, I went with a woman friend to the elegant courtyard of the Rex Evans Gallery. No one stopped us from climbing the stairs filled with plants to enter the gallery and mingle in the cocktail party in progress. I forget what show was hung on the walls. There was a separate living room space also displaying art. Next to a sofa there was a portfolio. I opened it. There were perhaps six or eight drawings of male nudes, each on large paper. The intimacy of the drawing form was a contrast to the large paper, the nude bodies, the lifelike genitals. These drawings were in a familiar pen-and-ink wash style. They were signed "Bachardy."

I found that Bachardy's first Los Angeles show had been in 1962 at the Rex Evans Gallery, operated by Evans and Jim Weatherford.[10] I was beginning to have what we now call discretionary money, and I decided to visit the gallery to buy one of the Bachardy drawings. I was hesitant to ask to see these nudes, but I did. Rex brought them out from their portfolio. This was probably late summer 1967, and in early 1968 I was sent to Vietnam. I mailed payments on the drawing as I could. Rex sent notes, giving news of Bachardy's being in the gallery, and offered to send me further photographs of the drawings if that were "allowed." Rex died in 1969 before I returned home.

When I did return from Vietnam, in 1970, there had been an entire revolution. Much of this social and cultural change came from Englishmen, or persons originally from England, like Isherwood. The Beatles had made smoking pot and following Eastern religions into a craze. Reyner Banham had begun his studies of Los Angeles architecture that finally brought the city recognition as a unique urban atmosphere and not a failed copy of somewhere else.[11] David Hockney had painted Los Angeles and made it legitimate subject matter. He had already painted and etched nude males, alone and together, in the beginning using the Los Angeles *Physique Pictorial* models as inspiration. The gay world had also changed. Stonewall had occurred in New York just as I was leaving Vietnam. I gradually found out about it. If, as Edmund White has written, it was not in the New York papers, it certainly was not in *Stars and Stripes.*[12] In that La Cienega area Don Johnson and Sal Mineo had appeared nude onstage in *Fortune and Men's Eyes.*[13] When I got back to Los Angeles to pick up the drawings, Jim introduced me to many of his friends and gallery artists, including Louis Fox, Don Solorzano, and Sheila Ross. As I met them or just sat in the gallery living room with Jim having a drink, listening to him reminisce about being gay in the army during World War II, I realized that I would never again worry about being homosexual.

Rex had written to tell me that Bachardy was to have another show at the gallery, but it never occurred. Bachardy moved to Irving Blum's gallery, a more "modern" space for showing. After the opening of Bachardy's one-man show in March 1970, Jim took me to the party at Tony Duquette's legendary West Hollywood space. Norma Talmadge had supposedly used it as a studio. I don't remember seeing or meeting Isherwood that evening. He may not have been there. But somewhere near Jennifer Jones holding court—could she have been wearing a red evening dress and sitting on a red velvet chair?—Jim introduced me to Don Bachardy.

I don't have a clear picture of him then, except as a person poised and charming in this setting which was somewhat awesome to me. I imagine that he was clean-shaven, unlike the image of longer hair and mustache he would have through the 1970s. I remember taking him to a gay bar, The Farm, on Santa Monica Boulevard. In contrast to the luxe and even outré Duquette interiors, it had a butch country motif, with barrels of peanuts in their shells and men dancing to whatever music was popular then.

I can't recall when I first sat for Bachardy. His studio was at their home at the top of Santa Monica Canyon, so perhaps it was there that I was reintroduced to Isherwood. The two were then "Chris" and "Don." I relished trips to their house. It was hidden on the side of a hill down from the street, but a tile roof in the Mediterranean style was visible. Down a steep driveway there were two sensible cars in a carport. Its back was one wall of Don's first studio, since remodeled. The stairs turned down through a space of hanging plants with a musty earthy odor and led to the wooden front door. Once inside, the space opened. Tall windows looked out over the canyon. A fireplace had bookcases on either side. From Gump's in San Francisco there were the elegant wicker chairs to be made famous by Hockney in his painting of Chris and Don.[14] There were a large sofa and coffee table with more books and art. I couldn't have guessed that before long I would take off my clothes to lie nude in a window seat for a drawing, or lie on the sofa, or sit in one of two patterned upholstered chairs that shortly after this time were removed.

Through the 1960s, it had been difficult for me to come to terms with

Don Bachardy: *Dan Luckenbill, August 23, 1970.* Pencil on paper. 14″ × 11″. Copyright ©
Don Bachardy. Used by permission.

being homosexual and to find others who were. There were not even the
concepts of role models or mentors at that time. Rex and Jim had served
as such at long distance, but Rex had died, and I didn't really experience
the two of them together. So, as for many others in Los Angeles, Chris
and Don became that model couple. I felt a great privilege in seeing their
domestic life. I remember Chris saying that one must make an effort of

the will every day, whether it be meditating or getting down to work on something quite difficult. Don and he got up early but didn't necessarily get themselves ready for the public until later. If I arrived in the morning they might each be in a long robe. They appear in these robes in a Hockney etching.[15]

In February 1970, I began to work at the UCLA Library. That May, I met Dan Clay, a history student just finishing his undergraduate work. In 1971 and possibly 1972, Don did nudes of me, of Dan Clay, and of the two of us in a style he used only briefly—a line in ink without shading but rendered with perspective and volume. It was perhaps after one of those sittings that we were invited to dinner, along with Jim Weatherford, I believe. I recall Don in the kitchen making a spinach salad. Seen through glass like a Hockney California idyll were Chris and Dan barbecuing lamb out on the deck off the dining room. Chris made an immediate impression on Dan. He wrote me after these early meetings: "I always feel Chris sees, understands, knows everything, instinctively."

During these times of going to their house and posing for Don, I became a writer. Giving drafts of stories to them provided discipline for me to finish them. There was almost no market for short stories at that time. Any market for gay short stories was completely unknown to me. To talk about the first story, they stopped by my apartment on La Brea Avenue on a hot weekend afternoon, unusual for them because they worked every day of the week. In the story, I had transposed a gay experience of mine in Tangiers onto a woman character. They didn't like the story.

Chris didn't mind when Don asked him to leave while Don talked to me about writing. Their relationship accommodated such a request. In fact, Chris enjoyed his walk and his observations of my neighborhood built largely in the middle to late 1920s. Around my building, which was in the exuberant Churrigueresque style, there were mainly small Spanish Colonial bungalows, most of them unremodeled. Even the streetlights had not been replaced. Chris was one of the first writers to convey the textures of life in Los Angeles, and he expressed his pleasure in his city when he said that it was as if nothing had changed since he was first in Los Angeles in 1939.

I also showed them some ribald passages from a story about the rowdy men in my army barracks. Chris liked this sketch. No one had written about being a gay lieutenant in Vietnam. I took this to mean I should write more gay stories of this kind. I used showing these stories to them as a weak excuse for stopping in on them and soaking up the warm atmosphere of their house and their lives together as a gay couple. Chris's table talk consisted in part of ruminations for the speeches and interviews he was beginning to give. I would often see these comments published later somewhere.

There are records of many of these events and interviews in the *Los Angeles Times* and the *New York Times,* and more of them appeared in lesbian and gay and local alternative publications. Chris was even on the cover of some of these, and I remember that he was pleased when his face would appear all over Los Angeles in the dispensers of these publications. Some of this reported talk would find its way alongside the gay publication's centerfold model. Though Chris found this juxtaposition amusing, he wondered whether we should be "saddled" with things like the classifieds in the *Advocate.* This has been a recurring concern in the community, but Chris then answered himself, "We must not get nicey-nice."[16]

His wit and wisdom are preserved in these articles. From them we learn, for example, that he was not comfortable with the word "lover": "Lover implies *he* loves me but doesn't express how I feel about him." He also didn't like the term "gay": "I prefer the words used by our enemies . . . 'queer' or 'fag.' It makes heterosexuals wince when you refer to yourself by those words."[17]

Chris appeared often at the Gay Awareness or Gay Pride events that began in Los Angeles in the 1970s. There was a feeling of daring in assembling as gay and lesbian people. He was careful later not to deny his privilege—his age, his income, and his long relationship with Don. But other writers with similar security did not necessarily come out. If they did, fewer still put themselves in public for further scrutiny. Chris's feeling of duty to the gay community had begun early. When my friend Ginger Harmon interviewed him for *Los Angeles* magazine in 1980, he spoke of this awareness as early as his time in Berlin: "I suddenly realized or gradually realized through meeting Magnus Hirschfeld that we [homosexuals] really were a cause, that we were part of something which seemed very important and had a meaning and was not just my private affair but there were lots of us and we had rights and that one should agitate for them."[18]

Chris and Don were generous in introducing young friends, carefully mixing their interests, even inviting them to dinner at their home. Before one of these dinners, I had a drawing session with Don. It took well over two, if not three, hours. Don and I were in the studio as it became dark. Chris appeared at the door irate to ask if we were ever going to finish and come in to dinner. We had no doubt missed the cocktail hour, although I suppose I caught up with the guests, among them W. I. (Bill) Scobie, Ralph Sylvester, and Stathis Orphanos. Bill had covered one of Chris's "gay pride" appearances, at Long Beach, and had done the *Paris Review* interview. But because of the Greek American Stathis, a bookseller, writer, and photographer, talk moved to Greece and the painter Tsarouchis, whom Stathis had not met. Later in the 1970s Ralph and Stathis became publishers, their first work the signed limited edition of *Christopher and His Kind.* Currently they are working on a portfolio of Tsarouchis's works with tributes by Hockney and Stephen Spender, among many others. It would be some years after that meeting before Stathis and I could settle on a project that would bring together our many interests. In 1990, I curated a UCLA Library exhibit, *Sylvester & Orphanos,* focusing on their publications, including influences from Tsarouchis to Isherwood and Bachardy. It included portraits of Chris by Stathis and by Don.

Chris's lectures at UC Berkeley in 1963 were called *The Autobiography of My Books.* In our 1965 UCLA class he referred to this idea as "a sort of autobiographical book from the point of view of the subject matter of my books." He said he owed the class a great debt for help in clarifying his ideas for these projects. He stood fast when some students challenged him for not being "modern" enough. He said, "Well, I shall finish my life doing what I do, you know. I don't foresee any great branchings off. I have a tremendous lot of stuff that I want to tell still, and I will just go ahead and do that the best way I can."[19] We students couldn't know that from "everyday things"—his mother's and father's diaries and his own—he would create his last books with the difficult poetry of precise observation and concise statement.

It was Don's idea to title the Berlin and Europe memoirs *Christopher and His Kind.* And it's a most clever wordplay, in the manner of that critical "ambiguity" that was popular when I was a student. It harks back to Chris's own ambiguity when praising Gore Vidal's *The City and the Pillar* as "one of the best books of its kind." So "kind" first suggests "homosexual" or "queer" or "gay" and serves as a code word for those who lived through years of disguise or hiding. The final subtlety of the usage is that there is actually no end to Christopher's kind. The book is about gay and straight and other, male and female and hermaphrodite, English and American and German, Christian and Jew and Vedantist. The word visually suggests the German *kind* or child, and the book treats Christopher's works as if they are his children. And the word extends to the many of us who have been his students or "children."

One of the last times I saw Chris was at an opening of Don's at the James Corcoran Gallery when it was on Santa Monica Boulevard in West Hollywood. I went into one of the large gallery rooms where Don's acrylic paintings were hung like colorful banners in some enormous guildhall. There was a mix of portraits and nudes of his friends, of actors and writers, and always of Chris. For a moment, the crowd was elsewhere. Chris stood almost alone in the room. I took that moment to talk to him. He seemed ill. And though I knew better—perhaps even he had warned me, don't ask about a writer's current difficult work—I heard myself asking him about his writing. I thought that he had begun making a book from the Hollywood diaries, as from previous ones he had made *Christopher and His*

Kind and *My Guru and His Disciple.* When I saw Chris's reaction, I knew I had made a great mistake. He answered me politely, "Oh, you know it's enormously difficult. Difficult." I had never been so sad in his presence. I felt that he couldn't complete this work, this fascinating part of his "tremendous lot of stuff."

I've never been able to see enough images of Chris. Snapshots enable me to live that different life I had wanted since Illinois: the one lived by Auden and Spender and Isherwood in Germany or by the lovers Heinz and Chris in Portugal. Fortunately we have portraits that give us new ways of seeing him. In the portrait of Chris by Stathis, his first of a famous person, the black background seems to swallow the subject, but Chris defies the void with the force of his clear, all-seeing vision.[20] One eye is strongly lit and focused, the other is not. The photographer has depicted in his art the dual vision writers have seen in Chris's works. As Edmund White has written, Chris saw "close and far."[21] Chris is best known for his clear analysis of what was around him—Sally Bowles, or China in the 1930s, or Los Angeles in the 1940s, or Kenny in the surf. There is also a seeing beyond the present and the corporeal to the spirit of himself and us all, shared with us through his works on meditation and Vedanta.

If for me and for fortunate others there had been a physical nearness to Chris, his body must retreat and he must remain where we had first met him, in the various essences he created of himself in his own work and as he is reflected in the work of others. As Dan Clay wrote me, we may "live life differently for what Chris has given all of us." Joy now resides in our memories of Chris and our times with him, what Don recently called "those wonderful bygone days." Our work now lies in what we can recreate of his life and influence, or what we might create through that influence, what he sparked us to do through his example of steady work, his support of others' work, and his bravery in coming out and living openly gay with Don.

Notes

1. The epigraph is from a lecture at UCLA, probably April 1965. Author's notes.

2. John Van Druten, *I Am a Camera,* in John Gassner, ed., *Best American Plays Fourth Series, 1951–1957* (New York: Crown Publishers, 1958), xvi. The recording is *Christopher Isherwood,* Columbia Literary Series, no date.

3. "Playwright Isherwood Conducts Writing Course," *UCLA Daily Bruin,* February 2, 1965, 3.

4. Notes by the author. It is unclear which lecture these were from, perhaps from one entitled "What Is a Novel?" given May 17, 1965.

5. Taken from transcripts of six lectures by Christopher Isherwood, given at

UCLA, April–June 1965. Transcripts in the Department of Special Collections, University Research Library, UCLA, hereafter referred to as Isherwood, *[6 Lectures]*. For an article about the class with quotes from Isherwood, see Russell B. Frizzell, "Isherwood: A Noted Author's Semester at UCLA as Regents' Professor," *UCLA Alumni Magazine* 39, no. 5 (May/June 1965): 10–12.

6. Quotations about Sally Bowles from the author's notes. The quotations do not appear in the transcripts, so perhaps the first one or two lectures were not recorded or transcribed. The discussions transcribed begin with the plays, leaving out the earlier works. On *F6*, Isherwood, *[6 Lectures]*, April 27, 1965, 12; on the arts, see May 4, 21.

7. Note by author. On homosexuality, see Isherwood, *[6 Lectures]*, May 11, 15–17; on Waldemar, May 18, 6.

8. Isherwood, *[6 Lectures]*, May 18, 1965, 7.

9. William P. Smith, "The Lotus Kick" [review of *Down There on a Visit*], *Commonweal* 76, no. 8 (May 18, 1962): 214.

10. For more background, see Dan Luckenbill, "Rex Evans (1903–1969): Memorabilia and Photographs from His Cabaret, Stage, and Movie Careers," *UCLA Librarian* 37, no. 3 (March 1984): 19–21.

11. Reyner Banham, *Los Angeles: The Architecture of Four Ecologies* (London: Allen Lane, 1971).

12. Edmund White, *The Beautiful Room Is Empty* (New York: Knopf, 1988), 199.

13. Photographs of the production appear in "Rape on Stage," *IN Magazine* 1, no. 1 (July 1969): 4–9.

14. Reproduced widely in, for example, *David Hockney by David Hockney*, ed. Nikos Stangos (New York: Abrams, 1977), 156.

15. Reproduced in John Lehmann, *Christopher Isherwood: A Personal Memoir* (New York: Henry Holt, 1987), unnumbered pages between 70–71.

16. Richard Stanley, "Christopher Isherwood: A Candid Exchange," *In Touch* 24 (July/August 1976): 82.

17. On "lover," J. Moriarty, "Christopher Isherwood: 'Love Is a Miracle,'" *Advocate* 142 (July 17, 1974): 38; on "queer," W. I. Scobie, "Christopher Isherwood: A Lively Exchange with One of Our Greatest Living Writers," *Advocate* 179 (December 17, 1975): 8.

18. From notes by the interviewer. Interviewer's collection.

19. Thanks given Isherwood *[6 Lectures]*, June 1, 1965, 15; other statement, May 4, 18.

20. The portrait, which appears on page 48 of this volume, is reproduced in Dan Luckenbill, *Sylvester & Orphanos* (Los Angeles: UCLA Library Department of Special Collections, 1990), 33.

21. Edmund White, "A Sensual Man with a Spiritual Quest: Christopher Isherwood," *The Burning Library*, ed. David Bergman (New York: Knopf, 1994), 87.

3 *Stathis Orphanos*

In the Blink of an Eye
Evolving with Christopher Isherwood

Christopher Isherwood has been a major influence in the development of two of my life's endeavors. He was the first author I photographed. Over a hundred have followed. The first book I published under the imprint of Sylvester & Orphanos was a limited, signed edition of *Christopher and His Kind* in 1976. Farrar, Straus & Giroux supplied the sheets; Don Bachardy created original art for our edition; and Max Adjarian, a fine binder for UCLA and the Getty Museum, hand-bound 130 copies of the book, 100 in raw Indian silk and 30 in leather. Chris and Don signed the colophon sheets, and with this elaborate first venture my partner, Ralph Sylvester, and I forged our firm. We have since published twenty-four books. Works by two Nobel laureates (Nadine Gordimer and Odysseus Elytis) are on our roster, as is the last work Tennessee Williams saw through publication. Because of Chris's involvement with us, Graham Greene, Gore Vidal, David Hockney, Paul Bowles, James Merrill, and Sir Stephen Spender all gave us works. They, along with other major authors, are now part of, as Gore Vidal once embellished, "your publishing empire." What is not an exaggeration, however, is that due to Christopher Isherwood we had an auspicious beginning, and for all that followed we are indebted solely to him.

I first photographed Chris in 1972, after having known him for five years. This was my first sit-down session with a celebrated subject, and a

43

milestone in my career as a photographer. Until then, I had shied away from photographing well-known people, assuming that their fame would overwhelm their portraits. Though I still believe this premise to be true, I have come to realize that intimidation, especially during those early years, was also a cause of my timidity. In any case, these assumptions, trepidations, cost me sessions with Dorothy Parker, my unlikely schoolmarm at a local college, and, while still in my teens, with Marilyn Monroe. I had been invited by an anxious, equipment-encumbered, young photographer to assist him on a closed set of one of her final films. He promised to let me take photos with my camera as long as I kept his cameras accurately metered and loaded with film. I relinquished both opportunities, and it wasn't until I photographed Christopher Isherwood that I was able to transcend my apprehensions.

My association with Christopher Isherwood began in the early 1960s, when I chanced upon a rather waterlogged copy of *Goodbye to Berlin* at a garage sale. I was inspired by the novel's clean, crisp style and by its vital, eccentric characters (their idiosyncrasies incisively conveyed), and within days I read everything of his that I could obtain, mainly from my local library. Much of his work was out of print, even some of the New Directions reissues of his early novels. Books that were not in the library, such as *Prater Violet* and *The World in the Evening,* I found in thrift shops— old paperbacks, dog-eared, sometimes split, and priced no higher than a dime.

At this time, I enrolled in a class at California State College at Los Angeles. It was titled "The Angry Young Men" and was being taught by a D. Parker. I had no idea that *the* Dorothy Parker would end up being my professor and that, during a previous semester, Christopher Isherwood had also taught there. The head of the English Department had arranged for celebrated writers to conduct classes, and for a few semesters the series was a success. Until, that is, some of the authors began to vilify the institution. Dorothy Parker was among the first to lob a volley. Her tenure was contentious from the start. She was disdainful of academics and skeptical about the curriculum and, especially, teaching modes that were in vogue at the time. She refused to analyze the works of the rebellious young men she had selected—Osborne, Pinter, Albee—and instead had us read from their plays during class time.

One student asked, "But, Miss Parker, don't you think that Albee's choice of naming George and Martha after the Father and Mother of our country means something?" To which she replied, "I have no idea. I just like his cadence—and his ear." Students complained that they were not being taught. Though by now a fragile old lady, with a tremor and a deceptively beleaguered demeanor, Miss Parker was still a formidable foe. There was strife in the class, and aptly targeted students began receiving Parker barbs.

Her discontent became quite well known. During an interview with the *Los Angeles Times* she was told by the reporter that the school was erected over unstable ground, that its buildings were sinking a few millimeters a year, and that within a hundred years or so the entire college would disappear into the tar-pitted bowels of the Los Angeles basin. Her response: "Not fast enough for me!"

I was quite taken with Parker's class and felt that, by refusing to interpret works, she demonstrated how writers sometimes assess the work of their peers, i.e., intuitively and by their "cadence." For my final, I wrote a quick piece on Albee and included, unsolicited, my own story based on a boyhood experience during a trip to Greece. Miss Parker gave me an undeserved A+ on the Albee piece, written in the hallway just prior to the class, and bestowed a rare invitation to her office to discuss the story, which I had labored over. She advised me to expand it into a novel. Later, when she saw my work as a photographer, she offered to sit for me with her poodles. I procrastinated. Within weeks, her husband, Alan Campbell, died, and she moved back to New York.

Christopher Isherwood's *A Single Man* was based partly on his experiences teaching at the same institution. When I told a student who had taken both writers' classes that I regretted having missed Isherwood's, he suggested that, since Chris had been exceptionally congenial, particularly with students, I should call him. He was listed in the Santa Monica telephone book. I finally contacted Isherwood after two years. Over the phone I expressed my admiration for his work and hoped that I could meet him one day. He offered to inscribe my books, which now numbered dozens of hardbound first editions, and told me to bring them by whenever I was in the vicinity. Less than two weeks later we had our first meeting.

Much has been written about how youthful Chris appeared, even well into his seventies. Though one could detect, even into his eighties, a semblance of the Isherwood depicted in photographs from his Berlin days, there was a wizened quality to him as well. His face was tanned and lean but was also quite lined. It was this venerable Isherwood, peering from beneath a cascade of white brows, that I would eventually capture in my photographs. Years later, when I showed Graham Greene one of the portraits, he commented that it was the only photograph of his cousin that he had ever seen in which Chris did not look like a schoolboy.

By the time I met Isherwood, I had already completed the Greek novel Dorothy Parker had encouraged me to write and was working on the final draft of a novel set in Los Angeles. Harold Ober in New York and David

Higham in London became my agents. There were many close calls with
publishers but no takers; and, though the Ober Agency retained me as a
client for quite a while, I never submitted anything to them again. It wasn't
until I had known Chris for a while that I spoke to him about my writing.
I had pretty much given up being a novelist. Still, he asked to read one of
the manuscripts, and I gave him the Los Angeles one, which I had written
in just three weeks. I don't believe that he liked it very much, though he
commented favorably on the second half and on my ability to make a
relationship between two disparate characters credible. He suggested that
I revise the entire novel from first person to third, and he confessed that
he wished he had written all his novels in the third person. He also revealed that he regretted allowing New Directions to combine *Goodbye to
Berlin* and *The Last of Mr. Norris* into *The Berlin Stories,* a delineation
that was not only incorrect but also impugned the works as individual
creations, as novels.

During the months that followed, he was always willing to see me, to
sign my ever-expanding Isherwood collection, and even donated several
rare editions from his own library. Review copies, foreign editions, and an
occasional author's copy, bound in leather by the publisher, joined my
own scarce English firsts. By the time Chris died in 1986, he had signed
over five hundred items for me, the rarer books bearing full-page (or
longer) inscriptions.

Greed sets in when an author is so accommodating—and guilt too. As
brash as I was, bringing him boxes full of books to sign, he, in turn, was
obliging. Chris must have noticed my shame, for he would disarm it by
reiterating that having so many editions of his books amassed in one place
was beneficial to him as well. On several occasions this indeed proved to
be the case. When the BBC dispatched an English crew to his Santa Monica house to film a documentary on Isherwood after Berlin, a full array of
my rare English editions was depicted in the film, each tome leisurely
zoomed to full-screened grandeur. Because Chris possessed very few copies of his own early books, many of mine were essential for illustrating the
film, including a rare separate edition of *Sally Bowles,* a first issue (salmon
colored) of *The Memorial,* and a pristine copy of *Goodbye to Berlin,* which
was exceedingly scarce due to the destruction caused by the blitzing of
London during World War II. When Bernardo Bertolucci was interested
in reading *Down There on a Visit* for a possible film, Chris sent him to me
for an Italian edition of the book, which he borrowed and returned in
perfect order. Several journalists, needing to research out-of-print Isherwood articles or prefaces, were also put in touch with me; even after Chris
died, Don Bachardy borrowed my Random House first edition of *Goodbye
to Berlin* to be reprinted in *Where Joy Resides.* The New Directions reissue

of *Goodbye to Berlin,* still in print as part of *The Berlin Stories,* had textual differences from the first English and American editions, and Chris had never been content with them.

I first met Don Bachardy during one of my early visits to Chris in Santa Monica. Don had been swimming at a nearby beach and was returning home as I arrived. He wore only a skimpy black bathing suit with a towel draped around his neck. His wet hair, prematurely gray, streaked the side of his face. He was slender, well built, and had muscular arms and legs and a tapered abdomen. Even after seeing many photos of a younger, equally handsome, Bachardy, I still believe that at this more mature time in his life he was in his full flowering. He was in his early thirties.

Chris suggested to Don that he draw me, which in turn prompted photo sessions with both of them. If they would sit for me—I got up enough nerve to suggest—then I would pose for Don. On a subsequent visit I showed them samples of my work and received favorable comments, and we set up our appointments. I believe that Don drew me first, prior to their individual sessions with me. There were two portraits, in ink, pencil, and wash—a medium, with deftness in line and shading, that Don perfected and made his own. No one has ever done it better. I appeared intense in the first drawing and, after hours of posing, pensive in the second. Don let me choose one for myself, and I selected the second.

I photographed Chris first, using only one roll of 120 film and my Hasselbladt. The session produced a single, definitive, photograph of which I am very proud. I judge my photographs as if someone else had taken them, and, in truth, I recall very little of an actual shoot. Impulsively, I used a close-up lens inches from Chris's face and focused on that legendary camera eye. Though elusively reflective, it sees all without judgment, the very eye that had focused on the foibles and eccentricities of friends and foes and, for decades, transformed them into traits that shaped such memorable characters.

I was elated with the result of this, my first celebrity sitting. Previously, by concentrating on snapping my Hollywood chums, mostly young actors, I had attained enough technical expertise with spontaneous, available-light sessions to facilitate all my future endeavors. I used everything I had taught myself about photography, about not fearing the unknowns of setting, subject, and shine, traveling without lights, trusting the patience of sitters—all of it—within this one session. Chris was compliant, even as a 150 mm Hasselbladt lens extended perilously toward an eye; compliant, as I fumbled with meters and lens; compliant, as I dealt, at times despairingly, with the tedium of focusing, the maddening mechanics of hand-set gauges; compliant, as I wrapped him in black cloth and spun him round and round to facilitate a light that, streaming harshly through a large win-

Stathis Orphanos: *Christopher Isherwood, 1972*. Photograph. Copyright © Stathis Orphanos. Used by permission.

dow, etched his face with the tarnish of his years. The stark lone result from that session is still one of the best portraits I have ever taken. Chris never commented on it, though I believe that Don is fond of it. It is a favorite of authors I've photographed who may not like their own austere portraits but admire similar ones of others.

Don was next. I took many rolls of him, and, though the effects were varied, they convey little of the real Don Bachardy, who is certainly more fervent and discerning than the impassive stranger I inexplicably captured. They are attractive portraits and, therefore, easy to appreciate, as I appreciate his handsome, but equally impassive, second portrait of me. Still, with his first—rather ardent—depiction, he succeeded in getting a more perceptive rendition of me than I ever did of him.

I saw much of Chris and Don during the seventies. As the years passed,

Stathis Orphanos: *Don Bachardy, 1972.* Photograph. Copyright © Stathis Orphanos. Used by permission.

I was invited to several dinner parties and to all of Don's art openings. Through them I met Dan Luckenbill, who mounted a definitive Sylvester & Orphanos exhibit at UCLA in 1990 and wrote the text for its sumptuous catalogue. My photographs were included in both the exhibit and the catalogue, and the entire affair was a momentous occasion for our firm. For the catalogue, Graham Greene wrote an introductory piece,

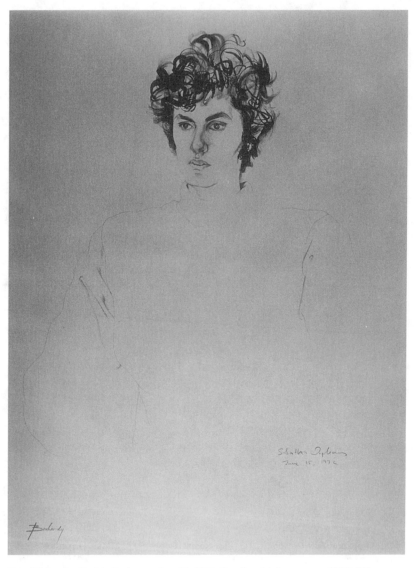

Don Bachardy: *Stathis Orphanos, June 15, 1972*. Pencil and ink on paper. 29″ × 23″.
Copyright © Don Bachardy. Used by permission.

50

Melina Mercouri, as Greek minister of culture, praised Ralph and me as publishers in a special tribute, and Julie Harris, Lizabeth Scott, and Esai Morales honored me as a photographer. What began with our edition of *Christopher and His Kind* and an initial photograph of its generous author had evolved into a major retrospective of twenty-four publications and a comprehensive display of my literary portraits.

Three memorable exchanges highlight my association with Christopher Isherwood. The first occurred in 1974, when he called me from the Vedanta Temple and asked if he could stop by for a few minutes. The temple was in the Hollywood Hills, and at that time I lived a few blocks away. When he arrived, he requested one of my copies of *Exhumations.* He sat at my desk, asked for a pen, and then proceeded to write at length on the endsheet. When he finished, he closed the book and, as he rushed away, told me that he had inscribed it with a poem that, composed many years before, he had committed solely to memory, but now wanted me to have. "For Stathis—here's a poem I wrote sometime in the 1930s." I have chosen to keep that poem to myself for all of these years. That I collected his books, "indefatigably," as he once put it, was not perceived by him as a superficial bond; it was what brought us together; it was what made it all happen.

Our second memorable exchange occurred when he asked me to drive him from his Santa Monica home to the Vedanta temple. Don had a prior appointment, and, due to a suspended license, Chris was prevented from using his car at that time. Whenever Don drove, Chris would lie across the back seat, his head resting on a couple of pillows, but with me he sat in the front. As I drove into Hollywood, Chris began to speak about Prabhavananda, his swami, and then, at length, about Vedanta. It wasn't long before I began to suspect that there was more to this request than just a ride, a realization that caused me to resist the seductiveness of his reflections, none of which I now recall, and then to reappraise, for the first time in years, the religion I was born into. Greek Orthodoxy is a denomination that, with spiritual *and* secular constraints, has become the nucleus of Greek American life. It is a denomination—domination—that I have been impervious to since childhood.

As we arrived at the center, Chris asked me if I wanted to come in and meet the swami. I have since been told that this was a rare invitation. I blurted out some excuse, and Chris, leaning over to give me a hug, whispered, "That's all right; you'll get it by osmosis anyway."

To present me privately to so venerated and shielded a religious leader was, perhaps, a perilous endeavor. I was already anathema in one Greek American community for a near catastrophe that occurred during my sole encounter with the Greek Orthodox equivalent of an eminent swami. When I was about eight and visiting relatives in New York, I was asked to substitute for an ailing altar boy. I had never participated in a service before, and, as the liturgy droned on, I accidentally allowed a large candle I had been holding to tip forward. I inadvertently set fire to the gold-threaded vestment of Athenagoras, archbishop of North and South America, a cleric higher than any Catholic cardinal, and second only to the ecumenical patriarch of Constantinople, the "Greek pope"—a primacy that, having survived me, Athenagoras the First eventually ascended to himself.

Nevertheless, I regret not having met Prabhavananda and have often wondered if my life would have been different had I accepted Chris's invitation. Perhaps, this time, I would have been set ablaze—with a religious zeal that might have either consumed or liberated me.

It was about this time that Chris began to devote a significant share of creative energy to works dealing with Vedanta. And though *Ramakrishna and His Disciples* and *My Guru and His Disciple* are major Isherwood books, reviewers were not impressed. The general criticism was that Christopher Isherwood should be writing novels, not mystical treatises. There was ridicule, too, as epitomized by a scathing David Levine caricature, in the *New York Review of Books,* of Chris with Ramakrishna sitting on his head. Chris showed me the caricature. He was not amused. I don't believe that he answered his critics directly, though he did respond in writing to a reviewer's reproach that, by embracing Vedanta, he was simply grasping at straws. "If that's the case," Chris said to me, "then these straws have kept me afloat for decades."

Our final exchange occurred a few days before Chris died. Julie Harris had spent an afternoon at his bedside and phoned to tell me that the end was near. I called Don and was invited to visit Chris for the last time. Ralph and I spent nearly two hours with them both. By now a mere shell of himself, Chris lay on his back. He did not talk but seemed alert. Don sat beside the bed and presided over what quickly evolved into a colloquy about Greek sailors, American marines, and military pursuits in general. There was much laughter, more from Don and me, less from Ralph, and none from Chris, who remained attentive but immobile. Was he in pain? There was not even a sign of mild discomfort, nothing of what was captured by Don in his remarkable final drawings. Toward the end of our visit, Don left the room to answer the telephone. It was a lengthy call, and Chris became agitated. I asked him if there was anything I could get him. Without much movement, he gestured toward a bottle of orange juice. Don had been feeding him toast, and, as I held the bottle for him, he managed to drink it, as he had eaten, without raising his head. That he did not choke I found extraordinary. I asked him if there was anything else I could do for him, and he answered, in a surprisingly powerful voice, "No."

I now believe that he was in pain, that his stolid demeanor and that single, strong, response were meant to assuage emotions during what could have been a dire final meeting. The wanton talk, too, was a diversion, initiated by Don for Chris's benefit. If a recalled vision of amenable Greek sailors, loitering in luminescent summer whites within the secluded thickets of an Athenian park, was enough to temper, even slightly, the agonies of a dying man, then I was happy to evoke erotic images of past encounters to console him.

When it was time to leave, I bent to Chris, kissed his brow, and ran my hand through his hair. I caught his glance and paused. He stared at me and then, with four distinct blinks, opened and closed his eyes. The emphatic resolve expressed by this gesture—the intense contortion of the face, the total release, repeated four times—convinced me that he was signaling something to me and, thereby, conveying an enigmatic transcendental clue that, though incapable of being *comprehended,* was somehow *fulfilled.*

When I related this to a skeptical Gore Vidal, who had last visited Chris about the same time, he assailed my deduction with a disdainful drawl: "He was just clearing his vision!—Nothing more!" Years later, I asked Don, who had been present, what he thought. Without hesitation, he agreed that Chris had beckoned something mystical to me.

Chris died shortly after our final meeting. There was no funeral, no memorial service. His body was donated to UCLA for medical research. This, however, was not the end of Christopher Isherwood in my life. Within days of that last visit, I began to experience a surge of energy, a vitality that, coupled with a renewed incentive, made it possible for me to return to my own endeavors, which I had been neglecting. I was able, for the first time since the formation of Sylvester & Orphanos, to work diligently at the firm and return to my own artistic quests. Between publications, I set off on a series of photo odysseys across America, resulting in a major share of my work, and I have not stopped taking photographs since. I also completed a trilogy of related novellas, and I have not stopped writing since. I am certain that Chris is responsible, that his final farewell to me was charged with an arcane power that transformed my very existence.

Drafting this memoir a decade after his death, I still find it difficult to comprehend my last moments with him, let alone to relate them. Suffice it to say that his charge is still with me.

4 *Michael S. Harper*

Ish circa 1959–1963

Memories are old identities.
W. B. Yeats

I met Christopher Isherwood in the fall of 1959 in a class he taught, "Literature between the Wars." The class met on Tuesday and Thursday mornings, and I was working graveyard shift at the downtown terminal annex post office. That meant I had to make an early decision to attend class or to collapse for the next tour of duty. It became clear to me, sitting in the back of a tiered classroom in the music building, that "Ish" was no traditional teacher. Our reading list began with *Goodbye to All That* by Robert Graves and included a smattering of Wilfred Owen, Edward Thomas, Rupert Brooke, and Siegfried Sassoon. There was no mention of Ish's father, who died in World War I in 1915.

Ish, in and out of the classroom, never bored you. He was excellent "savage" company, for a pacifist. Watching a living writer, an Englishman, reading from the assigned texts with an impish comic bantering was a show in itself. His costume was usually penny loafers and a woolen tie worn with a workshirt. Ish was quick on his feet with the zest of an athlete about him. He maneuvered his bushy eyebrows in expressive wit encouraging us to enter the give-and-take of the classroom. Students of that day were in awe of celebrity and, in the main, did not read books unless they were assigned. None would admit they had not seen the film *I Am a Camera,* and though *The Berlin Stories* was on a reserve list in the campus library, copies were hard to come by.

On the whole Ish did not assign his own books, but he did bring his famous friends to class. He would spring them on us with little fanfare. We saw a procession of the likes of Aldous Huxley, W. H. Auden, Stephen Spender, Gerald Heard, Charles Laughton, Elsa Lanchester, and others as part of the hidden agenda of Ish's first semester at L.A. State College. Auden appeared in slippers, deeply hung over, and Ish called on me to address him. Fortunately I had read *The Shield of Achilles* and so was able to ask him to recite "September 1, 1939," and he complied without text and recited his poems for forty minutes. For me, a fledgling English major who'd just transferred from L.A. City College, Ish was a bonanza. I was a failed premed student with 120 units of core classes in everything, and I was to discover later that Ish had studied an abbreviated medical program in London before going to Germany and that he never considered himself any kind of student.

I did not call Ish "Ish" to his face. In the casual manner of a would-be aristocrat, he insisted that we call him Chris, which helped put his students at ease. "Ish" was for me a secret allusion to Ishi, a lone Native American, the last member of his Oroville, California, tribe, and an allusion to Ish's emigrant status.

With Ish you were equals, particularly if you wanted to become a writer, even if you didn't know it yourself yet. I can't overemphasize how important "equality" was for me in the late 1950s, or as Robert Lowell called them, "the tranquilized fifties." I was trying to write one-act plays, mostly involving characters who spoke the idiom of jazz as a shorthand and set in the places I knew best: jazz clubs, the airmail section of the post office, the locker rooms of the city swimming pools, and the library. I wrote these efforts on the bus and trolley en route to the L.A. State campus, a two-and-a-half-hour jaunt from La Brea Avenue through downtown and East L.A. and along City Terrace.

After much hesitation, I made an appointment with Ish and told him I was trying to write plays. Encouraging my work, Ish would pop up from his seat, glide to the window, turn, and say, without any hesitation, "You should send this to *Encounter*." I did not know the magazine, or that Spender was the editor, but that did not deter Ish. When I was courageous enough to send a sample (with return postage), I never told Ish about my reception, even though I often got these efforts back in a week or two.

I read Ish's collaborations with Auden—*The Ascent of F6* in particular—and I remember to this day the closing song by Auden, also known as "Stop All the Clocks." Ish loaned me many books, including plays by Arnold Wesker, essays by D. H. Lawrence, and novels by William Golding published in England but not in America. I wish I had the marginalia from Ish's copies of these books. Although papers were expected in his literature classes, if Ish knew you wanted to be a writer, he paid little attention to deadlines on assignments, thinking it more important that you focus on your own writing.

In my final year at L.A. State, I felt like a fish out of water because Ish's contract had not been renewed, and the best student prose writer, my friend John Stewart, left for Stanford's Writing Program. Stewart, a Trinidadian living on the margins of campus, wrote a story called "Blues for Pablo" which was published in the campus literary magazine. John took the title from an album we cherished, Miles Davis's collaboration with Gil Evans, *Miles Ahead!*

In January 1961, I was ready to leave for Paris when I received a draft notice in the mail. Paris in the sixties was for me what Berlin in the thirties was for Ish. I had hoped to take what little I had saved and go to Paris like so many musicians and artists had before me. I was determined not to go into the Army, and so I decided to continue my student deferment by going to graduate school. Two of my writing teachers at L.A. State, novelist Wirt Williams and poet Henri Coulette, were alumni of the Writers' Workshop at the University of Iowa. They both agreed to recommend me to Paul Engle's workshop, and they suggested that having a recommendation from Ish would be a coup.

My application was a hurried affair, but I called Ish at home and told him the story, and he came quickly to my aid with a handwritten letter. Though I would find out later that Ish did not believe in writing programs of any sort, he kept this from me at the time in order not to discourage my efforts. He invited me to lunch at MGM, where he was freelancing. This was the first image I had of how frustrating an artist's role can be when he is at the mercy of a director or a producer. Ish kept his cards close to his vest in the area called "the movies."

During my drive to Iowa City my car broke down in Needles, California, so I returned to L.A. and flew to Chicago and then to Iowa City on Ozark Airlines—the mail run. Later I met Paul Engle in his office in a temporary Army barracks near the river. Soon I met poet Philip Levine's Asian-American student, Lawson Inada, who had a better jazz collection than I did. I shared an apartment across from the police station with a black medical school student. I was taking six units of writing—fiction and poetry—and one seminar in contemporary fiction. Philip Roth taught several of my courses, and in the fiction seminar I wrote a report on Golding's *Lord of the Flies*. I was the first volunteer in a class full of critics, and after I read my twenty-page paper, I waited for criticism, which I did not receive. All Roth wrote on my paper was "B−" in the margin. So I made an appointment with him, and he accused me of plagiarizing my paper. I thought of Ish and his lending me the English editions of Golding.

Since the only criticism of Golding published in America to date was in the *Partisan Review* in 1957, and that issue had been stolen from the library—the same one that contained James Baldwin's "Sonny's Blues"— Mr. Roth and I agreed to disagree about what I knew and didn't know. In his fiction workshop, I turned in a novella which was heavily influenced by James Joyce's *Portrait of the Artist as a Young Man* and *Dubliners,* and Roth accused me of writing a pornographic novella. Case closed.

Roth's reading list included Giovanni Verga, Isaac Babel, Pierre Gascar, Isaac Singer, and of course Golding. I found I'd read most of his list even though I was not an alumnus of the University of Chicago, and I had Ish to thank for this. I told Ish in a postcard that things were moving along, but I did not tell him about Mrs. Lemme, the black woman who rented rooms to black musicians on the road: that Iowa had no fair housing laws, that students from SNCC were raising money for their Freedom Rides, that I could not hold hands with classmates at Iowa singing "We Shall Overcome." I told him none of this.

I flew home for the summer, took and passed a lifeguard exam, and began my job patrolling the traffic in the Coliseum swimming hole, the site of the 1932 Olympiad, licking my wounds from the workshop experience and biding my time. Late in the summer I called Ish, and he visited my parents' house on Orange Drive. He entered our home in his patrician ease, and he and my mother hit it off immediately. They had tea, and he admired my mother's plants. My mother did not tell Ish about her ambivalence toward the English clergy, which stemmed from the tales told to her of her grandfather's efforts to raise money for the poor in Bermuda, but she did tell him of her love for John Galsworthy and the Brontë sisters. Ish was relaxed and enjoyed himself while I gnashed my teeth. Ish asked my mother whether I would return to Iowa City despite the problems with Roth. My mother answered matter-of-factly, "Of course. With you behind him, what does he have to worry about?" My mother was just as patrician as Ish. My father later said that L.A. State had finally paid off. "A great writer came to my house to see my son off to his nemesis."

Winter 1962. I was back at L.A. State enrolled in a certificate program for training junior college instructors and also completing another master's degree in English. I needed some kind of job while I was in school. The options were limited: I took the civil service exam to qualify for county work. Another option, if one had aptitude in math and science, was to work in the private sector, in particular in the aerospace industry. In almost every case, I tested higher than the job required, and in almost every case, I was accused of cheating and was retested. I usually made a higher score the second time. At job interviews, I would be told I was on the waiting list or that I had failed the physical, even though I had been a city lifeguard over several seasons. I was in touch with Ish through phone calls and an occasional lunch. When we discussed my situation, Ish immediately saw the possibility of a screenplay—a series of short scenes which heightened the comedy of what I told—and he always saw equivalences to his own experiences which he shared in cryptic asides. Whenever we went to lunch, Ish paid. I did not discuss with him *Giovanni's Room* or Proust.

Some of the books Ish recommended to me—the Ramayana, the Upanishads, E. M. Forster's *Aspects of the Novel,* D. H. Lawrence's *Studies in Classic American Literature*—did not seem translatable to the American context because they did not take the subject of race into account. Race was ever present on my mind, in the literary context especially after reading Melville's *Benito Cereno,* Twain's *Huckleberry Finn,* and Ellison's *Invisible Man.* I had borrowed Irwin Swerdlow's copy of *Invisible Man,* with Ellison's inscription, written while Swerdlow taught at Dillard University. Swerdlow had helped me make connections between European serfdom and American slavery in a course called "The Epic of Search." He had been connected with the Provincetown Players and Eugene O'Neill and shared the same draft board with Richard Wright in Brooklyn. Swerdlow was more flamboyant in dress than Ish himself, and I could quarrel with him about O'Neill's *All God's Chillun Got Wings* and T. S. Eliot's negative review of the play. When I told these stories to Ish, he would laugh because he was no admirer of "Possum."

Ish was an elusive animal—outsider, stranger, interloper—especially in conversation. He was always outside of the Establishment in our minds, mostly because he had to live by his wits, earn money, and keep a steady exposure to the movie business that I thought he despised. He hid mysteriously behind his accent.

As a professor, Isherwood had a strong but varied impact on a wide range of students. Among them was Stephen A. Black, who later taught nineteenth-century literature at Simon Fraser University in British Columbia. He read all of Ish, and we discussed Ish's various narrative strategies and what Black called Ish's style of "failed disclosure." Fred Berwick, a classmate of mine in American literature, later taught at UCLA and once interviewed Robert Hayden. Gene Woods left L.A. State to work in publishing. L. Ronald St. John also went into publishing, and he read and collected Ish's novels and plays. John Stewart went on to Iowa and eventually earned a doctorate in anthropology at UCLA. Stewart has written about the ideology of race and white supremacy from a global perspective. It was John Stewart who wrote to me that Ish was the only one of our teachers at L.A. State who treated us like men with no sense of condescension.

I was writing at this time about West Venice coffee shops, bistros, the Renaissance Club on Sunset (which had the best matinee jazz features), and Shelley's Mannehole, a club co-owned by the jazz drummer Shelley Manne that was one of the few places where interracial folks were welcome. These pieces were little vignettes that I prepared as I entered, by necessity, the teaching world. My first teaching appointment was at City College in Los Angeles (LACC), on the Vermont Avenue campus of L.A. State, the scene of many of my earlier lost educational battles. The most memorable was with my zoology teacher, who told me that I would never qualify for medical school and should not take another more deserving person's place in the premed program. I taught remedial composition to immigrants who needed to become proficient in English to hold a job or get promoted, and I had them write about their personal histories in an effort to help validate their identities. Ish had taught me that identity American-style was always about the "who" and that this was every American's problem. As an Englishman, Ish had a thousand years of tradition in literature to buttress his exiled identity in America. But we did not talk about that.

Nor did we talk about Ronald Reagan as governor, the Black Panthers in Sacramento, San Francisco State College student protest, S. I. Hayakawa, or the free speech movement at Berkeley, all of which I witnessed. Ish refused an invitation I made to him to speak at Contra Costa College. He refused, I suspect, because the money was paltry and he was busy commuting to UC Santa Barbara. Much later, in 1976, I sent Ish a postcard from London, while I was part of a bicentennial exchange with Britain. I had bought postcards at the National Portrait Gallery—one of Ish and one of Auden—and sent Ish his own image, circa 1936. At a London reception at New Zealand House in the middle of Hyde Park, I thought of what Ish had done for me. He couldn't know that I would visit the moors (his favorite site in England), stay at the White House in London (without knowing it was a cathouse for oil moguls), or study the annals of the slave trade in Bristol which allowed me to trace my great-grandfather's steps while he campaigned for funds for the AME church. I sent Ish his postcard with my timely London greeting; the postcard of Auden I sent to Hayden, who had studied with Auden at Michigan in the early 1940s.

In 1972, I won an award from the National Institute of Arts and Letters. Ish was an honorary member, so I hoped to see him at the annual event. But I was told Ish never attended these meetings. Years later I was invited to L.A. State, now called California State University at Los Angeles, to give a talk and receive an award. I visited the English Department and saw that one of Don Bachardy's portraits of Ish was featured in the outside office, right next to one of Dorothy Parker by Bachardy. I was a student in the first class Parker ever taught, on popular literature, in 1962. On the first day, she stood birdlike and frozen, unable to speak. After a few minutes, I approached her, put my arm around her, and told her we would wait until she was ready. Before long she found her voice. The portrait reminded me of her as a teacher, but it also reminded me that upon her death she had left all of her money to Martin Luther King Jr.

A portrait of Ish for me is about support, order, and grace. For aspiring writers Ish always had a ready answer: Keep writing! Sooner or later you will have the text they might need. This was optimism of a very high order and came from Ish's spirit of adventure and the need to record that he personified for his charges, known and unknown. Ish holds a singular place in my career. He gave me an appreciation of the craft and art of "making," in the Greek sense of the poet as maker. As a comic writer Ish was deadly serious in his observations, his recall of puns and slights, and his mastery of detail in camp. I believed in Isherwood because he believed in me.

5 *Michael S. Harper*

Reading from Isherwood's Letter circa 1959–1963

March 21. Saw Dr. Lichtenstein again yesterday evening. He assures me
that my scar is healing normally. Many small nerves are cut through
when the flesh is cut, and these are bound to hurt for a while. So I should
just ignore the whole thing—and I will try to.

Last night we went to a goodbye party for Terence Rattigan, given by
Hecht-Hill-Lancaster—more specifically by Hill, who is having an affair
with Rita Hayworth. Because of this affair, apparently, Hayworth has
been forced on to poor Terry as one of the stars in the movie version of
his *Separate Tables.* She is somewhat spectral, now, but still, in a grim
way, beautiful. Judy Garland looked like a cook, in a small white glittering round pie-shaped hat and a black dress that didn't fasten behind,
because she's so fat, and that looked as if it might have come from the
Goodwill. Lenore Cotten talked and talked and the two coons from Trin-
idad sang, while one of them scraped a gourd with a nail until all but
the strongest nerves were ready to snap. Cedric Hardwicke's young wife
insisted on sharing my chair, as she told me that Hardwicke was the kind-
est of husbands but that she has more fun when he's away.

March 1957, *Diaries* 1:687

In a crammed postcard, during the bicentenary
exchange with Britain, I sent you word

of yourself, around 1936, as a memento to your goodly
instruction, in what could not be taught:

the landscape of the Brontës' Moors, Sussex as an outpost,
"the White House" in elegant London

as a whorehouse, for the Arab oil-moguls
(T. E. Lawrence on his motorbike over country lanes)

a reading list of mostly friends whom you brought to class:
Huxley, Auden, Spender, Heard, Laughton, Lanchester

as a platoon to vestrypacifism
encampment on Adelaide Drive

the impish vestigial laugh and pain in the gut
you disguised most ably when in company with Wystan

private vanities on the subject of Korea and Vietnam
the test of infantry hymns and foxholes between the wars

in Germany: pennyloafers and woolen tie with workshirt
as a costume of the writer who has not written

lunches in the canteens of 20th, MGM, Warner Brothers
and the spread of forbidden fruit at Trader Vic's

Fred Shroyer's TV novel class with you as guest of honor
one-act plays in which the agents were musicians

who grew up on the Watts local, worked at Terminal Annex,
discussed Chopin and Debussy on the graveyard shift

of airmail, special delivery, and helicopter to LAX
the swimming pool in which the blackbird lifeguard chastens the
    metronome-

count in laps of the LAAC corpus of the Olympic team,
varsity across the street from USC and Exposition Park

and learning to serve at some distance as Pancho Gonzales
gave "free lessons" to the "colored" kids at Rancho Park

next door to the Coliseum: All-City Track Meet the race rituals of the
    Department of
Recreation and Parks telling jokes about "coons"

falling off diving boards onto concrete and not breaking
their skulls, and not learning to butterfly either

the Renaissance Club on Sunset Boulevard, where Dexter Gordon,
just out of Chino, came in to play the Sunday matinee

"with his ax and porkpie hat" in imitation of the President, Lester
    Young:
Dexter Gordon in the joint because of a stash of Marijuana

which he inhaled; years of inhalation from Anniston, Alabama army
    barracks
until Lady Day saved him from race riots with her song.

When you deliver newspapers in the white section of Baldwin Hills,
the *L.A. Times* becomes the paper of editorial delight

subscribers would meet your speeding car, downhill,
to pluck the ads and headlines from beneath the sprinklers

which were sprocketing their veiled spray over the grass,
rhododendrons, jacaranda, geraniums, Japanese gardeners

and at the end of the paper route, the sunrise, at the reservoir
and some fixation on the sprawl of L.A. going west, to the ocean

when, on bright days, you could see Catalina:
no paper allowed to be wet from grass or sprinkle

no actresses allowed to talk with Rochester
who kept Jack Benny in stitches, whose son,

Billy Anderson, made the '48 Olympic team as a hurdler,
who played defensive back for the Chicago Bears,

who ran the high school hurdles at Dorsey High School
in combat boots; who could broadjump from a standing

position over 20 feet, who highjumped backwards,
who was a terrible student made eligible by his grace alone

remember Howard Rumsey's All-Stars in Hermosa Beach
the Pasadena Playhouse, reading at Huntington garden archives

Swerdlow's O'Neill seminar, "Epic of Search" class,
his lending his signed copy of *Invisible Man,* a tour at Dillard

how he was in the draftline with Richard Wright,
in my hometown, Brooklyn; Calamus Club in *Invisible Man*

how James Baldwin wrote *Giovanni's Room,* on Bessie Smith records
"artists are here to disturb the peace" he said

introducing Malcolm X to the congregation on Central Avenue
the sickness of the westside, for negroes, was gerrymandering,

the Santa Monica Freeway, and the Watts Riot
which I predicted lifeguarding at Willowbrook, in Compton,

at South Park, the Watts Poetry Workshop, Bud Shulberg's
contribution, *not making Sammy run anywhere*

but to early publication and sacrifice
to the media; remember Faulkner's admonition about *Soldier's Pay*

while "on the dole" writing scripts, and your hatred
of the tab you were on keeping you from your own novels, Vedanta

and *solemn meditation* with the elements in the last search
unknowable essence of the Swami P.

You taught me the fables of William Golding on loan (in England),
refuted Philip Roth's accusation about voyeurism

loaned me Arnold Wesker's plays, fought over *possum*
in Coulette's *War of the Secret Agents*

fought Aristotle ("some men are natural-born slaves")
when black Alcibiades raised by Gilgamesh and Enkedu

after gangfighting in Peloponnesian Wars
white betrayal (all God's chillun got wings)

black assassination (the Emperor Jones)
the intellect betrayed in Milton's *Paradise Lost*

in Pico Police Station cellmate 33rd degree Mason
the career of the book now prison

to rescue the father as continuous bail
without the prism of *Black Orpheus* (the film)

the first act of liberation (*Benito Cereno*)

is to destroy one's cage—(*My Bondage and My Freedom*)
in jail, out of jail, or no damn jail at all.

6 *Robert Peters*

Gay Isherwood Visits Straight Riverside

In the spring of 1966, the appearance of Christopher Isherwood on campus for a fifteen-week stint as Distinguished Visiting Writer facilitated my shift from a heterosexual life (wife, four children, a cat) to the homosexual life I had craved most of my adult life. I was in my early forties, a tenured professor at the University of California, Riverside, publishing Victorian scholarship and writing poetry. When I proposed to my department that we invite Isherwood, the prospects seemed dim. Few of my colleagues read contemporary fiction, believing that almost nothing written since World War I (Joyce being the exception) matched up to the great nineteenth-century authors they taught and theorized about. Their wives, the brainier ones, were enamored of Isherwood's generation, adored Virginia Woolf and Katherine Mansfield, liked saying "W. H. Auden," and regarded Isherwood as a mainstream writer of much consequence. They all loved quoting Gertrude Stein's remark about a rose.

My wife was one of the enthusiasts, and I counted on her to convince other wives to work on their husbands to approve Isherwood's appointment. And there was some urgency, for no other candidates were forthcoming, and rather than lose the money offered by the dean of the school, who might send it over to the Citrus Research Station for their use, and aware of the prestige Isherwood might bring, the department invited him. There were no dissenting votes. Moreover, the English faculty believed that in order to attract students—Riverside was the least popular of all the University of California campuses—we needed to energize our writing courses, attracting students to continue as English majors. A trio of faculty wives with pretensions to being novelists and poets had assembled a dozen students, free spirits all, as a nucleus for fledgling authors. Isherwood, if he gave just one stunning campus address, would do much to illuminate this barely visible darkness. Though the handful of bizarre writing students would have preferred Jack Kerouac or William Burroughs, they liked the idea that an author of Isherwood's stature would be present to fraternize with them and to read their work.

My sponsorship of Isherwood was not without self-interest, for I was in the midst of struggling over a failing marriage and increasingly vexing homosexual urges. A few months before he arrived, Allen Ginsberg appeared for a reading and proved controversial. He had brought his lover Peter Orlovsky's feeble-minded brother along, positioning him on a thronelike chair in the midst of adoring, stoned hippies. Ginsberg's unwashed look, the Big Mac overalls, the long twisted black hair, and the chanting accompanied by finger cymbals proved arcane fare for Riverside's conservative academic souls. Most of the English faculty failed to show up, as, I might add, they failed to show up for Isherwood, in part because of homophobia. Isherwood, as one of my colleagues specializing in the work of French modernists observed, "will look conservative. We can't get too upset about that."

Though I had not yet met Isherwood, I had read most of his novels and saw him as a brilliant but conventional novelist who had been a witness to international crises and who was both anti-Franco and anti-Nazi. I had seen photographs of him in magazines and knew that he occasionally addressed gay groups. In his photos, he was always clad either in a suit or in a tweedy jacket with casual trousers. He was never without a tie. I revered him as a gay man who prospered in a homophobic world. Straights accepted him, and his books sold and were taught in modern literature courses. With a quiet ebullience, he moved through both straight and gay worlds.

"You see, Bob," he said during an early chat in his office, "I like wearing a suit and a tie." He laughed, raising his hand. "It's my uniform. And it has little to do with my being English and having gone to Cambridge." He was wearing a natty red wool tie sprinkled with silver diamond shapes. He saw his dress, and pointed to his tie, as a badge of entry into the realms of straights. As a political statement, he was saying that gays are nonthreatening. "You could take one of us home for tea with your grandmother."

"You are rare, Chris," I said. "I'd assume that homosexuals would continually have to face hostility and isolation."

He believed that if by subduing our image we could exploit the straight world, so be it. We need those editors, publishers, readers, and critics. Straights, excluding religious bigots, always seemed comfortable with him, and he'd been fortunate to have mainstream publishers in both England and the United States. It always delighted him to know that his books were read and discussed in colleges and universities. The success of *A Single Man,* the most overtly gay of his novels to date, particularly gratified him; if heteros liked the novel, they would modify and perhaps even abandon their homophobia. He was particularly keen to address fledgling college gay groups—to appear before them as a benign and positive force, possibly diminishing their regrets at being gay. He worried much, he said, about the plight of gay high schoolers with nowhere to turn for counsel and for positive images. "I don't even care," he said, "whether they read my books or not."

The following week, though reluctant to impose on his time, I approached him about reading my poems. Since no professional writer had so far seen them, I feared they were dreadful. Most were about the death of my son Richard; the others about the love affair I was having with Gary, a former student.

Christopher's desk faced a white wall. He swung his chair around to face me and the only window in the room, one with a view of a parking lot fringed with palm trees, beyond which rose the Box Spring Mountains.

"Have a seat, Bob."

I drew up the chair he reserved for advisees.

"You've got your work there?" He reached over for the manila envelope.

"I put these together last night. Bruce Leary, editor of *Empty Elevator Shaft* in San Francisco, is interested."

"Leave it with me," he said.

The following week, I met with Chris again. "I've read your poems," he said. "There's a lot to talk about. Can you come to Santa Monica Saturday? I'll treat you to lunch. There's a good French restaurant. And I want you to meet Don Bachardy. He's a painter, as much younger than I am as Gary is than you. You'll like him."

Chris took me to lunch at the Bellevue, on the corner of Santa Monica Boulevard and Ocean Avenue.

We were led to a secluded table for two near a window facing the street. Subdued French music wafted through the room now filled with merry upscale diners. The tables were spread with heavily starched lavender linen cloths. On each was a bulbous, transparent cut-glass vase, each holding a single yellow rose and a spray of baby's breath. Linen napkins, matching the tablecloths, were big enough to cover my lap.

Chris gestured for me to sit where I would have a view both of people passing in the street and of the well of the restaurant. "You'll see a number of older men here," he observed. "The place is very popular with queers." He laughed. "My guess is that these waiters can be had for a price." He shuffled his menu. "Oh, incidentally, the food's excellent. So have anything you want—my treat." He paused. "We'll start off with some wine. Red or white?"

"White, thanks," I said.

The menu was *très authentique* to upscale diners, including those who knew little more French than the students who failed to move past the *la plume de ma tante* level of high school French, yet loved feeling elegant. To accommodate my tastes, betraying my Wisconsin farm origins, I combed through the menu (managing the minimal French I was able to read) and found an approximation for what I assumed was good old pot roast . . . boeuf roti. I asked that it be well done. Chris chose prawns steamed in wine smothered with mushrooms, crushed garlic, and scallions.

We touched glasses. Chris appeared to study me, and I felt uneasy, but not in a sexual way. My timidity, I felt, reflected my feeling intellectually inadequate to this accomplished man. He had enjoyed friendships with Thomas Mann, Charles Laughton, and Stephen Spender, among others. No matter how much he seemed to like me—and he exuded warmth—I never felt totally at ease. Any effort I made to be clever in the sophisticated way of his fiction failed, and, lacking the necessary reach, I settled back, accepting my cloddishness.

"Your poems are good, Bob. They differ from your first set, 'Songs for a Son.' Less traditional, more like rock songs, especially those about Gary." He paused, smiling. "You are writing about yourself?"

I explained that Gary was still in my life and had spent a month living with me when my wife visited England. The ostensible reasons I gave for Gary's moving in were that he had no car, lived far from campus, and was a student needing help. Gary and I shared the same bed. I insisted to myself that my older son did not know what was going on.

"I'm wrestling with leaving my family, moving to Laguna Beach, and getting a divorce. Gary will probably remain in my life."

"I see, Bob. None of this is simple."

"I envy you, Chris. You convince me that a gay life can be something to celebrate rather than feel guilt-driven about. I'll always be grateful."

"I'm touched," he said, with a caution that I alone must make decisions. He would not presume to tell me what to do. I would like his lover, Don Bachardy, he said. Years ago Don, his brother Ted, and Chris played musical chairs. Chris had met Ted on Santa Monica Beach, had an affair with him, then met Don. They hit it off. He was only eighteen. He and Don remained lovers and partners until Chris's death.

"I wish you were at Riverside permanently," I said. "There's no colleague I can really talk to."

"What about Don Howard?"

A young and brilliant Chaucer scholar, Howard was a man of sardonic wit who skewered writers and colleagues as often as he admired them. His style of conversation was shaped by William Congreve, Oscar Wilde, and Gertrude Stein. He was, as I later discovered, tactfully gay, a fact Isherwood knew. Don eventually moved to Stanford, where in his forties he died of AIDS.

"Though Don and I swim together in the campus pool a couple of times a week, nothing overt is ever said."

"You don't write a book on Chaucer and teach medieval literature without developing subterfuges, academic and otherwise," Chris observed. "I'd guess that Don is toying with you—if you've shown him these Gary poems. . . . "

"He's read them and edited some of the overwritten lines. His own poems are more conventional, academic—"

"But you must feel a kinship with him?"

"I don't feel, though, that I can discuss these issues with him. He's not married and wouldn't understand the impact on one's kids and wife, no matter how wretched the marriage. He wouldn't be able to advise me on these."

"Well," he laughed, "I've never married either."

Then Chris said, "Let's assume that Don Howard is gay. As a professor in a good university, isn't he a model for young queers? He can charm the most homophobic colleague or faculty wife, and he's more intellectually astute than most of them. He comes to Los Angeles and has dropped by our house on occasion. If you tell him I told you any of this, I'll deny it!" He laughed and drank some wine.

Even though I felt doubtful about my own sexual sophistication, Chris tried to reassure me. "Sex pretty much should take care of itself. The mind, though, is tricky." He believed that some gays have a residual distaste for their homosexuality, one bordering on hate. "Do you see what I'm saying?" he asked.

"I think I do."

"If you do decide on a gay life, Bob, that will be an irretrievable choice. But keep writing. Of course, I'll keep an eye on your progress in both areas—I hope we'll have other visits." Touching my hand, he said, "We've gotten too serious." He shoved his plate to one side. "Now, how about some dessert. They have a splendid chocolate gateau topped with a fresh raspberry sauce."

Because of Isherwood's example, I no longer felt that all gays, no matter how successful as writers, actors, or artists, were automatically either alcoholics or social pariahs, incapable of finding a place for themselves in a homophobic world. Isherwood proved to me that one could be revered by both straights and gays. I admired the fact that his books, particularly *The Berlin Stories* and *A Single Man,* were successful and were taught in university courses. After knowing Chris, I was no longer so frightened of my homosexuality. I could, I felt, absorb the guilt over leaving my family. I still think of him often and remain encouraged by his loving example.

My Isherwood, My Bachardy

I can lay claim to no more than a footnote in Isherwood's biography, and I doubt that his current biographers will concede even this claim, but I stand behind it. Certainly, Isherwood was more than a footnote in my life, not much more, but what he was is worth noting, particularly since the portrait he creates of himself in his recently published journals renders his kindness to me unlikely. He mentions in his journal that "people bore me pissless," and he must have been remarkably pissless after meeting me.

It was uncharacteristic of me to ask to meet him in 1970 when I was in Santa Monica on other business. I do not believe in meeting writers, convinced that it is far better for readers to content themselves with texts and not contaminate their admiration with views of the imperfect author. Certainly I did not at that time know of his familiarity with movie stars and what I would have seen as his inevitable refusal to meet me, the nobody. I asked to see him because I had written a monograph on him for a series on modern writers the Columbia University Press was publishing (1970), and having little experience at that time of how bored one can become with studies of oneself written by young academics, I thought he might wish to discuss my monograph with me. Ah, youth, even at forty plus!

These days, I am often asked why I wanted to write a monograph on Isherwood, why he appealed to me as a subject, for the choice of whom to write about was mine. The monograph is out of print and unavailable; at least, I certainly hope so. I chose Isherwood for a number of reasons: I admired his writing, and particularly his use of what I called the "documentary" form; today it would, I suppose, be called a memoir. My monograph opened with the wonderfully declarative sentence: "Since Christopher Isherwood has been denied, or spared, the gifts of widespread fame or fashion, it is appropriate to begin with the pronouncement that he is the best British novelist of his generation." I went on to define "generation" narrowly enough, as those born in the twentieth century before World War I. This generation's experience of being just too young to fight in the war reverberated with me because, I now suspect, as a woman I too felt that I was somehow destined to miss the important action of my time: the modern feminist movement was just underway, and I was to become one of its oldest adherents.

I was attracted to Isherwood also by his admiration, which I shared, for E. M. Forster: "*My* 'England,'" Isherwood had written during World War II, "is E. M.; the antiheroic hero, with his straggly straw mustache. . . . While the others tell their followers to be ready to die, he advises us to live as if we were immortal. And he really does this himself, although he is as anxious and afraid as any of us, and never for an instant pretends not to be" (*Down There,* 162).

Isherwood was, moreover, associated in the public's mind with Auden, a poet whose work I relished and would quote widely in a detective novel I published (anonymously) in that same year.

But probably, above all, or so I now think, it was Isherwood's search for a spiritual life distant from English or American established religions, and the fact that he had found one, that propelled me into seeking him out.

That he and Don Bachardy consented to see me and Jim, my husband, marked a kindness that would continue over the years. When I think back at how I dropped my spiritual angst, like an unwanted female Chinese baby, at their feet, to have that bundle returned to me with grace and something close to understanding I, even at my advanced age, squirm with embarrassment. At the first meeting, however, I simply listened and admired. Isherwood and Bachardy had us to supper, which they barbecued on their terrace, and treated us with amazing generosity. Knowing little of California, I was dumbfounded to see, from that terrace, their view of a precipitous valley, and to learn that part of their front lawn regularly fell away.

At that dinner—fish and parsnips—Isherwood mentioned that he had worked on a movie, *Rage in Heaven,* with Robert Montgomery in which they had to contrive the plot to fit into the actor's rather mad conception of his role, but somehow I thought that was an unusual, possibly unique film engagement (*Diaries* 1:133–34). My ignorance and naiveté were due, in part, to the fact that we seldom went to the movies in those days, and that I have never had the smallest interest in acting as a profession. During subsequent conversation, I was not so much shocked as astonished to hear Isherwood remark to Bachardy that some man he did not like was a "cunt."

I knew, of course, that Isherwood was homosexual; I had said so in my monograph. Certainly he had claimed his homosexual status often enough, pronouncing the word in that wonderful English way which makes it sound like a rare achievement. But *Christopher and His Kind,* and the newly energized gay movement so soon to instruct us all, were still in the future. I, furthermore, was a simple creature, without prejudice or knowledge, content in the belief that the act of loving was more important than the sex of the object of one's love. If I sound too guileless to be believed, let me assure you that the innocence and naiveté of my genera-tion—those born between the world wars—to say nothing of our faith in authority, was immense. In later years, I was to meet a woman professor, only slightly older than myself, who had been married to (among others) a Frenchman to whom Isherwood had gratefully dedicated one of his books. This act of appreciation had terrified the Frenchman, so his ex-wife told me, because he feared to be thought homosexual like Isherwood.

I knew, also, that Isherwood did not like women, certainly not women who were neither young nor outstandingly attractive; that distaste was early evident in our meeting and was never to become less so. In my mono-graph I had quoted passages from J. R. Ackerley and Isherwood to show their almost identical disdain of women. In both paragraphs, men would enjoy an all-male society (in the spirit, no doubt, of the former Citadel and VMI), and women would be relegated to harems or breeding farms. Women, Isherwood's character declares in *Down There on a Visit,* are all Lesbians (capitalized), evoking chills of horror when portrayed by Ingres and such. Yet, I must have thought, he will not despise me because I have written about him. One groans at remembering. Isherwood was, in any case, fair-minded enough to recognize that it was ordinary middle-class women—the kind most likely to be despised—who had fought hardest against California's entrenched homophobia. Don Bachardy did not seem to share Isherwood's loathing of women; he had been, in his youth, an adorer of actresses, and he drew portraits of many women among his far more numerous male models. On that first visit, learning that Jim was a balletomane who had followed Balanchine's company from its earliest days in New York, Bachardy gave Jim sketches he had made of Balan-chine's dancers; we have those sketches still, framed and daily appreciated. We also have, hanging in our foyer, the original of one of the sketches of

Isherwood Don Bachardy made for a book jacket; Don sold it to me at an outrageously low price. In the picture, Isherwood's hands are on his cheeks, and the rest of the body is barely sketched in. Our children referred to it as the drawing of a man holding his own severed head in his hands.

It was at my meeting with Isherwood the day after the dinner in his study, where my monograph revealed itself in a grocery box filled with such tributes, that I asked him for spiritual help, or at least guidance to the help he had found from the Vedanta Society of Southern California and his admired swami. I don't know what he said to me—I remember best his remarks on D. H. Lawrence—but probably in despair he sent me on a visit to some sort of monastery in the desert some miles from Santa Monica. With Jim to navigate, we made the trip, of which I remember only a pleasant monk, clearly warned of our arrival, talking with us as we sat on a terrace. He pointed out a beautiful hummingbird, but I could see only a small brown creature. "Not that one," I remember him saying, "that's just a plain female; over there."

What on earth did I want from the monk, or the swami, or Isherwood? I had been brought up in a Christian version of Vedanta (as I now recognize) and was at that time in search of some spiritual sustenance. Isherwood said his swami was too old and frail to meet me (how he must have quailed at the very idea), but he suggested a man in New York who headed a Vedanta group. I went to see him and found him unsatisfactory; he kept speaking of famous writers who had consulted him, which I thought a kind of betrayal, and he was in no way the sort of man I could have honored at any time. Before meeting him, however, I had the only unearthly experience of my life. Waiting to cross the street to reach this man's building, a private house, I was surrounded, almost engulfed, by a foul odor. I looked about me; no one, nothing that could have caused it, was near. After I had left the man's presence I understood it had been a warning; where from? Nothing like this has ever happened to me again, nor, I am certain, ever will. I am of the earth, earthy, and distrust all so-called psychic phenomena.

Some years later, when Isherwood was delivering a talk on homosexuality to an audience at the Modern Language Association convention in New York City in, I think, 1973, I went to hear him. He was in his element, talking on his favorite subject, holding the audience spellbound. He wore red socks which, for some reason—his trousers may have been too short, and he kept raising his arms—were constantly evident and bespoke his mood. Afterward, I went up for a word with him and Don Bachardy, and they kindly went with me to an empty meeting room and tried to comfort me as I explained my sense of emptiness and purposelessness. They did not, of course, succeed—no one could have comforted me—but they did not spurn me, a memorable act of goodness which remains with me now long after my spiritual angst has melted away.

Through the MLA I was able, some years later, to repay Isherwood— although that puts it clumsily—to suggest to Isherwood by my actions my admiration for his work and his kindness to me. The Common Wealth Awards of Distinguished Services, financially generous and prestigious, were given annually in many fields, including literature. The MLA had been chosen by the trustees of the Common Wealth Fund, the Bank of Delaware, to select the recipient of the award in literature, and did so from 1980 until 1992, when their choice for the award was turned down by the Bank of Delaware. The bank expressed its dismay with many of the MLA's choices for the literature award, which were too often either not American, or not conservative (i.e., they were gay), among other complaints. The last two chosen by the MLA to receive the literature award were Aharon Appelfeld and Adrienne Rich, and the Bank of Delaware dug in its heels. They wished to give the award to James Michener—indeed, they did so— and the MLA refused to be a party to this.

Back in 1983, when I was about to become the next year's president of the MLA, the committee agreed with my suggestion that the award be given to Isherwood. Indeed, his name met with unanimous enthusiasm; the tradition was to honor the choice of the incoming president if possible. I called Don to tell him of the award and to ask if he thought Isherwood would accept it, but Isherwood himself answered Don's phone, so I had to speak with him about it. He said he was pleased because he hoped to accumulate enough money to leave Don, thirty years his junior, financially secure at his, Isherwood's, death. And so the two of them came to New York and received the award. It was presented, not by me, but by that year's president. (The following year I was to present the award to Eudora Welty, who was frail and could barely hold up the heavy, steel object given together with the money; there is a picture of us both more or less holding it.)

By the time of the Common Wealth Award, I had outgrown my need for Isherwood's spiritual counsel, but Jim and I did have lunch with him and Don in New York. Isherwood was clearly failing; Don had to tell him what to order, and I recognized in Don the situation of the Victorian wife, much younger than her husband, bound to him during the years of his slow, palpable decline. At lunch, they spoke of a tower being built in the valley so as to block their view, and the fight this was involving them in. It was not an easy meal to endure as we remembered the Isherwood we had first met. In the end, Don survived the last painful year of Isherwood's extended death by drawing him each day. These powerful sketches have been published as *Christopher Isherwood: Last Drawings* and are part of my complete Isherwood collection.

I saw Don Bachardy once again after Isherwood's death. I was in Los Angeles, researching my biography of Gloria Steinem; I had sent Don a postcard saying that I would be there. He invited me to have lunch with him at a restaurant Isherwood had liked, and we ordered the crab cakes Isherwood had favored. Don told me how, after Isherwood's death, he had read the journals recording their relationship from its beginnings; Don had not seen them before. Now, Don said, he lived with a man thirty years younger than he, as he had been thirty years younger than Isherwood. So he now had the experience from both ends, as it were, and from both his and Isherwood's account of it. I suggested that he write a book about this. In the end, he drove off in his Volkswagen, the same sort of car he and Isherwood had always driven, perhaps the same car, and that was the last I saw of him.

He and Isherwood had served, for no reason they could possibly have understood, any more than I understood it, as touchstones for me. To them I had explained my spiritual hunger, and they did not refuse to listen.

"Write It Down or It's Lost"
Isherwood as Mentor

I begin this essay at the period before I knew Isherwood, in the spring of 1977. My first novel, *Birdsong,* had been published quietly by Copper Beech Press at Brown University. Edwin Honig, the poet, publisher, and my friend, did me a great favor. I was promoting the book myself, sending copies to various people I knew, when I came upon a list of well-known writers and their addresses. I sent *Birdsong* to a number of these authors, omitting any whose works I was familiar with and didn't like, assuming they wouldn't like mine, either.

Soon after, I picked up my mail at the Oak Lawn Post Office in Dallas and received a postcard from Isherwood. I took the letters home and laid them on the table. Later my wife told me, "That's a wonderful comment from Christopher Isherwood. He's a very famous writer." I'd never heard of him before seeing his name on the list. I wrote, thanking him for his card and asking if we could meet since I was planning to visit L.A. Yes, he answered.

Several months later I flew to L.A. I was at a friend's apartment when I mentioned visiting Christopher Isherwood that evening. "Never heard of him," my actor friend said. "That shows what you know," his roommate said. "He's only one of the most distinguished writers in the world."

I had not read Isherwood's work when I drove to his home at the crest of a hill in Santa Monica. I got out of my rented car and walked along the driveway to the garage. A door opening to steps and leading to the house below was open. Along the steps grew a profusion of flowers.

I walked down the steps to the front door and knocked. The heavy door opened, and a short man with a big grin and blue eyes stood in front of me. "James White?" he asked. I nodded. He didn't invite me in or stand back. "You're going to become a great writer," he said. "I was just rereading your line, 'his head was absurd with love.' That's what love is, absurd." He laughed, then stepped back, and I was taken completely off guard. My nervousness increased. "*Birdsong* is going to make you famous," he stated.

Who was the man who told me this?

I was prepared for Isherwood to be reserved, even haughty, but not this. Isherwood's being so generous at that moment startled me.

He led me into the white stucco room hung with many paintings. Outside, the Pacific lay in clear view. "Have a seat," he said. "Would you like a drink?"

I watched him go out of the room. I have always thought he bought this house with the twenty-five thousand he made from *Cabaret,* which was based on *Goodbye to Berlin.* Liza Minelli, I've heard, made a million for her role. This house made more than either, worth two million probably in today's market.

I brought a list of topics to talk about in case I got tongue-tied. Instead, when Isherwood returned to the living room, I began to ask about the house and the view. Really, we were looking each other over, and who was I?

"You know I have in my date book that you were supposed to arrive at this time last week," he said. "We have dinner plans, but if you could go, I will call to see if we can include you. We're going to a studio preview of *A Death in Canaan* with Tony Richardson."

That evening I had my first glimpse of Hollywood, watching the picture at the studio, then listening to a discussion of the film by the vice president of the studio, Tony, Chris, Don Bachardy, and Tony's two daughters, who made more interesting comments than the vice president. Afterward we ate at Musso and Frank's and saw several stars who made a point of speaking to Chris.

I really don't remember the dinner or the dialogue. I strongly remember the sharp hill leading from where we parked afterward up to Richardson's house, which had been rented previously by *Deep Throat* star Lynda Lovelace. The walk was strenuous, and I had difficulty keeping pace with the seventy-five-year-old Isherwood. Again, he spoke, although this time in a drunken voice: "You're going to become a great writer."

After his death in 1986 I had the opportunity to read his private journals and turned to the entry for that afternoon, ready to be flattered. He made no reference to my novel, starting his entry with "The rather sweet James White came by today. . . ." This entry shows more about the nature of his journal than it does about Isherwood. He wrote his sharpest, perhaps harshest observations there, privately.

On the flight home, I thought, why not move to L.A.? I had a wife and five-month-old son, but recently had sold a commercial Nazi novel I'd co-written with Anne Reed Rooth. I decided yes, that evening. And when I returned to Dallas I joked with friends that I was going to move to L.A. and make Christopher Isherwood my closest friend.

Once I was living there, my situation reversed dramatically. The well-paying job my wife got initially was cut, and I decided quickly that I disliked being told that my film ideas were "soft." I hunted and, within a week of looking, was hired as general manager of two new French bakeries, in Westwood and in Fox Hills. The proprietor had owned a large business in Iran but had left the country and was opening these in L.A. I got the job because the franchiser's son, a student at Brandeis University, wanted to be a writer, and the franchiser liked the idea of saying that he *hired* writers.

Isherwood and I, in one sense, took the job together. He had told me he could find me "some writing job" in Hollywood, but I said no. Regardless, he was interested in my observations of the Iranian emigrés.

I told him, for example, that although they bought the businesses they counted on the Iranian situation changing at any moment, when they would return home, leaving the businesses. The man I worked for owned a car lot, too, which lost a lot of money. His sons went to auctions to buy the cars, and since every car was cheap compared to its relative price in Iran, they paid too much. The lot stayed full, as did the driveways of the various Beverly Hills homes he bought.

It would be difficult, I suspect, to know Isherwood well without being at a dinner party with him. I preferred just Isherwood and Don Bachardy and my wife with heavy drinking in an atmosphere where I think any of us could have said almost anything and it would have been accepted.

I have always thought that since Isherwood wrote much of the day, he was eager to go out in the evening. Don Bachardy, a disciplined artist, was in the same situation. In his journals, Chris complains about the dullness and frequency of parties, but he was drawn to company because of his curiosity about people. Often, Isherwood would express to me that he hadn't wanted to go or that the evening was wasted and he was on "rote."

I never saw Chris quiet at a party. He was very polite, as a host or guest. There was none of the bad-writer syndrome in him. Rather, he avoided hurting anyone's feelings. He put up with being personally bored. One evening at dinner at his house, a TV executive who didn't realize what she was saying leaned across the table and asked, "Tell me, Mr. Isherwood, do people still read your books?" She had no idea this was insulting. He responded immediately with "I hope so!" and contagious laughter.

He always would tell me who the other guests would be and mention their work. I think he would reread something by them beforehand if possible.

At the dinners with Isherwood I attended or hosted, both of us drank too much. It was not very unusual to have a scotch or two before dinner, a bottle of wine each at dinner, and an after-dinner drink. Several times the next morning, having gone to bed with the room swirling, I would wake up sick, hearing a ringing telephone. Chris was calling to thank me for the evening, his voice vibrant.

He told me that when he and Bachardy first lived together, they used an outdoor patio table in the dining area, and there they would eat crowded knee to knee—with Auden, Maugham, Garbo, whomever. By the time I knew him, the dining table was oak, with high-back matching chairs. A wall was mirrored on one side, and a glass door overlooked the Palisades and the Pacific behind where Chris sat.

Usually there were ten or twelve at dinner, a number I felt was awkward for conversation. But the guests included celebrities, which created immediate interest. I met many accomplished artists—writers, painters, directors, actors—at Chris's, but their best work was in the library or at the store, not in their conversation.

Isherwood's personality, however, was as interesting as the most accomplished of his work. When you met him you met Herr Issyvoo, which makes sense because he wrote extensively about himself. He was the narrator he used—observing, making comments to himself, but always proper. He never set limits upon what you could say—the more personal the better. He wasn't full of himself as Spender was or defensive as Tony Richardson was. At the end of my first and only evening with Spender, I asked him to sign a book and heard him whisper to Don, "What's his name?" I write this critically, aware I could do the same thing, but Chris couldn't have. He would know whose book he was signing.

The most critical Isherwood got was in his diaries, where years later you discovered he stated things that you disagreed with but had no means to redress. For example, after I moved to Mobile, I would talk with him for hours weekly on the phone. I always asked if I disturbed him, and he would say, "*You* never disturb me. Call whenever you like." If I didn't call for a long while, he would answer and say, "Oh, hello, Jim," as if absolutely nothing was wrong, but his nonchalance showed his awareness that I hadn't called. In his diaries, I came upon a passage where he writes of my calling one afternoon, "His incessant chattering drives me . . . to distraction." Yet many times Chris and I would be talking and Don's phone would ring in the other room. Chris would say, "Hold one minute," while he answered Don's and got back to me. He easily could have ended our conversation if he wanted. My pique about this comment is exactly what makes the diaries so good—real life to the smallest detail.

Clearly there is an element of hero worship in my relationship with Isherwood. I knew successful artists, but none struck me as more impressive personally. Isherwood's U.S. reputation lagged behind his accomplishments because of how he was stereotyped. In the States he was considered a British, not an American, writer. In Britain, since he emigrated just before World War II, there was prejudice against him and particularly against the novels he wrote while in the States. Too, he was openly gay. He did not join the New York establishment. He chose to live in Los Angeles, where few literary novelists resided. He became a Hindu when a scant few in the United States knew much about Eastern religion. What Isherwood chose was freedom—from the British and New York literati, the Anglican church, and the more homophobic parts of the world. It was comparatively easy to be gay in Hollywood.

The stereotypical way of looking at him has made him a neglected writer in the States. While his early support of gay rights has been recognized (in 1974, he charged a thousand dollars to give a talk, but he spoke for gay causes for no charge), his translations from the Sanskrit with Swami Prabhavananda have been relatively ignored. These translations of the Bhagavad Gita and other works are as finely honed as his fiction.

He had a spontaneous generosity shown in his first note to me—"I *hate* disliking things," he wrote, thanking me for my novel because he liked it. Months later, when his publisher turned down reprinting my book, he told me, "I could find another publisher."

Those who knew him realize how many people were struck with him as a person. I couldn't count the number of people who have told me that he impressed them more than anyone else they ever met. People saying this varied from close friends to individuals who met him only once.

I quit managing the bakeries because the Iranian owners overpaid me, as they did everyone else, and I had quickly saved enough to live a few months without income. I taught novel writing part-time at UCLA, and then I was hired to build the new master's in professional writing program at USC. I organized the MPW and hired many new faculty. Frequently I would ask Chris for a suggestion about whom to hire, and he would call me back with a first-rate candidate—such as screenwriter-novelists Harry Brown and Ben Masselink. USC's administration was liberal and experienced, and we created a program focusing on film, fiction, poetry, drama, technical, and nonfiction writing.

During this last period, Chris and I already had gotten to know each

other well. When he called my office, everyone got nervous. Our reception-
ist, talking to him the first time, begged me to tell him she wasn't as stupid
as she sounded when she took the call.

My wife and I left Los Angeles in 1982 for Mobile, Alabama, to rear
our son, Jules. It was traumatic leaving USC, but the smog, violence, and
expense of L.A. convinced me. In a telephone conversation shortly before
I left, Chris asked, "What would it take to make you stay in L.A.?" "If we
stay, we'd never own a house," I said. "If I found one you could afford,
would you stay?" he asked. "No," I said. "Very good," he said. "But let
me read your writing you're complaining about." He referred to my complaints that I had no time and my writing suffered. "Okay," I said, having
refused before, and showed him the unrevised pages. He had no response,
and when I asked him for one later, he said sardonically, "Oh yes, I could
read it all day," an unusual put-down, although he was certainly right.

Next we move into my favorite period of knowing Chris. At one point
he would wisecrack to Don, "Jim is immobile in Mobile," which was true
considering how happy my family was there, and how disaffected I became
for a number of years. During this period I would call Chris, talk, hang
up, and often say to my wife, "That's all I need."

Occasionally, after these conversations, I would go to class and teach
his work. So I would ask Chris to open to a page in a particular novel,
and then I would question him. "What does that word do?" I'd ask, or
"that and that?" He would be stumped. When I suggested an answer, he'd
say, "Yes, I agree. Your students are lucky. I'd love to be in your class."

When we talked, if I said something that we both laughed at, he'd often
say, "That would have brought Broadway to its knees, Jim." He used the
term "love" as an endearment the way the British do. "Yes, Love," he'd
say. "No, Love." He had a special "hmmm" that came from between his
teeth when he was especially pleased. I remember one time I called and
asked, after he said hello, "How's the greatest writer in the world doing
today?" and he gave the "hmmm," appreciating the gesture.

We would talk about historical topics such as Napoleon, often remembering few hard facts, and about what happened to everyone we knew, as
long as we had some detail. We were talking about the infinite variables
of human behavior and were amused and shocked.

We seldom spoke of philosophy or spirituality. I did not read his Hindu
translations until after he died. Nor was I much aware of his Commonplace Book. From time to time, I'd say, "Chris, isn't this what life is," and
he'd agree. We dealt with the fascination of life, not its meaning.

Once, when he was speaking enthusiastically about *My Guru,* he said
to me, "Jim, I never should have written a novel." I gave that short shrift.

And much later, during his last months, I called and he did not recognize the title of a book of his I mentioned. I then listed his novels, and he recognized about half of them.

A few weeks before he died, I visited him in Santa Monica, and we sat on the terrace overlooking the Pacific. We had a long conversation in which he spoke of his mother, Don, Auden, Forster, and others. Then I realized that he was about to cry. Chris was always strong, stoic. Six months before, he'd had back pains as he was getting out of my car and I offered my hand to help. He waved it away. "The moment you give in, it's all over," he said. But on the terrace it was different. His tears were completely out of character. I got up out of my chair and went to him and awkwardly put my arm around his shoulders. "The people that I've known, they've touched me," he said, "they've *touched* me." These words were a summation of so much I know about him.

I visited him later, but he was in a comalike state, not sure of what was going on around him. His face was shrunken and had an ethereal look. Seriousness was everywhere in the room, reflecting his inner struggle. As I was about to leave for Alabama, I went in to say goodbye although he would not know me. I stood over him and said, "Goodbye, Chris." He opened his eyes. "Hello," he said. "I'm leaving," I said. "I love you," he said and closed his eyes.

When Don called to say that Chris had died, I felt numb. It would take years for me to experience my grief. Anyway, my relationship with Isherwood was far from over.

After Isherwood died I catalogued his personal papers. Don was in Europe, and I took days going through everything, making a bibliography of the papers, which I published with my small press, the Texas Center for Writers Press. In going through these manuscripts—reading all of his diaries and looking carefully at letters from Forster, Auden, Spender, and a macrocosm of celebrities—I found a version of the Commonplace Book. This work contained handwritten paragraphs taken from mostly spiritual sources—passages that meant something special to Chris from all the reading he had done. Later I would discover that this shorter version was more focused on spirituality (although not exclusively) than the whole, which had equal emphasis on literature, psychology, and philosophy. Reading the Commonplace Book and the sources from which he had quoted brought me closer to Isherwood's thought and made revolutions in my own thinking.

When my son, Jules, was three, one evening I was reading to him as he lay beside me on his half of the bed. He put his arm across me so I wouldn't fall off. When I told Chris this he said, "Write it down or it's lost." He had the discipline to record what happened, and he recorded what he was reading. For years he listed the books he read and wrote about many of them. These special quotations in the Commonplace Book run as long as ten pages in his neat handwriting.

I began reading the book with curiosity and no expectations. I had never read religious material and frankly had no firm beliefs. The shorter version of the Commonplace Book was written into a hardback blue notebook. The entries included excerpts from Fenelon's letters, *The Tibetan Book of the Dead,* Lao Tzu, Bishop Hedley, Helen Waddell's *The Desert Fathers,* and others.

Although I tried to read dispassionately to collect information, the selections interested me. Discovering that no one wrote more purely and clearly than Fenelon, or more convincingly than Meister Eckhert, or with deeper insight than Lao Tzu, lured me on to read the works in their entirety. These books were as new to me in 1992 as they were to Chris in the 1940s. Unfortunately many are not widely known, such as the work of Vivekananda or the booklet *The Path to Light.* I read with diligence but took no notes, often continuing for eight or nine hours at a stretch, frequently reading at the Tulane library, where I located many works.

The Desert Fathers by Helen Waddell describes the goings-on of the earliest Christian hermits in the Egyptian desert. *The Way of Zen* by Alan Watts is a good introduction to a subject few knew about at the time of its publication in 1945. I then read Bishop Hedley's *Christus Veritas,* in surprised absorption. I chose to pursue this material, realizing it was a kind of dialogue between Isherwood and myself. It gave me endless questions I'd wished I'd asked him.

If Isherwood were alive, I would ask him what he thought about God and about mortality. The closest I came was once on the phone when I had a bright idea.

"All right, Chris," I said, "now listen to me. I'm completely serious. This moment, if you'll tell me what you've learned in life, I'll listen." This meant that my mind was wide open, with full attention and ready. He got silent. "I mean it," I said. "Tell me what you've learned and I'll believe it."

His voice changed in tone, becoming thick, full like a gong that went deep. "Nothing," he said.

We both laughed and felt a kind of happiness that perhaps came from not knowing. However, he never spoke with me about the Commonplace Book. I think that at the time the manuscript would have bored me.

The full manuscript contains 150 references and includes philosophy, psychology, even quotations from songs and newspapers. It presents key passages from Jung and Freud and quotes psychologists such as Kretschmer, who was popular at one time. A microscopic panorama of twentieth-century thought is created by these quotations, yet Isherwood's personal touch prevails.

As a result of compiling the bibliography of his papers and perusing the manuscripts, I could not help but know him better. A part of him was deeply religious, and from 1940 on he practiced Vedanta regularly. His translations with Prabhavananda illustrate this—the Bhagavad Gita, the *Crest Jewel of Discrimination*—as well as his editing the volume *Vedanta and the West* and his biography of Ramakrishna. His papers include typed notes he took on Prabhavananda's talks at the Vedanta Center. His classic spiritual work *My Guru and His Disciple* describes the relationship he had with Prabhavananda. His commitment to Vedanta was not purely an abstract one; he practiced meditation, made japam, and contributed in important ways to the Vedanta movement in the United States.

His papers were well organized, the letters alphabetized and in good order. He kept his datebooks and was able to look up any period to determine what he did each evening and with whom. Again and again in his journals he describes the problems of being a hypochondriac, of enduring society when time is wasted, of his need to work on his art. The personality that comes through is very honest, critical of himself and others, able to write, when he discovers he has cancer: "It's no shit."

The journals are replete with references to his friends, many of whom were famous. I would ask myself, why are so many of his friends famous? Was it accidental? He did not particularly admire celebrities and had critical opinions of them. I came to the conclusion that he was friends with celebrities—and he had many friends who weren't—because he was interested in their work, whether they wrote novels, acted, directed, or sang.

Chris was the first person I observed in the process of dying. He had always said he wanted to go quickly, with a heart attack or in a sudden accident. But his death was painful and took months. He said over and over to me during this period how he felt complete happiness because of Don. But he was in extreme pain. During the last few dinner parties he gave, he would unexpectedly scream at any point, then act as if nothing had happened. His guests, surprised and upset, pretended to ignore the outburst.

It was important for him to move about, but he would scream in pain as he was helped on to the terrace to sit. The pain grew, disfiguring him, and he shrank up so that his false teeth no longer fit, and, ultimately, he lay unaware of what was going on around him.

His death was not easy. At the end it took him a long while, even in severe pain, to let go. I remember asking him several times what he would want to be if he lived again. He always answered the same, a writer. His choice suited him, and he knew he was good at it.

The publication of the diaries furthers his reputation. They are both literature and a unique three-thousand-page social history of the period. His translation of the Bhagavad Gita has been in print for over fifty years. His novels have not diminished in reputation, despite the stereotypical view that his British work is superior to his American work. I suspect that what was true for me was true for most people who knew Isherwood: my life was changed because of how he thought.

PART II
ARTIST AND COMPANION

Stathis Orphanos: *Don Bachardy and Christopher Isherwood, 1972.* Photograph. Copyright © Stathis Orphanos. Used by permission.

Our life continues to be marvelously harmonious. I hardly dare breathe on it or even glance at it, though. It's like an organ of the body whose operation must never be interfered with by the conscious will.

Diaries I:667

Isherwood ends *Christopher and His Kind* with himself and Auden arriving in New York City. Playing the part of a fortune-teller, Isherwood looks into the future to see whether he and Auden will be able to find the "ideal companion to whom you can reveal yourself totally and yet be loved for what you are, not what you pretend to be." Auden, he says, will find his partner within three months. Speaking to himself in the second person, he continues, "Christopher, you will have to wait much longer for yours. He is already living in the city where you will settle. He will be near you for many years without your meeting. But it would be no good if you did meet him now. At present, he is only four years old" (340). When they finally met, Don Bachardy was eighteen and Isherwood was forty-eight. As Isherwood's diaries attest, the two spent much of the early part of their relationship concerned about Don's ability to form an individual identity and to find a vocation.

With few models to emulate, Isherwood and Bachardy developed their relationship as lovers, partners, friends, and collaborators. In spite of the notoriously homophobic environment in the Hollywood of the 1950s, they insisted on defying the prevailing culture and lived their lives in the open.

We believe that to talk about Isherwood, especially the American Isherwood, without paying serious attention to his relationship with Don Bachardy—their working together and their influence as a gay couple on their friends and associates—would give an incomplete account of Isherwood's life and work. So we begin this section on their collaboration with Bachardy's own voice. Excerpts from his diaries not only reveal that he is a talented writer and a keen observer but also provide an occasion to compare Bachardy's perspective with Isherwood's accounts of the same events. These excerpts concern the mid-1950s, when Chris and Don traveled together to Philadelphia and to Europe.

An interview with Bachardy from 1997 provides a more contemporary perspective on their literary collaborations. Scholar Niladri Chatterjee also discusses Bachardy's relationship with Isherwood and Bachardy's understanding of Isherwood's relationship with his own family and with England.

The last three essays in this section focus on two of the collaborations Isherwood and Bachardy completed. Katharine and Robert Morsberger offer an analysis of Isherwood's writing for film and television, an area that gets scant attention. In 1973 Isherwood and Bachardy wrote the script for a television adaptation of *Frankenstein*. The Morsbergers analyze the script in relationship to the original Mary Shelley novel. They focus on the chief difference between Shelley's text and the teleplay, which is, perhaps not surprisingly, Isherwood and Bachardy's emphasis of the homoerotic elements implicit in the novel's relationship between the artist and his creation. The Morsbergers' reading of the adaptation suggests that Isherwood and Bachardy's personal relationship can be seen in various onscreen relationships among Shelley's characters, especially between Frankenstein and his monster and between Frankenstein and Clerval, his collaborator.

Edmund White and Donald N. Mager write about a most unusual collaboration: the drawings that Bachardy did of Isherwood as he was dying of cancer. A selection of the drawings and accompanying diary entries by Bachardy were published in 1990 as *Christopher Isherwood: Last Drawings*, and several of the drawings are reprinted here. White, a close friend of Isherwood and Bachardy, discusses their last project together in terms of the relationship they had developed over many years, characterizing Bachardy's vision in these drawings as displaying a primal connection with his longtime lover. In a more theoretical analysis of the drawings, Mager offers an analysis of what he calls the "queer eros" inherent in them. Looking at the emotional complexity involved in this project, Mager addresses the potential for cruelty between the artist and his subject. Bachardy avoids this problem, in Mager's view, by eventually focusing on the process, on "working," rather than on the product, "the work," suggesting a lesson learned from Isherwood's writing on the Vedantic approach to life.

9 *Don Bachardy*

A Life Open to Art

3 March 1955

The day after the opening of Cat on a Hot Tin Roof *in Philadelphia.*

Carson McCullers, like Chris and me, is in Philadelphia for the opening of *Cat.* We saw her yesterday evening at the St. James Hotel before the play. Her physical appearance made one of the strongest impressions on me of anyone I've met. She is tall and pale-faced, with lavender circles around her wet-dark, puppy-dog eyes. Though her hanging cheeks, like swollen jowls, are doglike, too, she is essentially an Olive Oyl type. Her body is lanky, her arms and legs thin and elongated, her movements disjointed. She's recently had some kind of stroke and been partially paralyzed. At the end of one arm and making it next to impossible for her to get her overcoat either on or off, there is a metal hoop inside of which her splayed hand is wired by each finger. It's on her right hand, because she absentmindedly proffered me the hoop when we were introduced.

Chris and Carson had met before but only briefly. Both fey and avid, she was pleased to be in his company. While hungrily attending to him, she showed no real interest in me and deftly conveyed that her shyness limited her awareness of her surroundings, and particularly of strangers. Her childlike vulnerability allowed me to excuse her lack of interest in me, but still I dread her. The very expression on her face promises entangle-

91

ment in her defenseless dilemma, even if it is only helping to get that metal hoop on her hand into or out of her coat sleeve.

We also met William Faulkner this morning. He was brought to our breakfast table by Jean Stein in such a glow of triumph that a fanfare might have accompanied the scene. Small, impassive and inaudible, if in fact he said anything at all at our table, Faulkner has a remote air and his dark, hooded eyes suggest a blind man with Jean as his seeing-eye dog.

9 March 1955

We saw *Cat* again last night, and after the play we had drinks in the hotel bar with Faulkner, Marguerite Lamkin, and Jean Stein. Both encounters with Faulkner were difficult for Chris. There are many books of Hemingway on his shelves, and most of Fitzgerald, but only three books of Faulkner. Besides *The Portable Faulkner,* there is only *Light in August* and a paperback edition including both *Sanctuary* and *Requiem for a Nun.* Though he is far from Chris's favorite writer, Faulkner is certainly somebody he respects and to whom he wants to be friendly.

Faulkner, however, is not in the least forthcoming. Gray-haired and compact, he is like a gentlemanly veteran of the Great War who, suffering from shell shock, has learned to get along without communicating much with those around him. Perhaps in his drinking days alcohol encouraged him to speak more. During the long evening with us and the two women he occasionally sucked on a pipe, perhaps to console a mouth which has been deprived of most other uses.

Chris never protects his ego at the expense of others, and accepting his dharma, he willingly plays the roles of charmer and entertainer, even jester. Seldom at a loss to get somebody to talk, he clowns if necessary and usually manages to make even the most tongue-tied offer at least a few words. He's especially good with teenaged boys and young men, probably because he's particularly interested to know how they feel, how they see themselves, him, others, life.

As used as I am to this side of Chris, I was still impressed by his attentiveness to Faulkner. Coaxing rather than prodding, he was like a concerned doctor inducing his prize patient to speak the first words to end his catatonic isolation.

The five of us were in a cozy, wood-paneled booth next to a window and watched the beginning of a heavy, deadly silent fall of snow which gradually mounted in the street as the night wore on. As well as attending to Faulkner, Chris, I knew, was worrying about our departure early the next morning.

"I never fly when it snows," spoke the taciturn Faulkner finally. Even though it sounded like a Cassandra's warning, no one carped about the only clearly audible sentence he'd uttered the entire night. *Faulkner had spoken.* It seemed like a miracle Chris had wrought, and it had a cumulative effect. We were all pleased, even Faulkner. Yes, his fire burns low, and he is no magpie, but there is something sympathetic about him, even kindly.

19 December 1955

St. Jean de Cap Ferrat, France [for Isherwood's version of this occasion, see *Diaries* 1:558 —Eds.]

Spent our first night in the Villa Mauresque with Maugham and Alan Searle. As we came up the grand and green drive to the house, I was wondering if Maugham would still be alive when we got there. Then the car stopped at the open front door and I saw him standing in the hall alone. He was so unmistakably Maugham that I felt it was more a picture of him than the real thing and was surprised by how relaxed I felt. Warm and friendly but not exaggeratedly so, he had such a natural air that I didn't lose my ease until I reached the drawing room when, suddenly, the whole shock of meeting him hit me and I didn't know where or when to sit.

I think he and Alan only shook hands with Chris. They both said "How do you do?" to me. Alan, alert and quick, then said to me: "Would you like a *Bacardi?*"

Last night Willie (he asked me to call him by his first name) surprised me by asking Chris if he were making me keep a diary of my first trip to Europe. I felt flattered by the unexpected warmth of his interest in me.

In a terrible moment at dinner Willie had a very bad attack of the stutters and I thought I wouldn't be able to keep from bursting into laughter. That's when he seems oldest—his mouth opens and shuts with rasping attempts at words, his hands tremble, and finally his whole body shakes with convulsions. Sometimes Alan prompts him, and sometimes Willie manages to finish alone. But always he recovers, and immediately regains perfect composure as though nothing embarrassing has happened.

Willie will cross the room from one sofa to another for a cigarette instead of asking Alan, who is sitting beside the cigarette case.

Later. Willie said this afternoon that he and Alan never quarreled, although he had once "knocked Alan down" for throwing a *second* stone at a frog in order to make him move.

20 December 1955

I feel very restless today. Chris told me that Alan had confided to him his fear of the future after Willie's death. Alan feels people in England hate him and think of him only as Maugham's familiar, or his guard, and he would be afraid to go there without him. Also, Willie's family hate Alan.

How true it is—the friends, familiars, companions, guardians, all in fact who take the trouble to have an intimate relationship with any famous artist, almost always find themselves universally suspected, bitched, even hated, and, finally, ignored. Frank Merlo, Walter Starcke, Chester Kallman, Robert Craft—they all suffer this treatment and in their turn put off those who try to be their friends—even those in similar situations.

We had a lovely walk this afternoon with Willie and Alan on the hill above their house. We followed very rocky, often steep and slippery paths with Willie leading the way very quickly. He often tottered and sometimes barely missed falling, but he managed to keep his footing and after a considerably long walk was not out of breath. We shot some movie film of them. Alan was shy and reticent to be photographed.

We passed a mimosa tree in luxuriant blossom and I commented on its beauty. Willie turned to me and said significantly: "All beautiful things last a very short time." Neither compliment nor threat, his words were more like a lesson.

Alan is very much the twinkling-eyed, saucy Cockney, and not nearly as simple and unimpressive as he pretends to be. I think he is sincerely fond of Willie and very concerned for his welfare.

Willie said about the countless manuscripts he receives: "So many people think they can write without being educated."

7 March 1956

To Graham Greene's apartment in the Albany last night for the first meeting of the John Gordon Society, an elaborate conceit devised by Greene specifically to oppose a columnist named Gordon and generally to attack everything that Gordon supports. The official meeting, what there was of it, was over, but many people were still standing around in two big smoke-filled rooms. We talked to Greene for a few minutes. He doesn't look quite as ravaged as he does in his pictures, but he is strangely unappetizing. His face is pink and splotchy, his eyes bloodshot and watery, and the inner rims of his lips are blackened. He is quite lively and easily engages in superficial, ordinary chit-chat. I saw his smooth charm and a facility for handling people, but I don't think he was enjoying the party. We also talked to Angus Wilson, who seemed pleased to be told that I had read and liked his play, *The Mulberry Bush,* and very pleased when Chris then praised his book, *Anglo-Saxon Attitudes.*

31 May 1956

Another sudden and inexplicable scene with Chris yesterday. I don't really know why I make these scenes—the least little thing seems to set me off. I was reading Chris's 1939–41 journal on the balcony, and Chris came up from his study, still wearing his shabby, yellow terry cloth robe and feeling ill again. (He's been sickish for more than two weeks now.) He dragged himself to a sun couch and, with great preparations and groans, awkwardly lay down on his back facing me.

Coldly perfunctory, I asked him: "How do you feel?" He moaned and shook his head, vaguely indicating a few centers of pain. I told him, half-wanting to provoke him, what a deplorable character he had made of Gerald Heard in his journal, and that now I could never like Gerald again. "What does it really matter 'liking' people?" said Chris. "It's a matter of pure subjectivity." After a moment he continued: "When I was young I was famous for liking people and being liked, but it was only because I took trouble to flatter them—that was all." Chris's inference, it seemed to me, was that I would like Gerald again if he flattered me enough. This irritated me, and as I sat looking down at Chris, I was revolted. He looked so old and felt so bad and talked so cynically that I hated him for a moment. I left the balcony and got ready to go to the beach.

That was all, but this incident started me smoldering. By the time Chris joined me on the beach I was full of resentment and rebellion and made a scene. First accusing him of possessiveness and a lack of genuine interest in me, I then said that I felt bored, lethargic and useless and wanted to go to New York by myself. I blamed him for everything that was wrong with me and, by exaggerating my unhappiness, made him feel I hated him without really saying so. When I get carried away in my despair and confusion, I want to wreck everything for no good reason. Then I cry, and make Chris cry. Afterward I feel guilty, and so silly, and just as unsatisfied as usual.

[For Isherwood's version of these events, see *Diaries* 1:618–25 —Eds.]

5 June 1956

Have just finished reading Katherine Mansfield's *At the Bay*. I don't get the ending. Am I dense, or haven't I read enough to know the form and lingo of such writers? The last paragraph is obviously symbolic, but I don't know what it means. However, I think Mansfield is terribly exciting. She creates such mood and atmosphere that it hardly matters what she is writing about, if anything at all. Until her I've never enjoyed aimless descriptive passages about landscape and light and flowers. Reading Mansfield makes me want to write more than ever before.

I told Chris tonight that I wanted "more than anything" to write. As soon as he encouraged me to start on something *tomorrow,* I wished I hadn't spoken. What can I write about? A dozen tiny snippets of ideas and bits of scenes passed vaguely through my head, but where to begin, what to write about? I must learn to concentrate, to think things through, to come to conclusions, to make decisions.

Chris seems better today, and his eyes are less jaundiced. [We were early pioneers of hepatitis, which he had caught from me.] Again I arrived at the hospital in an extremely tense state and immediately flew off the handle because Ted and Bob [my brother and his partner at the time] were coming up to the room unexpectedly, and after they'd left, I went into all my old complaints: no friends of my own; I don't fit in with Chris's friends; I'm not taken seriously as an individual; I have no interest or profession to work at; I suffer terrible fears and lack of energy. I sometimes wonder if any of it is really true. My mood changes so suddenly sometimes, especially after unloading all my grief onto Chris, that I ask myself sincerely, what *is* all the fuss about?

28 June 1956

Three more days before I start at Chouinard Art Institute. I dread it so, and yet I know I must go, I must try. If only I can succeed! I dimly hope it may be the answer, that my whole life will open to "art," take a new direction, etc. But I mustn't put too much significance onto this effort because it will make failure all the more crushing—and I'm so afraid already that I will get cold feet in the middle of the first day. One class from nine until four! It sounds too awful. If I loathe the class right off, there will be no hope of relief for hours and hours. I dread my own determination, and the sheer effort it will take to carry it through.

10 *Niladri R. Chatterjee*

Portrait of the Artist as Companion
Interviews with Don Bachardy

When I was awarded a Fulbright Fellowship to go to the United States to research Christopher Isherwood, I decided I would go to Santa Monica to interview Don Bachardy at least once. However, I had no idea what kind of questions I would ask him. My reading of Kathleen Isherwood's diaries at the Harry Ransom Humanities Research Center in Austin, Texas, and the release of the first volume of Isherwood's diaries took care of that. I was delighted to learn that Bachardy himself would be coming to the Harry Ransom to speak at an exhibition of some of his drawings. Thanks to the wonderfully cooperative staff of the Research Center, I was allotted about forty-five minutes. Having interviewed him there, I expressed my desire to see the house that had been celebrated in two different paintings by David Hockney. He said that he would be very glad to receive me at the house he and Isherwood shared for twenty-six years. So I interviewed him again at his Santa Monica home.

On both occasions my prime objectives were to understand as clearly as possible the relationship between Isherwood and his mother and to ascertain the importance of Vedanta in Isherwood's life. But there were also queries about the publication of the diaries and other miscellaneous matters that I wanted to explore. For the sake of clarity, I have edited these two conversations into one narrative.

97

CHATTERJEE: *There has been much criticism about the first volume of the diaries. Many people are of the opinion that it could do with some rigorous editing. But you absolutely insisted that every single word should be published.*

BACHARDY: I don't think it should pretend to be anything other than what it is. It wasn't written as an entertainment. One critic said, "Why do we have to read this? Why hasn't it been edited? Why are repetitions allowed?" And there's a critic who takes to task those reviewers who claim that it was too long and repetitious, saying that it's not pretending to be a novel. I also think it gives a completely different aspect of Chris as writer. Because all of his published work was very highly polished by him. He wrote draft after draft of every novel, and he polished until he got everything just as he wanted it, whereas these diaries are written totally spontaneously. There's no rewriting and no correction. The first two sections he did polish in the mid-forties. But after 1944 everything was quite spontaneous, the first draft. You look at the manuscripts and there are very few corrections, very few things crossed out. He would cross out a word if he misspelled it and rewrite it above. Otherwise very neat, very legible handwriting. Six of the twelve manuscripts are handwritten.

CHATTERJEE: *When I read the diaries I have this inescapable feeling that somewhere at the back of his mind Isherwood is thinking of a reader. He really has this idea that maybe the diaries will be read someday. Is that a correct impression?*

BACHARDY: He never gave me any instructions about the diaries. I read only the first two volumes, the polished ones, up to 1944, because they were written before I knew him. The third volume includes our meeting, so I'd never read anything after 1944. . . . He never told me how to publish, whether he wanted them to be published or not. But he was a professional writer, and he realized that anything he didn't destroy would probably one day find its way into print after his death. He did destroy the work he didn't want other people to read. But he didn't destroy the diaries. So I took that as an indication that he was prepared to have them published. The diaries seem to me to be written to please himself. In fact he often laughed when he read the diaries of other writers, because he felt they betrayed themselves clearly: they were writing for a public rather than writing to satisfy their own desire just to keep a record. I think that Chris is very convincing as a diarist. He was writing out of an inner need to record his life. His diaries don't seem to me nearly as self-conscious as those of most writers.

CHATTERJEE: *When I was reading through Isherwood's mother's diaries, I sometimes got the feeling that his Vedantism grew out of his father's interest in Buddhism and his mother's exposure to Indian culture. She attended Indian plays, read books on India, attended lectures by Jiddu Krishnamurti, whom Isherwood himself met eleven years later. Did he ever talk to you about these connections?*

BACHARDY: I don't think he himself knew [that], but both of his parents were highly cultured people with a wide variety of interests. And yes, he seemed very surprised by his father's interest in Buddhism.

CHATTERJEE: *But Kathleen Isherwood never mentioned the fact that she had met Krishnamurti in any of her letters to Isherwoood?*

BACHARDY: I don't think so. Chris read her diaries when he was preparing to write *Kathleen and Frank,* but I think he didn't read much beyond the period that he was intending to write about. And that more or less goes up to the end of World War I. I don't know that he read her diaries after that.

CHATTERJEE: *This particular lecture that she attended by Krishnamurti was in 1928.*

BACHARDY: I don't remember whether or not Chris knew that she'd been exposed to Krishnamurti. We both knew Krishnamurti. We had lunch with him in Malibu in the early sixties, probably 1963. And we went to a lecture of his in Santa Monica after that. We both read several of his books, but I don't think he would have shared his interest in Vedanta with Kathleen. I think he probably assumed that she wouldn't have been interested or wouldn't have really approved. I think he assumed that she was very conventional in her Church of England interests.

CHATTERJEE: *I get a sense that Isherwood was a lot closer to his mother than he allowed the public to see. Would you agree?*

BACHARDY: Of course he was very involved with her. He called her "Mummy" all his life. It's interesting that when she is referred to in the diaries she becomes "M," I think because he was embarrassed to write "Mummy." So yes, he was very involved with her. But, you know, in a way, I think he felt even more intimate with the nanny who raised him. I've often thought that it was his nanny who got his most basic love. He was emotionally involved with his mother, but when he spoke of his nanny I heard a loving tone that I didn't hear when he spoke of his mother.

CHATTERJEE: *What do you think could have been the reason for that?*

BACHARDY: That he felt a greater affection. I don't imagine that Kathleen was a very physical woman. I don't think she expressed her affection physically, and I suppose that his nanny did. He valued that kind of physical affection. It was a very basic part of the bond between us. We were both very physical with each other. And we always slept in the same bed and always slept very, very close to each other—arms and legs intertwined. We often woke up in the morning not knowing which arm belonged to whom.

CHATTERJEE: *Would it be wrong to suggest that he was unwilling to talk much about Kathleen's varied interests because he didn't want the public to see her as the remarkable woman she was?*

BACHARDY: I think he felt she was a remarkable woman, but he also felt that she was very reactionary and that she expressed an English attitude that he himself found distasteful. It seemed to me in many ways that the England he wanted to escape was the England that his mother represented to him. That was a very strong part of his motivation for leaving England. He had always wanted to come to this country, to see the American West, and he loved movies from an early age, and he always wanted to go to Hollywood and do a film. And that's how he found his home.

CHATTERJEE: *But he didn't burn the bridges. He still kept in very close contact not only with England but with his own mother.*

BACHARDY: Yes. But whenever he went back to England, after a week or two he was very ready to leave. He felt that it might get him again. In fact, I lived there for most of a year in 1961, and I liked it very much. I had my first exhibition in London, and that made me think that really I would like to stay on, to live in London maybe for a few years. And I came back to California to propose the idea to Chris, but he absolutely didn't want to go back. If I insisted he probably would have resigned himself to it, but he really didn't want to go. And I didn't want to put him through that. No, he felt that he had escaped England. Auden wanted to go back. He missed England. He felt he could return. But Chris never wanted to.

CHATTERJEE: *Kathleen's diaries describe the two of them sitting by the fire reading aloud. Did he read aloud in later life?*

BACHARDY: He was a wonderful reader of prose and poetry.

CHATTERJEE: *Was this a performance that he really enjoyed?*

BACHARDY: Yes. He loved the theater, you know, and knew how to read to get the dramatic quality in a piece of writing. That was in his bones. I never had much pleasure from reading poetry, but as soon as he read it to me, oh, then I got the point. For my birthday or when we had anniversaries, he asked me what would I like, and for many years I asked him to record the poetry that he loved—to record it on tape so that I could play it in the studio while I am working. And I have hours and hours of his reading all kinds of poetry. He was a great reader of Auden, of Shakespeare, Housman, Hardy, all kinds of people. It's wonderful, and I'm so glad I got him to do it.

CHATTERJEE: *He once said that he was a frustrated actor. Why do you think he said that?*

BACHARDY: He had a very well developed theatrical instinct. He was taken to the theater at a very early age. He saw Sarah Bernhardt onstage. And he went to the theater a great deal as a young man. That's why he became fascinated by Charles Laughton. He saw him in all kinds of theatrical appearances in the twenties in London. And he was also a moviegoer from a very early age and loved movies. I think that's what he meant by that comment. He had a great appreciation for actors. And I think any artist who loves the theater identifies with actors and is capable of feeling like a frustrated actor.

CHATTERJEE: *In your day-to-day life, did you think that even when he was telling stories or meeting someone for the first time he dramatized or sought to produce an effect?*

BACHARDY: He told stories very well, and he always had a very clearly developed theatrical sense. And of course it was a great help to him in writing plays and screenplays, which he did a lot of in this very house.

CHATTERJEE: *Did he often play the famous writer?*

BACHARDY: Well, he knew what the part required, and he also knew how not to overplay it.

CHATTERJEE: *Let's talk about Swami Prabhavananda. What, apart from the obvious, attracted him to the swami?*

BACHARDY: He believed in the swami's belief—yes, he believed in him. He believed that he had extraordinary experience and that he was capable of a profound love. Chris was a very, very shrewd judge of character. I never met anybody I would trust as I trusted him in judging the character of other people. And all his talent as a novelist was brought to bear on Prabhavananda. He tested him time and time and time again, and he always rang true. It was largely instinctive belief. The whole of his experience was behind it.

CHATTERJEE: *What was your first impression of Prabhavananda?*

BACHARDY: As Chris says, he had a very endearing animal quality. He was small and compact, and he had great charm. But he also had his severe side. His conviction was very impressive. I knew Prabhavananda for a period of many years, so it was a gradual getting to know him, and so much so that it is really difficult for me to remember now just what or how I felt. But I did sense even at that very early age that it was very important to Chris that Prabhavananda and I should meet, that Prabhavananda accept me. I think Prabhavananda knew it too. So we were always on our best behavior, because we both loved Chris, and we didn't want to make any trouble for him.

CHATTERJEE: *If Isherwood had had his way with the biography of Ramakrishna, how differently do you think he would have written that book?*

BACHARDY: I think very differently. He'd never before done anything like that: allowing his work to be edited. It was a great mark of his love and respect for Prabhavananda that he allowed the team of swamis at the Belur Math to pass on what he wrote.[1] I think Ramakrishna seemed to him a much madder character than he was allowed to present. All kinds of behavior—dressing up in women's clothes—and he was fascinated by it, but, of course, Belur Math saw such behavior differently. They were acting in the role of censors, as it were. Then, of course, it's never, ever a good situation for a creative writer to have any kind of censorship exerted.

CHATTERJEE: *Do you think that would apply to other Vedantic writings he did?*

BACHARDY: No. Because I think the nature of the translations was quite different. He and Prabhavananda were working toward accuracy, and they were united in their objectives. And all of his Vedantic writings about his own personal experience, how he came to Vedanta, that was all done by himself. There was no censorship exerted.

CHATTERJEE: *Do you think Vedantism gave him a new perspective on writing as such?*

BACHARDY: Oh yes, I do. I think it affected his writing. You can see it in *Prater Violet.* You can certainly see it in *A Single Man, A Meeting by the River.* I believe it changed his life profoundly. I think it gave a support, a courage to go on that he might not have had without it. It was very, very necessary to him.

CHATTERJEE: *In the book* Christopher Isherwood: Last Drawings, *Stephen Spender writes that you and Isherwood "were utterly dependent on one another." Could you talk a little bit about this interdependency?*

BACHARDY: It was symbiotic rather than dependent. We both chose freely, and it seemed to me that we strengthened each other rather than depended on each other. Stephen was such a split personality. . . .

CHATTERJEE: *I am interested in what your influence on Isherwood may have been, because you too were an artist.*

BACHARDY: If he hadn't encouraged me, I would never have been an artist. He gave me support, both financial and emotional. And he took a very real interest in my work. Every day when I came home from art school, he would say, "Oh, let me see what you did." And he would go through my drawings and say, "Oh, now that is real advancement, that one!" Well, you know, that's just golden! I mean, how many people take that much interest in one's work? Because I was very young and I lacked confidence in myself, he was continually encouraging me and giving me pep talks. And his own example was itself an encouragement to me.

CHATTERJEE: *What qualities of your drawing would you say Isherwood liked?*

BACHARDY: The aliveness. He claimed that my drawings were never dead, that there was a quality of animation in them. And he felt I had an uncanny knack for likeness. Both of those qualities I put down to the fact that I only work from life. I can't work any other way. And I never touch anything I do after my sitter leaves. So it's all spontaneous, and it's all a collaborative effort. I can't possibly work without my sitter. And that's what I attribute the alive quality in my work to. The fact that it's all done from life.

CHATTERJEE: *I see an affinity between your drawing and his work. Just as you try to capture people with a few lines, Isherwood tried to do that same thing with just a few sentences.*

BACHARDY: I've always had an interest in people, you know. And we both had this urge to record our experiences. My work really amounts to a kind of visual diary. Chris wrote his diaries, and my pictures of people are my diaries. They are signed and dated by their subjects. So if you give me a date, I'll look that date up in my archives and produce pictures of people that I was spending the day with. I've been doing that for forty years. We were both instinctive recorders of our experience. Chris also advised me to keep a written diary. That was in the first week that we knew each other, and I did begin because he never gave bad advice. And I keep a diary still.

CHATTERJEE: *I remember you telling me that Isherwood had a great sense of humor. How important do you think that was when he liked or didn't like literature? Did he lose patience with writers who were grim, humorless?*

BACHARDY: Oh, certainly he did. I think his humor is a great key to his own writing. He wasn't somber about writing. He made it into fun for himself and therefore fun for the reader. He was acutely aware of the reader, and he felt keenly the obligation to entertain and amuse as well as give the reader something of substance to think about.

CHATTERJEE: *You told me that he felt very close to his nanny, closer than he felt to his mother, but what did he feel about his father? Did he talk about him often?*

BACHARDY: Well, you see he lost him so early that he was really more of a mythical figure than a real personality to him. His father died in 1915, when Chris was barely eleven. That's awfully early. A great deal of those first eleven years his father was probably away from home. I think most of his relationship with his father was constructed on memory and myth as much as real, physical access to him. I think that writing *Kathleen and Frank* brought him in closer contact with his father than he had ever been and gave him a genuine sense of who his father was and developed in him a sincere admiration for Frank. I think he suffered as a young man from the fact that his father died a hero's death. He fought the obligation to follow that example, and I think it scared him, even terrified him at times. And I think that made him almost resentful toward his father in his early youth.

CHATTERJEE: *He acknowledged to some extent that his artistic temperament came from his parents, who were artists, didn't he?*

BACHARDY: Oh, very much. They were both astonishingly adept water-colorists. They both had a thriving interest in the theater. They both read and went to concerts and they saw to it that their son also . . . well, taking him to see Sarah Bernhardt! That made a great impression on him—something Chris never forgot.

CHATTERJEE: *What was it like for you to meet Kathleen? Did you connect with her as a fellow artist?*

BACHARDY: I was a budding artist, still in art school, and I would never presume to meet her on any sort of equal ground. Besides, I don't think at that time I'd even seen any of her work. But I remember that we got along. Chris was a bit apprehensive of our meeting for fear that she might be rude to me—but not at all. In fact, Chris told me that he had a very strong impression that she sincerely liked me, which was a relief to us both. Meeting the parents of one's lover is usually a harrowing prospect.

CHATTERJEE: *At one point Kathleen wrote in her diary that Isherwood had practically adopted you, which would make you her "grandchild."*

BACHARDY: He did eventually adopt me. I became his son legally, but that was long after her death.

CHATTERJEE: *I think she would have been interested to know that.*

BACHARDY: We were worried that, since there was no such thing as marriage between people of the same sex—and there still isn't—if he got sick, I might have difficulty even getting access to him in hospital. But as his legal son we circumvented all such difficulties.

CHATTERJEE: *When you met Kathleen Isherwood, did she really know that you were more than just a good friend of Chris's?*

BACHARDY: Oh, of course! There couldn't be any doubt. Chris simply wouldn't allow her not to face his homosexuality. He was determined that she should know and accept him as he was. He made no pretense to her and would not have tolerated any pretense on her part not to know exactly my status in his life. He was determined that she get her nose rubbed in it if necessary. [Laughter] So, yes, he wouldn't tolerate any kind of mystery on that question.

CHATTERJEE: *And do you think she took it well?*

BACHARDY: She took it because she knew she had to.

CHATTERJEE: *After seeing her three times in four years, do you think Isherwood was right in thinking about her in the way he seems to have thought of her, as the Evil Mother, the Domineering Mother?*

BACHARDY: I knew her only as an old lady in her eighties, so I couldn't judge her from any kind of reasonable vantage point. I had to take Chris's word for it. I do think that his understanding of her was much improved by the research he did for *Kathleen and Frank.* That book allowed him to feel more kindly toward her, to understand her better and to forgive her somewhat for what he earlier regarded as her crimes.

CHATTERJEE: *Can you recall the day when Isherwood learned of her death in June 1960?*

BACHARDY: It couldn't have been regarded as a surprise, because she was nearly ninety-one. He lived with the prospect of her death for many, many years. His younger brother, Richard, had telegraphed him to tell him that she had fallen ill, and there was every chance that she would die soon. But it was certainly an occasion of deep significance to him. He had a strong attachment to her. She was a very powerful figure in his life. He took the deaths of people close to him very, very seriously to heart. I don't remember him crying at the news of his mother's death like he cried when he heard of Auden's death.

CHATTERJEE: *Do you think Isherwood was right when he thought that his brother, Richard, was rather jealous of him?*

BACHARDY: Oh yes, of course he was. It was inescapable. And if you read some of the passages of the first volume of Chris's diaries, he stated very clearly what his attitude to Richard was. Chris took great pains to be kind to Richard and to understand him and to alleviate any kind of jealous suspicions that Richard might be harboring about Chris and not to interfere with Richard's possessiveness about their mother. . . . Chris regarded himself as the one who'd gotten away. Richard took the rap for both of them by getting stuck at home with his mother. Chris escaped. Well, Chris was so grateful to be the one to escape, he was all the more kindly toward Richard. He was glad not to be in Richard's shoes. And he took great pains to reassure Richard that he only had the best of goodwill toward him, that he in no way wanted to interfere with Richard's happiness or take away anything from Richard that he felt belonged to him. And in fact when Chris inherited the family money, he gave all of it to Richard. What better gesture of good intentions could he possibly have made?

CHATTERJEE: *Isherwood went to Calcutta in 1957 and in 1963. What were his impressions of the place?*

BACHARDY: We were together on that trip in 1957, and we were stunned by the place in both positive and negative ways. We stayed at the Guest House in the Belur Math on the Ganges. And to wake up at dawn and to go to the banks of the Ganges and see the people bathing and receiving blessings was extraordinary. I never forgot it. It made a huge impression on me, and I know it did on Chris. It was incredibly beautiful and significant. I remember my first experience of vespers in the Belur Math, the noise and the movement and the smoke. Oh, it was just a dazzling experience. We were both stunned by it. Eventually, of course, part of this experience was used for *A Meeting by the River.*

CHATTERJEE: *Could you tell me about your collaborative work with Isherwood, such as on your television adaptation of* Frankenstein *and stage adaptation of* A Meeting by the River?

BACHARDY: We discussed the story in detail for days, weeks. We worked out the construction together. We each had ideas, made suggestions, and developed from each other's suggestions until we had a general direction, a general sense of our characters and how they were going to interact. And then at that very decisive moment when the first serious words of the script were to be written, I took my place at the typewriter and Chris dictated to me. So in other words, I had all the fun without any of the responsibility. I was a very good typist and could keep up with his dictation. He was very considerate never to talk faster than I could type. We had a very symbiotic relationship. And that's always how our collaborations worked. We wrote many scripts. *Frankenstein* was the only one that got produced. We wrote a play based on *A Meeting by the River* and also a screenplay based on the material. So we were very used to working together.

CHATTERJEE: A Meeting by the River *was quite a success, wasn't it?*

BACHARDY: No, no. It was a disaster. We opened at the Palace in New York after a week of previews, and our opening night was our closing night. It was also done as part of an experimental theater program at the Mark Taper Forum in Los Angeles—I think a week or ten days of performances. We liked that production much better than the one in New York, and it was much closer to the original play.

CHATTERJEE: *Wasn't Isherwood himself of the opinion that the play is an improvement on the book?*

BACHARDY: Yes. I think he felt the screenplay was a further improvement. And one day I hope to publish a volume which will contain the novel, the play, and the screenplay, as they are all variations on the same basic material. All very different from each other, all written expressly for the particular medium.

CHATTERJEE: *You have already published two extracts from your diaries; will you publish all of your diaries at some point?*

BACHARDY: Oh, that I can't answer. I really can't think seriously about that until I have all of Chris's diaries published. Then I'll see. I'll reread my own and see if I think there's anything I want to publish and, if that's the case, find out if anybody is interested in publishing them. My main objective at present is to see all of Chris's diaries in print, and then I'll think about my own.

Note

1. The Belar Math, a sprawling monastery of the Ramakrishna Order situated on the bank of the Ganges due north from Calcutta, is the setting of a major part of Isherwood's *A Meeting by the River*. It was founded approximately a hundred years ago by Ramakrishna's favorite disciple, Swami Vivekananda.

11 *Katharine M. Morsberger* and *Robert E. Morsberger*

Frankenstein: The True Story
The Artist as "Monster"

When Christopher Isherwood and Don Bachardy were asked to write the script for producer Hunt Stromberg Jr.'s 1973 television version of Mary Shelley's *Frankenstein; or, The Modern Prometheus,* they "found . . . that the story [had] really never been told at all . . . the real interplay between the creator and the creature and what this means."[1] This was a bold claim indeed. Mary Shelley had created a multifaceted modern myth so potent and so compelling that the novel has never been out of print and, from 1823 on, has been retold on stage, on screen, and by other novelists. Though the title *Frankenstein: The True Story* was the producer's choice, it reflects the spirit with which Isherwood and Bachardy approached the project, creating a highly original plot, altering some characters and inventing others, while retaining Shelley's main themes and concepts.[2] Their version is the most literate and in some ways the most provocative adaptation of *Frankenstein.*

Isherwood and Bachardy tell the "true" story with a unique depth and subtlety. Their script works on its own merits as an adaptation rather than a precise rendering of the story in another medium. Both were longtime film enthusiasts. Isherwood's perceptions, particularly his feeling for realism in dialogue, were heightened by his experience in writing for film. Bachardy brought an artist's visual awareness and a deep appreciation and knowledge of film's technical side. Their retelling of the myth adds vitality

108

and insight into the Creature's perennial appeal. A powerful symbol of the outsider—whether artist, woman, or homosexual—the Creature is also, significantly, a symbol of human weakness and feelings of rejection shared by everyone.

In 1973, it was extremely unusual for a script written and filmed for television to be made with the care and resources invested in a feature film. Stromberg and director Jack Smight's opulent production included a cast of distinguished actors, most of them British.[3] Though the novel takes place in the 1790s, the Hollywood films of *Frankenstein* were done in modern dress. *Frankenstein: The True Story* returns to the Romantic era and is meticulously accurate in period settings and costumes.

Isherwood enjoyed collaborative writing, and he and Bachardy worked together on a number of projects, before and after *Frankenstein: The True Story*. Isherwood approached screenwriting with a director's eye. He observed, "The person who matters in a film . . . is the director. . . . The writer and director should work in the closest possible collaboration . . . together from the very first day."[4] The camera may precisely record an image, but the subject must be selected, focused, and lighted, and the camera's angles chosen, in an attempt to put the director's vision on film. Isherwood and Bachardy's collaborations merged their respective angles of vision. In a cameralike method similar to Isherwood's writing style, Bachardy's portrait drawings are usually done with eye contact with his subject and in one sitting.

When asked how he and Isherwood worked together, Bachardy replied: "Chris always believed that the bones of a script were what mattered. We made an outline, knew where we were going, where it started, the middle, the end, and then when we felt we were ready to get something in type, on paper, I took my place in front of the typewriter, and he dictated to me. . . . The first typed version [of *Frankenstein*] was very rough, and he would often stop, and we would discuss, but always the actual writing was his words. . . . If I had suggestions, I made them. He always urged me; he wasn't the least bit possessive about the work. He wanted my input and often said, 'What do you think? Can you think of a word for this or that?' Yes, it was back and forth a lot, but always the writing was his" (Bachardy interview 1997).

Unfortunately, while *Frankenstein: The True Story* was being shot on location in England, there was a writers' strike, during which Isherwood and Bachardy were prohibited from revising or making further contributions to the script.[5] Many of the changes between the published script and the filmed version were minor ones, but there are considerable differences toward the end, which we discuss below.

Adapting Shelley

A dominant theme of Shelley's novel is the redefining and questioning of the complex relationship of Creator and Created. For a woman writer to address this question was an unprecedented challenge to religious authority. Shelley borrowed Milton's language for her epigraph—"Did I request thee, Maker, from my clay / To mould me man? Did I solicit thee / From darkness to promote me?"—drawing parallels between Victor Frankenstein and the Creature and the Adam-God-Satan relationship dramatized in *Paradise Lost*.[6] Shelley depicts a Creator whose skills are unequal to his Promethean ambitions, and who, terrified by what he has wrought, deserts his botched Creation. In his rejection and loneliness as a terrifying outcast, the originally benevolent Creature becomes vengeful, developing a demonic mind and spirit.

As an artist and a woman who has defied conventional sexual behavior, Shelley has much in common with the Creature, who speaks for the outsider, feared, rejected, hated, and pursued by society, desperately searching for a special friend to complete the self. Shelley's female characters, however, are all destroyed by the Creature, suggesting her ambivalence about a woman's role as creator. Victor's Creature becomes a symbol of the artist as an outsider in society and of a woman as doubly an outsider if she dares to create any "progeny" other than children.

The novel contains significant sexual subtexts, including homosocial, homoerotic, androgynous, and incestuous themes that become more prominent in Isherwood and Bachardy's teleplay. Isherwood's previous writings had dealt with most of the issues: the relationship of man and God; the relationship of creator/artist to his or her creation; the search for the "second self," often in a same-sex relationship; and the isolation of the "monster" as outcast. The women, problematic in the novel, become increasingly so in the screenplay: Elizabeth, Victor's fiancée, becomes the voice of religious authority, of social conformity, of conventional values, most significantly marriage and procreation. Victor, torn between religion and science, chooses science and his fellow scientist, Henry Clerval, rather than a conventional life with Elizabeth. Eventually, the Creature will be endowed with Clerval's brain and will form a fraternal and homoerotic bond with Victor. Mirrors become a symbol of the complex doppelgänger relationships among Shelley's characters, which reflect those among the Shelleys and Byron.

The most significant change in the adaptation, however, comes in the prologue, which was filmed but was cut from the telecast.[7] In their prologue, Isherwood and Bachardy provide a counterpart to the complex framework of the novel, introducing significant images and establishing identifications relating the actual persons involved in the myth's creation to their fictional counterparts. The action of the published script begins at a picnic with Byron, his personal physician Dr. Polidori, Mary and Percy Shelley, and their son William on the shores of a Swiss lake. Mary refers to a previous evening when the adults told tales of horror and each agreed to write a story. As she describes her idea, Mary Shelley turns her companions into actors in the drama—Shelley becomes Victor Frankenstein, Mary becomes Elizabeth, Byron becomes both Clerval and the Creature. Isherwood and Bachardy introduce the character of Polidori, the only character who is not in the novel, using an actual person for fictional purposes. From his initial appearance until well into the script, Polidori remains on the fringes of the action, a sinister figure who takes on the characteristics of Fate. In the edited broadcast version, Polidori does not appear until about a third of the way through, at the point where Victor and Clerval leave the hospital after examining bodies from which they will form the Creature. However, in the opening scene as written by Isherwood and Bachardy, Polidori and Byron share the role of detached observer and of Victor's "Fate." Much like *Don Juan*'s narrator, Polidori speaks with Byronic irony. In the telecast, as in Shelley's novel, Victor is obsessed by Fate, convinced both that he is powerless to deviate from following his fatal curiosity and that the subsequent tragedy is "Fate's" responsibility, not his own.

At this point, one of the script's central symbols, a butterfly, is introduced.[8] As Byron attempts to kill a butterfly, and Shelley carefully rescues it, Mary's "half-joking hostility" toward Byron becomes deadly serious as her character metamorphoses into Elizabeth's. As the script develops, Elizabeth herself takes on some of Byron's more ruthless characteristics. Byron, when he finds himself, against his will, "seeing" the story that Mary has begun, calls her a "witch" (13). Mary, becoming increasingly more cold and distant, demands an unquestioning acceptance of her authority as storyteller. Though Shelley cannot swim, Mary orders him and William to swim in the lake, where William drowns. The televised version opens with William drowning; the videotape version, with William's funeral. Later, Victor sees William's face briefly in the face of the young man whose head is chosen for the Creature, thus combining the religious, homoerotic, and incest subtexts.

The butterfly symbolism returns when Victor later demonstrates to Elizabeth the results of an experiment, bringing a butterfly back to life. Elizabeth is terrified of the revived butterfly, shrieking: "It's—unholy!" (51). She smashes it with the first object at hand, the landlady's Bible, which is ironic given that the butterfly is a symbol of the Resurrection. This scene connects to an earlier scene in which Elizabeth is appalled by

Victor's blasphemous response at his brother William's funeral service. "Why *God*'s will? Any fool with a sword or a gun can give death. Why can't we give life?" (19). Elizabeth says that humans can only give life within marriage. "So can a pair of animals," sneers Victor. "Life out of life—that's no miracle. Why can't I raise life out of death?" (19). Elizabeth calls this a Satanic temptation, and Victor responds, "If Satan could teach me how to make William live again, I'd gladly become his pupil" (19).

In Shelley's novel, Victor is a medical student, but in the screenplay he is a doctor, making his skill more plausible and increasing his knowledge and culpability. At the hospital, he meets Clerval, who drops his medical bag, revealing a severed arm. Through a conversation about a new science that offers power over death, he and Victor discover that they are kindred spirits. Later they meet in a Catholic church, where, after mass, Clerval alludes to transubstantiation by asking why life cannot be "brought forth from the lifeless" (35).

Clerval assumes a Godlike presence, masked in scientific "authority" and expressed in antireligious terms. He speaks of "gods," implying his own brand of pagan science-worship rather than a variant on Roman Catholicism: "Will you join the brotherhood of Prometheus? Will you defy the gods?" (43). Prometheus, in some versions of the myth, represents the sun, the essential element in creating life. Victor attempts to recapture his blind faith in religion and the status quo that had been so abruptly shattered by William's death. Clerval counters, "It's our upbringing—we've been taught to fear the punishment of the gods" (42), again modulating Christian guilt into pagan defiance. The religious overtones of their pact suggest both a new kind of "transubstantiation" and a new sort of "marriage."[9] Their partnership leads them to search for body parts in order to assemble their "creation." A parallel can be drawn between the scientist and the artist here: since the Renaissance, both artists and medical students had clandestinely sought out cadavers to dissect and thus establish "truths" of science and art.

Whether Christian retribution or punishment for hubris, Clerval is attacked by the arm used in his first experiment. Just as he is posturing before a mirror and giving an imaginary speech, claiming credit as "sole creator" of a "second Adam" (66), the powerful arm escapes from its vat and advances threateningly toward him. Appalled, Clerval breaks down, sobbing, "Oh, my God! My God!" (67) in tones of prayerful anguish. Barely able to recover his scientific detachment, he searches through his records trying to find the flaw in the experiment. As he begins to write that the process is reversing itself, the pen drops from his hand at the crucial word and Clerval falls to the floor, dead. When Victor arrives in the morning, he misinterprets Clerval's final note, "The process is r——," as "The process is ready to begin." Still under Clerval's spell, Victor whispers, "We're going on—aren't we, Henry?" Victor then decides to give the Creature Henry's brain: "Whatever may come of this—forgive me, Henry" (67–69).

At Clerval's graveside, the clergyman intones, "The dead shall be raised incorruptible" (69), an ironic counterpoint to William's funeral at the beginning and Henry's "resurrection" in the form of the Creature. After the funeral, Polidori appears as Victor's Fate. Uncannily sensing that Victor intends to use Clerval's brain for his creation, Polidori turns a seemingly trite comment on the weather into mockery: "We must make the most of the sunshine, mustn't we?" (70). Isherwood and Bachardy envisioned the Creature's being brought to life in a glorious burst of solar energy, a studied contrast to the "dreary night of November" (Shelley, 57) when the novel's Creature is revivified.

The Creator and the Creature

Although it is commonly referred to as "Frankenstein's Monster," Shelley as well as Isherwood and Bachardy call it "the Creature" from the beginning. Only Polidori calls it "monster" consistently. Victor calls it a "monster" only in moments of rage and frustration, and, when he does, Victor is being equally "monstrous." Shelley's Victor had "selected [the Creature's] features as beautiful" (Shelley, 58), and Isherwood and Bachardy's Creature begins as a strikingly handsome young man.[10] Arising from the wreckage of the operating table, the bandage-swathed Creature looks like a mummy, recalling the 1931 Boris Karloff film and underscoring the contrast between the two interpretations. From the Creature's viewpoint, "Victor himself looks like a monster with his dark glasses, smudged face, and singed hair" (74). The Creature removes Victor's mask; Victor then removes the bandages from the Creature's face, a mutual "undressing" charged with erotic wonder. Delightedly examining the Creature, Victor says, "You're beautiful!" and the Creature, "a perfect mimic," answers in a melodious voice unlike Clerval's, "Beautiful" (74). Victor then tells the Creature to "rest." These two words will resonate throughout the script. When Victor takes his "second Adam" outdoors, he points out the landscape as "your garden of Eden" (75). But already there are hints of flaws to come. As the Creature, "with a gesture of delighted vanity," looks narcissistically in the mirror and arranges its hair, it is "extraordinarily reminiscent of Henry when he stood before the mirror at the hospital" (81).

Despite having Clerval's transplanted brain, the Creature's mind seems to be a tabula rasa, and its initial personality, rather than resembling Clerval's sardonic one, seems Edenically innocent. While Shelley's Creature is articulate, Isherwood and Bachardy's speaks only in monosyllables except in moments of stress, when the voice of Clerval erupts and takes over. At first Victor treats and educates the Creature as he would a child, and in one scene he laughs with delight and embraces it after a particularly successful lesson, crying "Bravo!"—another word which will reverberate through the script. The Creature laughs and returns the embrace. By the time the Creature is ready for its first public appearance (at a performance of *The Marriage of Figaro*), their relationship is developing into that of older and younger brother. An officious "foreign lady" at the opera's intermission mistakes the Creature for William. Victor takes it as an omen that means "William didn't die in vain!" (84), and he looks forward to their being able to carry on conversations together. But Polidori also attends the opera that night, his presence indicating that Fate is about to intervene again. In addition to a sibling and a pedagogical relationship between Victor and the Creature, there is also a subtext of homoeroticism. Clearly enchanted with each other, and in the seclusion necessary for the Creature's development, they have a "honeymoon" period that will prove all too brief. Until the Creature begins to develop physical malformations, Victor entirely forgets about Elizabeth.

When the Creature does begin to deteriorate, as the process reverses itself, Victor realizes that he must smash all his mirrors or hide them from the Creature, who is puzzled and disturbed by their absence. As the days go by, Victor will not permit the Creature to venture outside, and the Creature becomes sullen and sulky, begging to go to the opera. Victor, his nerves on edge, becomes angry with the Creature. He returns to the laboratory, where he writes frantically in his notebook, "Here am I—imprisoned with this Creature I have made. . . . I see no way out" (98). The Creature, meanwhile, discovering the malformations of its hands and arms, desperately searches for a mirror in the wreckage of the laboratory. It finally makes out its deformed features in a shard of broken mirror.[11]

The mirror can be both falsely flattering and mercilessly critical. Again, a crucial symbol was introduced in the missing prologue. To Mary's "Surely, Byron, you need no mirror? You are reflected in the eyes of a thousand adoring females," he replies, "In *your* eyes, my dear Mary, I see myself more clearly than I like. I doubt if they miss a single fault" (10). Clerval's vanity is reflected in a mirror, as is the sun's power during the creation scene, suggesting a mirror image, an Adam-God relationship between Creature and Creator as well. Mirrors reflect the Creature's Eve-like delighted self-discovery, and finally its self-realization, as it frantically attempts to see, in the shards of shattered mirror in the laboratory, what it has now become.

In the novel, Victor and his Creature become doppelgängers, the Creature a distorted mirror image of his Creator: "My form is a filthy type of yours, more horrid even from the very resemblance," the enraged Creature tells Victor (113). Walton, the narrator for the novel's opening framework, introduces one of the its main themes—the search for an alter ego, a friend who would complete one's existence: "I desire the company of a man who could sympathize with me; whose eyes could reply to mine" (28). This concept of male friendship must have seemed dangerous to the film's producers, since, in Isherwood and Bachardy's teleplay, Clerval and Victor seal their pact with an embrace, but, in the broadcast version, the embrace is replaced by a safer gesture, the act of drinking a toast. Victor is later permitted to embrace the Creature, but in a father-child context.

Same-sex love resembles both the mirror image, the kind of friendship Walton so longs for, and the completion of the "unfashioned creatures, but half made up" that Victor perceives humans to be, unless "one wiser, better, dearer than ourselves . . . does not lend his aid to perfectionate our weak and faulty natures" (36). In mythic tales, it is the *absence* of a shadow or mirror image that implies the demonic. To the extent that the mirror image is symbolic of a same-sex relationship, it is in this mythic context "normal," not narcissistic. In the Britain of Isherwood's youth, dual identity was of necessity a way of life for homosexuals, whose actual selves were as inescapable as a mirror image.

In the script, after the Creature finally realizes how its beauty has been ravaged, it weeps in anguish, then stabs itself repeatedly with the scalpel. Failing to die, it runs into the woods and submerges itself in a stream, supposedly drowned. The scene is more overtly dramatic as filmed, however, as the Creature runs to a chalk cliff (an improbably long way from London) and leaps into the sea. Again unable to die, the Creature arises from the waves and walks off down the beach. Here the first televised episode ends.

In the second part, the Creature wanders into the woods and encounters the blind Lacey, who invites it to his home. In the Creature's experience with the Laceys, the themes of the nature of friendship, of beauty, of loyalty, of death and resurrection, and of conventional religion converge. It is a decisive point in the Creature's life, affecting all those directly involved with it. Lacey judges character by what he can hear and feel, and he intuits that the Creature is somehow different, that there is something not quite right about it. The Creature is greatly attracted to Lacey's granddaughter, Agatha. It listens outside the window as she reads the story of Jesus healing the man possessed by a devil. Like the Creature, the "unclean spirit" has extraordinary strength and says, "My name is Legion: for we are many" (108). In the subsequent scenes in the script, considerably cut in the telecast, the Creature clearly has fallen in love with Agatha, but when she and her husband Felix encounter the Creature, they are terrified, and, in the ensuing confusion, the Creature accidentally kills Felix, Lacey has a fatal heart attack, and the fleeing Agatha is struck and killed by a wagon and team of horses. Putting her gently on the ground, the Creature kisses her on the lips and says, "Beautiful. Rest. Victor" (117).

Evidently imagining that Victor may be able to revive Agatha, the Creature carries her body to the old house, where it is greeted by Polidori, who has been wanting to make a female creature. At this point, a complex realignment of identifications takes place. Polidori takes Victor's place as the Creature's mentor, but only through hypnosis, discovering in the process that the Creature has Clerval's brain. In response to "Who are you?" the Creature replies, "My name is Legion, for we are many," emphasizing the demonic theme so prominent in Shelley's novel. Polidori has a demonic side as well, but he does not have the Creature's power. He realizes that only Victor can help him with the project he has in mind, but Victor, believing the Creature dead, has married Elizabeth, reversing his earlier choice of science over conventionality. In an echo of the novel's threat from the Creature, "I shall be with you on your wedding night" (142), Polidori appears on Victor's wedding day, at first simply as a Satanic tempter, offering Victor the opportunity to make another creature. When Victor refuses to repeat what he considers a "crime," Polidori asks Victor to accompany him to a carriage where the Creature waits, disguised with an "Oriental" mask, more sinister and disturbing than the Creature's ravaged face.

Polidori's project is to make not an "Adam" but an "Eve," this time by a chemical "beauty bath." In the Christian tradition, Eve is often linked with Satan as the source of man's temptation and fall. Victor's male Creature, though flawed, is so far innocent; it never intended any harm to the Laceys, who were destroyed by accident. The female's smile is "somewhat uncanny . . . like the smile of a doll" (144), an image suggestive of an inhuman creature whose eyes seem to stare out from an unknown and threatening void. Polidori calls his female creature Prima, "the first of her species" (142). When Victor, who has left the outraged Elizabeth on their wedding night to collaborate in making the female Creature, returns from his delayed honeymoon, he is clearly sexually attracted to Prima. The implications of this relationship are complicated by the suggestion of a parent-child relationship between them. The Creature, Victor's other "child," is also attracted to her, since she has the face of the dead Agatha, thus completing an incestuous triad.

Meanwhile, Polidori tries to destroy the male Creature, and, after Victor prevents him from drowning it in a bath of acid, Polidori locks it in the cellar and sets the house on fire, gloating, "Burn, you traitor! Burn, Henry

Clerval!" (172). Thus the sudden entrance of the Creature at Prima's coming-out ball, even more hideous after being burned by the fire, is terrifying. Though it comes to Prima with its arms outstretched, in a gesture of affection, she attacks it like an animal, and the Creature, responding with an "orgasm of violence" (181), tears off her head and then leaves. The "wedding night" has been grotesquely consummated.

At this point there are many differences between the script (i.e., pages 181–93 in Isherwood and Bachardy) and the filmed version, and here we leave the film version behind. In the script, Victor and Elizabeth, hoping to escape the Creature, sail for America on a battered hulk named the *Ariel,* after the ill-fated craft whose wreck caused Shelley to drown. En route, they are horrified to find that both Polidori and the Creature, unbeknownst to each other, have stowed away on board. Passing Polidori's cabin, Elizabeth sees the Creature in the mirror on the cabin's wall, which recalls the previous mirrors pivotal to plot and theme. She locks Polidori in with the Creature, but after Polidori calls for help, Victor forces her to give up the key, effectively severing the bond between husband and wife. During a thunderstorm, the Creature hauls Polidori, who is terrified of lightning, to the top of the foremast, where a bolt envelops them both. Nothing is left of Polidori but a charred skeleton, but the Creature is unharmed. The crew desert, and the Creature lashes the wheel to due north, sailing into the Arctic.

Throughout the script, Isherwood and Bachardy retain Shelley's subtext of natural creation and artistic creation, which is manifested in a climactic scene. After Victor is knocked unconscious trying to save Polidori from the Creature, Elizabeth and the Creature confront one another over his unconscious body. Elizabeth demands, "What more do you want of him?" The Creature replies, "Victor made me." Elizabeth pleads, "God has forgiven him for that sin. He has a child, now. *Our* child!" (216). The Creature, dismayed, asks, "Child?" (217). When it attempts to touch Elizabeth's abdomen, she backs away, demanding, "What have you to do with life— you thing of death?" The Creature replies with Clerval's voice, "You still assume the authority of the Almighty, Miss Fanshawe?" It then strangles her and, ironically alluding to the butterfly she smashed with a Bible, says: "Poor *Brassolis astyra!*" (217). Artistic creation retaliates against authority with a vengeance.

Upon waking, Victor leaves the ice-locked ship and follows the Creature to an icecave, where, instead of raging against it, as in the novel, he begs its forgiveness. The only thing Victor wants now is his own death. The Creature offers Victor one of the captain's pistols. Victor pauses—it would be too cruel to leave the Creature alone in this wilderness of ice. But then he realizes that a gunshot will trigger an avalanche. In Henry's voice, the

Creature cries, "Well done—Victor!" and Victor, in joyful recognition, calls out "Henry—!" (221). As the icy cliff crashes down, Victor looks at the Creature, who seems to be "transformed . . . into the face as we first saw it: innocent, joyful, beautiful" (222). Now the Creature is the protector, and, as they are united in death, it puts its arm around Victor. As written, when the credits begin, time has passed, the ice begins to melt, and, with a strange sound, an ice floe cracks. The gulls fly off. The Creature's hand appears. The path of its departure still is free.[12]

Isherwood and Bachardy follow Shelley's ending much more closely than any of the previous films had done. Her Creature's final words—"I shall die, and what I now feel be no longer felt. . . . My ashes will be swept into the sea by the winds. My spirit will sleep in peace; or if it thinks, it will not surely think thus" (Shelley, 185)—are strikingly similar in mood and tone to metaphors of ocean and consciousness at the conclusion of Isherwood's *A Single Man.* But Isherwood and Bachardy have a more positive resolution for Creature and Creator than does Shelley. The Creature and Victor are reconciled. Their final scene together is a kind of homoerotic *Liebestod,* an affirmation of their emotional and physical bond as well as their creative collaboration. Their joint creation—with the Creature's body, Clerval's brain, and Victor's spirit—lives on.

Notes

1. Daniel Halpern, "A Conversation with Christopher Isherwood," *Antaeus* 13/14 (Spring/Summer 1974): 385.

2. Don Bachardy recalls that their preferred title was simply *Dr. Frankenstein.* Interview with Don Bachardy, Santa Monica, California, August 28, 1997. The authors would like to express their appreciation to Mr. Bachardy.

3. The cast included James Mason (Polidori), David McCallum (Clerval), Michael Sarrazin (the Creature), Leonard Whiting (Frankenstein), Nicola Pagett (Elizabeth), Jane Seymour (Prima), Ralph Richardson (Lacey), and John Gielgud (the magistrate). The published version of the script (Christopher Isherwood and Don Bachardy, *Frankenstein: The True Story* [New York: Avon Books, 1973]) has long been out of print, and the complete version of the original telecast is available only in the Museum of Television & Radio at New York and Los Angeles. It has therefore been necessary for the authors to clarify their analysis of the differences between novel and film with a fair amount of plot summary, as well as pointing out the differences between the script as written and as filmed.

4. Charles Higham, "Isherwood on Hollywood," *London Magazine* 8, no. 1 (April 1968): 33.

5. As a result, Stromberg made a number of changes in the script that Isherwood and Bachardy did not approve, and, consequently, they were not entirely happy with the finished film (Bachardy interview).

6. *Paradise Lost* 10:743–45. Mary Shelley, *Frankenstein; or, The Modern Prometheus,* ed. Johanna M. Smith (Boston: Bedford Books of St. Martin's Press, 1992), 19.

7. The complete version runs 200 minutes; the videotape, only 123 minutes. But part of the complete video includes an introduction to the film, with samples of what is to come, a recapitulation of Part 1 at the beginning of Part 2, and some previews of Part 2. Jack Smight does not know who reedited the film as a videotape (telephone interview, August 29, 1997).

8. Not only was the entire prologue cut from the original broadcast, but the page of text introducing the butterfly is missing from the published teleplay. Don Bachardy provided the missing page, reproduced here with his permission. After Byron's first speech, "In *your eyes,* my dear Mary, I see myself more clearly than I like. I doubt if they miss a single fault" (10), the missing page continues:

(*As Byron says these words, a butterfly starts to flutter around him. Finally, it flies right into his face.*)
BYRON (*striking at it*): Devil take it!
(*The butterfly flutters away from him and settles on the table cloth. Byron irritably picks up a plate to crush it.*)
SHELLEY (*with dismay*): Don't.
(*Shelley stoops down, carefully catches the butterfly in his cupped hands, takes it down to the water's edge and gently releases it. Byron finds this funny.*)
MARY (*defensively*): Shelley cannot endure to see any creature harmed.
BYRON: And you?
MARY: I make certain exceptions.
(*She looks straight at him. There is a certain half-joking hostility between them. Byron recognizes this, then dismisses it with a shrug, smiles, picks up a leg of chicken and sniffs at it.*)

9. Their Creature has an initial Byronic, compelling attractiveness to both men and women. Later, his physical flaws, though of course much more exaggerated, recall Byron's. The Creature merges literally with Clerval when Victor gives it Clerval's brain. Unlike Shelley's, Isherwood and Bachardy's Elizabeth is aggressive, controlling, and "masculine." The artistic control demanded by Mary's alter ego in the prologue turns into attempts to control Victor, and Clerval is equally demanding. Caught in the middle, Victor cannot marry them both. When Victor is unable to choose, Mary asserts, "*He* has chosen for you. . . . If I were a man, I think I should kill him" (54–55), underscoring the homoerotic element in the Victor-Clerval relationship.

10. Michael Sarrazin, who played the Creature, said of the role: "How often do you get a Christopher Isherwood script. . . . [It was] essential that the Creature not look grotesque. The change had to be gradual. . . . [He] should evoke sympathy, you should care about him." Cecil Smith, "Sarrazin: Leading Man as Monster," *Los Angeles Times,* November 26, 1973, 4:23.

11. The image is borrowed from the climactic moments in Henrik Galeen's *The Student of Prague* (1926), an expressionistic German film that Bachardy says had long fascinated Isherwood with its striking images and treatment of dual personal-

ity (Bachardy interview). In it, the devil buys an impoverished student's mirror image, representing his soul. After his mirror image has murdered a man, the student finally shoots the "image" of his evil self, when it deliberately moves in front of the mirror, baring its chest. The image disappears, the mirror shatters, the student finds his image again in the mirror's fragments and dies.

12. Percy Shelley, "Mutability," line 14, quoted in Mary Shelley, 156.

Edmund White

Pool in Rocks by the Sea
Isherwood and Bachardy

Seeing is always perceiving—an imaginative integration of memory, feeling, and anticipation all subsumed under the aegis of style, that haphazard
collection of conventions and intentions. But Don Bachardy in his book
Christopher Isherwood: Last Drawings gives the appearance of seeing
simply and purely more than any draftsman I know, which is especially
remarkable since what he is looking at is the man he has lived with for
some thirty years. Isherwood, when the drawings were made, was in his
last months of life, had for the most part stopped talking, and seemed
scarcely conscious of anything beyond his bodily suffering. With a paradoxically vigorous line, Bachardy recorded this collapse. Looking at
Isherwood cruelly, if cruelly means honestly, he made these drawings the
most disturbingly transgressive images I have seen of a man, a beloved
man dying and dead.

The pictures do little to remind me of any direct precedents. Their fore-
runners in practice, though hardly in visual look, might be the death
masks, even casts of the dead person's hands, made in the nineteenth century as pious mementos, like the snippet of hair you might carry in a
locket. But Bachardy has given us a series of perceptions, not fossils. As
John Russell writes in his introduction to the book, "Faced with a death
mask—glad as we may be to have so exact a record—we feel above all
that nobody's home. In these drawings we feel Isherwood is as much

at home as a human being can be." Other precedents might include
Joseph Seven's drawing of his friend Keats in death, or, from between 1913
and 1915, the Swiss painter Ferdinand Hodler's repeated drawings of his
mistress Valentine Gode-Darel in her gradual decline, showing her playing with their child, for example, though gaunt and ill, and finally rendering her after death in murky paint tones with graphic underdrawing. But
Severn's saccharine sketch suggests none of the agonies of the tubercular
poet, and Hodler, despite the closeness of their relationship, always drew
Valentine at a distance and seldom looking directly at him and at us.
Bachardy's pictures, on the other hand, record all of Isherwood's distraction, pain, sullenness, disorientation, and growing inwardness. Positively
invasive, they demand our complicity and refuse us the security of a discreet unchallenged distance.

With nasty wit, a line drawing of Isherwood in profile juxtaposes his
sagging chin, bushy eyebrows, and downturned mouth with an inverted
profile painted on his shirt of a young woman with fashionably plucked
brows and luscious painted lips. On the facing page the symmetrical black
brushstrokes describing his windbreaker suggest a bird's feathery cape below a face stormy with mental confusion. In the first picture everything is
rendered with a thin, dry, bounding line and contained white space; in the
second nothing is left blank except the surround. Elsewhere the humble
patience of dying is epitomized by clasped hands in a useless lap.

The closest equivalent to drawings like these may not be visual at all:
it may be the prose of Simone de Beauvoir, who recorded every moment
of Jean-Paul Sartre's final decline in her 1984 book *Adieu: A Farewell to
Sartre*. Childish drinking bouts, incontinence, memory lapses, bedsores,
false teeth, ridiculous errors in judgment—the woman who spent forty
years with this century's best-known Western thinker leaves nothing out
of her account of his moral and physical decay. Thus Bachardy in diary
entries excerpted in *Last Drawings* worries about what he is doing, using
words like "ghoulish" and "ruthless," but acknowledging Stephen Spender's comment on his pictures: "They are both merciless and loving." And
he writes of his art, "It is the most intense way I know of to be with Chris.
It is the only situation now in which we are both truly engaged." After
Isherwood's death he adds, "While Chris was dying, I focused on him
intensely hour after hour. I was able to identify with him to such an extent
that I felt I was sharing his dying just as I'd shared so many other experiences with him. It began to seem that dying was something which we were
doing together."

Bachardy met Isherwood when he was eighteen and the writer was
forty-eight, and they spent the next thirty-three years together. An early
photo of them is shocking since Don looks barely a teenager—real jail-

bait. But over the years a mysterious personality exchange took place: Don developed an Oxford stutter, and Chris became more and more Californian. Don seemed friendly but formal, Chris casual and noticeably friendlier. In fact no one was better company than this man who had accumulated decades of extraordinary experience but lived entirely in the moment. He had been a member of the gentry in England, had lived in Berlin in the 1930s, then had worked for Hollywood. A friend of W. H. Auden and Spender, he was a Hindu convert who translated the Bhagavad Gita. Just as his *Berlin Stories* created the myth of Germany between the wars, just as his *Prater Violet* is the best novel I know about the movies, his *A Single Man,* published in 1964, is one of the first and best novels of the modern gay liberation movement.

Bachardy did not regard as tragic the decline of this man's brilliant mind or his terminal cancer. A strange tropism oriented Chris to Don and Don to Chris throughout the last months of Isherwood's life from August 1985 to January 4, 1986, when he died. With wide-open eyes Don *looked* at Chris, who returned the gaze whenever he was not befuddled by the radiation and chemotherapy treatments. In this way Bachardy's portraits penetrate a face known to a wide public—through book-jacket photos, postcards of authors, David Hockney's paintings—and dissolve its exacerbated individuality into a kind of landscape. Isherwood himself, in *A Single Man,* wrote of the self as a part of the landscape, as a sea pool in the rocks:

Just as George and the others are thought of, for convenience as individual entities, so you may think of a rock pool as an entity; though, of course, it is not. The waters of its consciousness—so to speak—are swarming with hunted anxieties, grim-jawed greeds, dartingly vivid intuitions, old crusty-shelled rock-gripping obstinacies, deep-down sparkling undiscovered secrets, ominous protean organisms motioning mysteriously, perhaps warningly toward the surface light. . . . And, just as the waters of the ocean come flooding, darkening over the pools, so over George and the others in sleep come the waters of that other ocean—that consciousness which is no one's in particular but which contains everyone. (183–84)

This cosmic view of the self recalls the art that Bachardy's drawings do in fact remind me of the most—the paintings of the Chinese artists, especially the Buddhists who broke down the distinction between animate and inanimate and erased the differences among animal, vegetable, and mineral. In Sung dynasty art of the eleventh to thirteenth centuries a gnat-sized pilgrim often stares into an immense void which is as charged with energy as is his regard. Jointed bamboo in this art has all the calligraphic force and subtlety of—and is evoked with the same brushstrokes as—the poem that may be written beside it. Three persimmons in a row, or a spider monkey with her babies in a tree, are the moral equivalents to the old man in the mountains in Liang K'ai's thirteenth-century *The Sixth Zen Patriarch Tearing Up a Sutra,* who howls a laugh into the wind as he rips apart a sacred scroll, demonstrating the supremacy of sudden enlightenment over the useless accumulation of wisdom.

What is remarkable in this art is that individuals are rendered in all their peculiarity at the same time that they seem to be interchangeable, a sleight-of-hand made possible by the painter's calligraphic style in which strokes linked to drawing stone can also trace a nose or chin, and lines that classically render water, pines, or clouds can describe a robe, a wizard's eyebrows, or a young woman's floating hair. Bachardy has no such vocabulary of recognized conventions to draw on, but with his powers of improvisation he finds the protean exchanges between disparate components of matter—finds the skull under the face, reveals the relationship between bloated body and bony head, changes the inspired gaze of a seer into the angry grimace of a ruined old baboon. The character-revealing line beside the mouth metamorphoses into the downstroke of a wing, the flowing creases in the forehead become a river, the light that bleaches out the fixed stare emanates from the mystic's morning sun.

And yet the drawings are so quirkily individuated. Looking at them, it is hard to remember Isherwood's Eastern view of the self as a rock pool, a nonentity. That paradox—between the impersonal forces of cosmic energy and the patterns, unique as a fingerprint, through which that energy flows and that constitute what we call the individual—is the fertile contradiction that animates both Isherwood's fiction and the drawings of Don Bachardy.

Don Bachardy: *Christopher Isherwood, August 19, 1985.* Acrylic on paper. 30″ × 22″.
Copyright © Don Bachardy. Used by permission.

Don Bachardy: *Christopher Isherwood, December 13, 1985.* Acrylic on paper. 40″ × 32″.
Copyright © Don Bachardy. Used by permission.

126

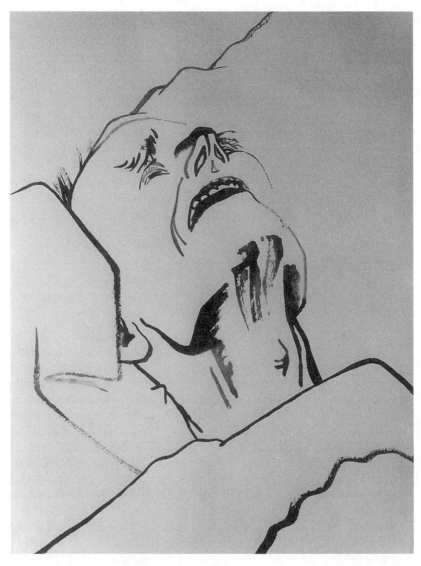

Don Bachardy: *Christopher Isherwood, January 2, 1986.* Acrylic on paper. 30″ × 22″.
Copyright © Don Bachardy. Used by permission.

13 *Donald N. Mager*

Deathwatch

For gay men and lesbians death has been inextricably linked to sexuality—on discursive, existential, and material levels—in ways unimaginable to straight culture. Heterosexuals have not been executed and murdered because of their sexual definition; heterosexuals do not commit suicide because of heterosexual panic or "heterophobia"; heterosexual movies and novels have not had requisite death-endings; and when heterosexuals die of sexually transmitted diseases, their sexuality is rarely seen as the cause. Because queers live in a world in which eros and thanatos are fused, where life and death are not oppositional, the community of the Names Quilt has been able to forge its multiple significances. The Quilt's life-rejoicing and life-bestowing imagery make it a celebration of life inseparable from its naming of loss and death. It is useful to contrast this communal remembering with the Vietnam Veterans' Memorial, a wall whose semiotic of names reduces the dead to an austere list where nothing of the person survives except the name.

Queer eros often encompasses more of life—it encompasses fuller possibilities of play and pleasures achieved—because at its core it is not bound to the procreative imperative which is often used to restrain or diminish straight eros. All sexualities, in their capacities to signify, are bound by taboos and permissions. Queer eros redefines taboo, thereby redefining the parameters of pleasure; therefore, even lesbians and gay men who experience guilt, repugnance, and prurience do so under the auspices of play and pleasure. Released from the procreative imperative and its culturally and mythically determined significance, all queer sexualities—including some heterosexualities whose pleasures are not proscribed by reproduction—are thrust into a space of redrawn taboos in which significance itself is created out of play.

In their groundbreaking collection *Death and Representation,* Sarah Webster Goodwin and Elisabeth Bronfen "read death," uncovering and recovering numerous iconographies that collapse sexual, gender, and death images upon and into each other. This rich inquiry begins with the already-dead body and reads the layers of sexuality and voyeuristic desire as encoded in the representation of death. The essays "unbury" the erotic content of the dead body. The Goodwin and Bronfen collection focuses on representations of death, not of dying. The medieval fascination with "reading" dying has nearly vanished in our culture, which insistently hides death and dying behind elaborate medico-religious practices attempting to shield the community from death's diverse manifestations. How different are cultures in which dying, like birthing, are integral to the life cycles of the home. In the advent of modernism, we find elaborate wakes and burials—from *Finnegans Wake* to *As I Lay Dying*—studies of grief and grieving and even metaphorical exchanges between the living and the dead. But extended displays of dying are rare until the recent appearance of AIDS narratives which focus on the protracted process, such as *Longtime Companion* and *Silverlake Life: The View from Here.* While Hollywood typically glamorizes dead bodies, dying itself has become a series of outlandishly stylized rote gestures. Both iconographies work effectively to unlink eros from thanatos and to suggest any linkage to be perverse and unnatural.

The most transgressive performance of queer eros in the process of dying is Don Bachardy's study of Christopher Isherwood in *Christopher Isherwood: Last Drawings,* which I call a deathwatch and which represents a fully lived death. This large-page book selects drawings that Bachardy did daily (often several a day) during the months of Isherwood's terminal illness. As Edmund White described it, "Bachardy . . . gives the appearance of seeing simply and purely more than any draftsman I know, which is especially remarkable since what he is looking at is the man he has lived with for some thirty years. Isherwood, when the drawings were made . . . had for the most part stopped talking and seemed scarcely conscious of anything beyond his bodily suffering. With a paradoxically vigorous line, Bachardy recorded this collapse" (345). The two men's symbiosis was complex. Despite considerable pain, Isherwood had agreed to sit for his artist-lover as his final action of giving and sharing. Isherwood—novelist, companion, model—has only his body to offer. At the same time, Bachardy is driven by a desire to capture and hold Isherwood as a material presence against the certainty of imminent absence and encroaching silence.

These wonderful drawings, despite the racking of Isherwood's mental and physical deterioration, are never laden with morbidity, sentimentality, or anger. I agree with White, however, that "these drawings [are] the most disturbingly transgressive images I've seen of a man, a beloved man dying and dead" (345). This quality results from the gaze that Bachardy is able to sustain. Because queerness invites us into an epistemology of eros and thanatos fused, it creates for us the possibility of a participatory gaze. Although gay men have learned the objectifying fetishizing gaze associated with straight mass media, a specifically queer gaze has been theorized in works such as Marlon Riggs's *Tongues Untied,* Isaac Julien's *Looking for Langston,* and Robert Mapplethorpe's photographs.

Rather than breaking the object apart, the queer gaze individualizes the object in its specific materiality and its history of pleasures shared between image maker and image. The queer gaze presupposes the possibility of participation. The straight gaze, on the other hand, projects fantasies of essential difference, separations, hierarchies, and exploitations; its images need not always enact these fantasies, for titillation itself directs the viewer's imagination toward unrealizable engagements. By contrast, the queer gaze, which Bachardy enacts, sees what is already known. It does not view so much as re-view, thereby seeing again. It is an eros not of wishing but of having. It engenders nourishment where the straight gaze provokes hunger. The pleasure it encodes is not of a future but of a presence.

Through the drawings, Bachardy's gaze records and delineates a known and pleasured body. As he re-views the older man's naked body, Bachardy's drawings offer a new view each time. His gaze never breaks that body apart to fetishize it. These drawings do not titillate us as viewers. Bachardy describes his project in his diary, excerpts of which introduce the book: "An exciting like-new experience for me. Also yesterday, after the first couple of drawings, I moved Chris's chair off the model stand on to the floor. Another good move. I must remind myself repeatedly to keep varying the experience. The merest change can make a vast difference. I don't get bored easily but there *are* limits, even to *my* endurance" (xii). When Bachardy isolates a section of body, it is synecdochic, not fetishistic, for it always signals the whole of the body extended beyond the frame. We can test this by asking whether we can imaginatively picture the weight of flesh, the lie of muscle and bone, beyond what is shown. And, of course, we can. With Bachardy and Isherwood, the desire or need of the viewer, if it can even be so named, is simply to hold the presence of time as long as we can even as we know it slips past us. Bachardy's drawings pull us into their narratives of re-viewing such that our willingness to participate does not seek voyeuristically to gain power over the images. The artist's gaze becomes ours. We do not assert power over the body we view, nor are we subjected and disempowered by it. Like the artist, we partake in having, not wishing; in presence, not postponement.

The artist's gaze is nevertheless relentless, some might even say ruthless. In a way our culture does not often teach us to see, Bachardy depicts the material presence of Isherwood's body. Consequently, these drawings are simultaneously invigorating and sobering—invigorating because even in the watch of death, life is celebrated in the site/sight of the body, and sobering because our culture denies us this particular view of dying and death. Like Bachardy's *Last Drawings, Silverlake Life: The View from Here* is a rare representation of the dying process built around a long-term relationship between two men. By celebrating living bodies even as they lay dying, both works transgress cultural taboos against taking pleasure from such images.

In spite of its apparent ruthlessness, Bachardy's gaze is detached—he never intrudes his emotions onto his drawing. Isherwood, the novelist of wryly detached and multiple-sited perspectives, seems to be reflected in and by the artist who now draws him. As sitting subject, Isherwood, even at moments of direct confrontation with the artist, never allows himself to take a pose. Thus he remains a subject rather than an object of the artist's gaze. Collectively, these drawings figure an exchange and a participation, as the following passages from Bachardy's diary detail:

21 September 1985 While Chris was sitting for me on Thursday evening, his eyes on me and the view of the ocean, mountains and canyon beyond me, he suddenly said: "There's so much to describe." His eyes filled with tears. He said nothing more. (xii)

30 December 1985 I drew Chris again last night, *at last!* After a whole three days without drawing, I was afraid I might not. It took all the strength I could muster to get myself to do it, and, even so, I didn't get started until nearly seven. I worked till around ten. I put the TV on close to eight and worked right through some show about a painter directed by Clint Eastwood, without being tempted once to turn around and look. I did stop for the second act of the Hitchcock show . . . and then somewhat to my surprise, went back to work with Chris for another hour and a half. It felt so right to be working again, looking at Chris intently. It didn't even matter that he slept most of the time. I was *with him.* (emphasis added, xvii)

Bachardy's diary, like the drawings, exposes us to an intimacy beyond the normal decorum of privacy. Nevertheless, because Bachardy has structured a site from which we can view the project, and share in it, we do not feel that we have invaded his and Isherwood's privacy, nor do we feel morbid or prurient.

Whether Bachardy lightly brushes the paper with fine lines or vigorously lays on thick blackened strokes, all of the drawings communicate immediacy and haste. Where revision occurs, traces of early drafts are not cleared away, as if time would not permit such an attitude of self-contained completion. One of Bachardy's stated objectives is to narrate the process of Christopher's dying. As with all narration, however, one asks: which are the episodes requisite for the story to be told and which the details, which the accidents, which the connections? At the same time, each drawing is a distinct event shared between the artist-viewer and his lover-subject. Are we to isolate each image and read it for the moment or hour it records, or are we to link it into a chronology of good days and bad days, of rallyings and weakenings, of waning alertness and mounting fatigue? Even as each image seems to freeze a moment of intimacy, it can only be held onto by stalling the relentless forward push of the deathwatch process to which the book so unabashedly invites us. Out of this struggle between the now of dying and the narrative of dying, and perhaps because of it, Bachardy crafts with a remarkable degree of surprise the particularity of a material body as it is and as it changes.

But given the conditions of Bachardy's viewing and re-viewing of Isherwood's dying, does his engaged and relentless gazing therefore partake of cruelty or sadism? Edmund White feels called upon to account for Bachardy's seeming cruelty, noting that the drawings are "positively invasive, [and] they demand our complicity and refuse us the security of a discreet unchallenged distance" (346). Bachardy himself acknowledges a degree of cruelty in the project:

26 December 1985 I did draw Chris yesterday, three drawings in the living room with him in the wine velvet chair and my board resting again on his knee. What *contact* this set-up provides, even when Chris is in his most distracted, unconcentrated state, as he was yesterday. We are face to face, so close that if we both leaned forward just a bit we could kiss. Though I feel each time we begin that I have exhausted the possibilities of this set-up, I can't resist trying it again. One *can* be addicted to something which is actually good for one. Yesterday's drawings are not bad, especially considering the state Chris was in—he vomited the moment I had got him sitting down, just about the entire dinner. (xvi)

Bachardy does not hide the discomfort that is exacted as perhaps unavoidable to the intimacy achieved. Isherwood submits to sessions of painful "immobility"—almost a kind of bondage—and Bachardy voices anxiety about the pain seemingly inflicted on the older man. In spite of the elements of intimacy and pain, the drawings lack any maudlin or sentimental gesture as well as any suggestion of sadomasochism.

Bachardy's drawings compel us to encounter the very structure of the gaze that initially produced them, which in turn positions our viewing of them. The key to understanding the elements of rigor, discomfort, and control is to view the artistic project as a record of "work" in progress in the most literal and fullest sense. Philosopher Vicki Hearne has meditated on work and the ethical demands it places on us. She contends that gentleness can be as unkind as cruelty, and that to equate all pain with cruelty is to misunderstand the full moral dimension of kindness, especially when one assumes the responsibilities of educators, trainers, parents, or workers in a shared task.

Bachardy and Isherwood can perhaps be best thought of as "co-workers." Each takes full responsibility for the work in progress, and therefore each bears a moral commitment to the other in that process. Hearne provides several analogies to describe this kind of collaboration: "This is complicated—something like the relationship between two dancers in a *pas de deux* when the decision is being made about the moment one dancer leaps for the other one to catch, or maybe something like the agreement between a conductor and an orchestra about when to begin— to say that the conductor is in charge is not to deny that the conductor must be responsive to the orchestra or that the lifting of the baton is only the most easily described of a web of gestures" (95). For Hearne, work is a thing in itself, an absorption not to be abstracted or transcended. It strikes one as another version of play, of a queer eros, as described earlier. From Hearne's point of view, both *Silverlake Life* and *Last Drawings* can be seen as engaging levels of communication, demand, expectation, and response too subtle to be translated into words. Unfortunately, all that is left to us is the product or representation of that work. The work itself is elsewhere.

Thus Bachardy and Isherwood have collaborated to produce a "work" whose *process* is the recording of a specific and immediate gaze. In each drawing, the body is extravagantly present to us. Should the deathwatch of Isherwood's body have been drawn in a more merciful way? Is the project's rigor inescapably abusive? Although part of him resists the work, Bachardy forces himself to continue the process: "*25 December 1985* No work done and now today, though I intended to work, I wonder if I can, what with Chris's cough and my revulsion to him in general" (xvi). A symbiosis of agony seems to be a necessary part of the sharing. In another entry, Bachardy writes, "I returned from a trip to my studio (just outside the house) to get more paint and heard Chris saying to Dan from his electric-chair-like position, 'Here comes the torturer again.' It was said in a wry playful tone of voice which he *meant* to be loud enough for me to hear. We all three laughed. It was such a pleasure to have a taste again of Chris's sly wit. The torturer then took up his instruments and he and his victim performed for another two hours, until the light went" (xv). I have called Bachardy ruthless; he and Isherwood refer to Bachardy as a "torturer." Stephen Spender has described the drawings as "merciless and loving," to which Bachardy replied, "I laughed too, quite agreeing with him. But then, all of my work is merciless and loving. And since *real* love *is* merciless, one might just say my work is loving—merciless is redundant" (xii).

To accept Bachardy's account of mercilessness, however, is not totally to absolve him, because of our complicity as viewers in this mercilessness. What account are we to give of our role? As we turn page after page, we are subjected mercilessly to the unrelieved immediacy of deathwatch, unbroken by glimpses of the transcendental or the maudlin or even the morbid as ways to escape the intense purity of this presence. What consummation to our watching do we expect? Are we breathlessly awaiting death's throes and agony? Do we want to see this body writhe and scream? I think not. We await, page after page, a view of this body simply at last delivered into death. Surely we expect that finality to register as an image only of the body. These expectations are "torturous." Bachardy has positioned our viewing well. As a "work" in progress, the project with its extremes of physical and psychic demands is an enactment of rigor; its ruthlessness, tortuousness, mercilessness are outside the bounds of the coherent communication through which work gets done.

The final queer move that this book invites us to make is to deconstruct the myth of the artist and "his" muse. I say "his" because the trope of artistic creation as progeny to the union of male artist and female muse has scripted the story of Western art. It seems especially inapplicable here. Inculcated by the art-as-procreation trope, the seemingly natural boundaries between artist and subject, draftsman and product, viewer and text, are predictable. Under Bachardy's pencils and washes, they simply are not there. In place of such venerable boundaries and such venerable ways of seeing and reading, a queer view opens before us. This muse and his rigorous artist or this artist and his rigorous muse—which after all dominates such an exchange? does either?—produce a knowledge through the drawing and sitting which breaks from the bounds and strictures of the heterosexist trope of creativity. What a queer thing to do. If we enter into these images at all, we enter into them with a gaze that is epistemologically grounded in an altogether other way of knowing thanatos and eros. Although Bachardy's drawings survive Isherwood's death, they show presence not transcendence. Bachardy gives to eros and thanatos space in which to fuse. He calls this fusion love.

Bachardy's written account of Isherwood's death seems in its unsparing understatement to express the quality of mercilessness that the drawings project.

4 January 1986 . . . I have had my death encounter with Chris. I have had that body all to myself all afternoon. I'm glad Elsie didn't notice the eleven drawings I'd placed on the table in the darkened dining room. . . . I was afraid she would think me ghoulish. . . .

I was deeply shocked by Chris's remains—their utter lack of connection with him, in spite of the nose, the eyebrows, the ears—but forced myself to go on and on, looking into those dead empty eyes where once such light had flashed. When drawing faces I am skillful enough in instilling a quality of life in them that I had to remind myself *not* to bring life to the drawings, but fear even so a few of them look as alive, almost, as last night's drawings. (I did six of them last night, from six-thirty to nine-thirty.) But already by last night he was on his way—those unblinking eyes half turned up under the lids. . . .

Looking back now on those last months of Chris's life, I know that I could not have got through them without breaking down if it had not been for my decision to do these drawings. It was the severest challenge I had ever set myself and my determination to do my very best would not let me quit.

Since I only draw and paint people and always work only from life, my working experience is one of identification with my subject. While Chris was dying, I focused on him intensely hour after hour. I was able to identify with him to such an extent that I felt I was sharing his dying, just as I'd shared so many other experiences with him. It began to seem that dying was something which we were doing together. That shared experience provided me with a greater understanding of what death is, and with it, a diminished fear of my own. Chris's last gift to me was one of the most valuable of many he gave me. It was characteristic of him to be generous, even in the act of dying. (xvii–xviii)

The "knowing" that grounds these words and the drawings that they accompany is surely the same knowing that grounds the Names Quilt and *Silverlake Life,* for in them we are invited to celebrate life in death and dying in life, with a future imaged as the known and remembered, not the unattained or merely transcendent.

Additional Works Cited

Goodwin, Sarah Webster, and Elisabeth Bronfen, eds. *Death and Representation.* Baltimore: Johns Hopkins University Press, 1993.

Hearne, Vicki. *Adam's Task: Calling Animals by Name.* 1986. Reprint, New York: HarperPerennial, 1994.

Joslin, Tom, and Peter Friedman. *Silverlake Life: The View from Here.* New York: New Video, 1993.

White, Edmund. "Pool in Rocks by the Sea: Isherwood and Bachardy." In *The Burning Library,* ed. David Bergman. New York: Knopf, 1994. [Reprinted in *The Isherwood Century,* pp. 121–24.]

PART III
THE WRITER IN CONTEXT

Don Bachardy: *Christopher Isherwood, December 17, 1976.* Pencil and ink wash. 24″ × 19″.
Copyright © Don Bachardy. Used by permission.

All I can offer them is this book, which I have written about matters I only partially understand, in the hope that it may somehow, to some readers, reveal glimpses of inner truth which remain hidden from its author.

My Guru and His Disciple, 338

Christopher Isherwood's reputation rests largely on his Berlin novels, *Mr Norris Changes Trains* and *Goodbye to Berlin.* To regard him as primarily a writer of the thirties, however, is to ignore his vast postwar work and the complexity of his vision and style. This section includes chapters that discuss the Isherwood of the 1930s as well as the influence of Isherwood's later work on contemporary American readers and writers. In conjunction with the final section, the chapters published here give a wider view of Isherwood's work than is commonly found in criticism of twentieth-century British and American literature.

James Kelley offers a new reading of Isherwood's second novel, using queer theory as well as Isherwood's account of his "real family" from *Kathleen and Frank* to reexamine familial relationships. In "Aunt Mary, Uncle Henry, and Anti-Ancestral Impulses in *The Memorial,*" Kelley's revisionist reading suggests that rather than ignoring Isherwood's sexuality, critics should read his fiction through his sexuality, which opens up new ways of understanding his work and his rebellious impulses against the dominant English middle-class value system. This iconoclastic element of Isherwood's personality is clear also in both *Kathleen and Frank* and *Christopher and His Kind.*

Antony Shuttleworth's essay, "In a Populous City: Isherwood in the Thirties," finds a new angle on the most-studied period of Isherwood's work. Shuttleworth tackles head-on the problematic issues of Nazism and aestheticism that have troubled critics and historians for over fifty years. Sometimes seen as ignoring the political events of the late thirties in favor of petty criminals and prostitutes, the Berlin novels, in Shuttleworth's view, arise from those very concerns. Shuttleworth argues that art becomes a lens through which important cultural events can be viewed and that "the Berlin novels account for how monsters are made when history itself becomes monstrous."

The collaborations between Isherwood and Auden are the subject of essays by William Ostrem and Marsha Bryant. In "The Dog beneath the Schoolboy's Skin: Isherwood, Auden, and Fascism," Ostrem analyzes Auden and Isherwood's plays in light of the fascination with and revulsion from fascism

139

that they, like many of their contemporaries, struggled with. Detailing their collaborative process, Ostrem shows how Isherwood's contribution to *The
Dog beneath the Skin* expanded the scope of the play beyond England to embrace the political situation of the European continent. In "Documentary
Dilemmas: Shifting Fronts in *Journey to a War*," Bryant follows Isherwood and
Auden to China in search of the fighting during the Sino-Japanese War. Bryant
uses postcolonial theory and gender studies to examine the position occupied
by the two writers as "documentary men" in a situation fraught with masculin-
nist assumptions about war, sexuality, and empire.

The final three essays in this section consider the question of influence: E. M.
Forster's on Isherwood as well as Isherwood's on other readers and writers.
Stephen da Silva examines a sometimes troubling aspect of Isherwood's and
Forster's work: their sexual objectification of men from lower social classes,
or different races or nationalities, from themselves. Da Silva confronts the psychoanalytic theory attributing homosexuality to arrested development, and he
recognizes the complexities of the two writers' simultaneous positions of im-
perialistic privilege and sexual marginality. Reclaiming the category of "minor
writer" as an empowering classification for Forster and Isherwood, da Silva
puts their position regarding British imperialism into a historical context.

In an autobiographical essay, David Garnes reexamines his reading of *A Single
Man* thirty years after having read it for the first time. Blending personal and
critical writing styles in a way reminiscent of Isherwood's own style of writing
from life experience, Garnes articulates what many readers of Isherwood experience. He finds surprising and perhaps even reassuring connections between his own life and that of the protagonist. Garnes writes an appreciation
of the novel and reflects on the significance of Isherwood's frank depiction of
homosexuality to gay readers.

Going a step further, David Bergman's essay, "Isherwood and the Violet
Quill," connects Isherwood not only to gay readers but to gay writers. Bergman shows the centrality of Isherwood's work, particularly his autobiographical fiction, in helping post-Stonewall gay writers find a way to write about the
everyday lives of gay men in the twentieth century. As Bergman demonstrates,
Isherwood's matter-of-fact presentation of the sexual and his attention to the
spiritual aspects of life provided a model for writers such as Edmund White,
Robert Ferro, and Andrew Holleran in creating fiction that allowed gay writers
to "tell their own stories."

14 *James Kelley*

Aunt Mary, Uncle Henry, and Anti-Ancestral Impulses in *The Memorial*

In late November 1970, upon seeing John Lehmann examine his collection of books on E. M. Forster, Christopher Isherwood commented: "Of course all those books have got to be re-written. Unless you start with the fact that he was homosexual, nothing's any good at all" (Lehmann, 121). Isherwood's insistence on reading the author's sexuality back into his works and using it as the point of departure for textual interpretation—an insistence found again in his assertively queer memoir, *Christopher and His Kind*—runs counter to the actual trend developing in Isherwood studies since 1970.

Isherwood's novels, from early to late, have been praised in most of these studies for their presentation of generational truths about post–World War I England or their treatment of some universal "human condition," even as such representational tasks are seen as ill suited to the homosexual protagonists of an author whose sexuality was becoming more publicly known. While these critics have recognized that Isherwood's later autobiographical writings, *Kathleen and Frank* and *Christopher and His Kind,* discuss the tensions between the author's homosexuality and familial relationships, they have generally failed to note that the author's earliest published novels, especially *The Memorial: Portrait of a Family,* raise these same problems and suggest strategies for developing a homosexual identity within and in relation to one's family of origin.

Of Isherwood's first novel, *All the Conspirators,* Brian Finney observes that by "underplaying scenes and events, . . . Isherwood was able to subtly undermine conventional moral values even while the narrative was ostensibly tracing their triumph over a younger generation's unsuccessful revolt" (70–71). Finney's observation applies equally well to the narrative of *The Memorial,* which "was to be about war: not the War itself, but the effect of the idea of 'War' on my generation" (*Lions,* 296). But underneath that cover story, one might trace a more subversive tale: an account of the formation of a young man's homosexual identity. The character's identity is established in part through his recognition of what Isherwood calls "Anti-Ancestors," other "queer" members of his extended family. This project of revisioning traditional models of kinship is not unique to Isherwood or the characters in his early works. "After coming out to themselves," Kath Weston writes in her 1991 study of the significance of familial bonds to gay men and lesbians, "some people report subjecting blood ties to new scrutiny in a search for gay relations. Great aunts, second cousins once removed, and blood relatives who might otherwise be considered genetically or emotionally distant in an ego-centered accounting of kinship suddenly assume prominence as gay or lesbian forebears" (73–74).

In Book 2 of *The Memorial,* dated 1920 in the novel and therefore chronologically the first of the four sections, Eric Vernon contemplates writing a poem about the tensions he feels when shuttling from his family estate to the house newly occupied by his paternal aunt and back again. Eric briefly considers using the conceit of a magnetized needle in this poem: "Chapel Bridge and Gatesley were like the two poles of a magnet. . . . And if you rode over from Chapel Bridge to Gatesley, from Gatesley back to Chapel Bridge, you were like a pin on a bit of metal filing, being drawn first by one pole, then by the other" (173). Alan Wilde has identified this passage as a key to "the novel as a whole" and writes that the choice for Eric, and for the younger generation he is said to represent, is one "between, on the one hand, an allegiance to the dead forms of the past . . . and, on the other, a liberation from them by means which are never made completely clear and toward a goal which remains tenuous at best, since none of the characters manages to make a complete break with the past" (37–38). The descriptions of the two homes here and throughout the novel support Wilde's conclusion. Chapel Bridge is "clean" and well ordered but also "dead" and "negative," seeming to offer little for Eric. Its owner and Eric's mother, Lily Vernon, quite literally worships the past: she kneels in front of a mirror, with candles burning to either side, as she writes of the house's history in letters to relatives and in her diary, just as she transforms her bedroom into a shrine to an irrecoverable era, one that died with her husband at Ypres (see *Memorial,* 77–78, 68).

By contrast, the "positive" pole of Gatesley—the house of Lily's sister-in-law Mary Scriven and her two children, Maurice and Anne—is chaotic and bustling with life. This is the environment in which Eric feels he can grow: "It seemed to him that, if he could always live with his cousins, he would expand like a flower, breaking out of his own clumsy identity, gaining strength and confidence" (172). Reading *The Memorial* in light of Isherwood's subsequent autobiographical writings clarifies the purpose and method of this liberating alternative to what Wilde has rightly identified as "an allegiance to the dead forms of the past." What emerges is a portrait of the author (the fictional Eric and/or the real Isherwood) revisioning rather than simply repudiating or unconditionally embracing his familial past.

In biographical terms, as critics have noted, Chapel Bridge strongly resembles Marple Hall, the family estate of the Bradshaw-Isherwoods, just as Gatesley is modeled on the home of the Mangeot family, the musical family for whom Isherwood worked in the mid-1920s and whom he treated "as a much preferred alternative" to his own family (Finney, 57). But the novel deviates from the biographical in at least one important way: the alternate family of Mary Scriven and her children is closely related to Eric Vernon, and these family ties make all the difference, for they enable the young Eric, like the young Isherwood on whom he is modeled, to read subversively within his family history in order to create an alternate lineage that fosters—in its emphasis on "queerness"—his emerging homosexual identity.

Aunt Mary is herself a queer character, if we take "queer" in the early twentieth-century meaning of "odd" as well as "homosexual." The word is used twice in the brief account of Eric's first impression of her (163). More central to her place in Isherwood's revised family network, however, is the "something odd or reprehensible about his Aunt Mary" which he can sense when his mother looks at her (162). Whatever scandal there had been involving Mary's love affair with Desmond Scriven is in the distant past and has been "tea-tabled," or purposefully downplayed, in the narrative and thus rendered easy to overlook and open to speculation. The precise nature of the deeds, however, matters less than the muted but powerful moral outrage evoked in both of Eric's parents. Of the older generation, only Edward Blake—himself an outsider, a family friend rather than family member—is adamant that Mary not be excluded from the family for her actions.

Older than Eric's own mother yet more energetic, rolling her own cigarettes and parodying the late Queen Victoria at every opportunity, Aunt Mary bears "the seal of strangeness" (164) and has passed that mark on to her children; Maurice and Anne are equally "strange" to their cousin

Eric (165) and present him with new opportunities for identification and desire, opportunities now outside of the nuclear family but still within the realm of blood relations. Indeed, in Eric's descriptions of the two, both drives seem to be at work, with identification shifting to desire and then back again as easily as his cousins slip from one conventional gender role to the other. Although daring, athletic, and mechanically adept, Maurice has also a "very feminine side"; he is "soft, like a girl . . . slim, delicate-looking" (169). His sister, Anne, by contrast, is "handsome, though not exactly pretty," and she possesses "a bold forehead, too broad for a girl, and eyes drawn down at the corners, giving her at moments a wise, kindly, rather masculine appearance." She is shown to be equally at ease managing domestic affairs and playing sports and socializing with Maurice and his male friends (171).

In *Kathleen and Frank,* Isherwood describes his real-life Aunt Mary, in terms similar to the ones he uses to describe Anne Scriven: "With her large serious grey eyes and interesting temperamental mouth, she would have made an attractive young man. . . . The heroine of one of her books wishes she had been born a boy and pleases her brothers by taking part in their games" (186). The Aunt Mary in Isherwood's life may not have been homosexual; he is not as certain about her romantic leanings as he is about his Uncle Henry's, of whom he would later assert: "Uncle Henry became my first known adult homosexual" (*October,* 75). But, Isherwood claims of his aunt, "she never showed any inclination to marry," just as he points out that she found in a member of her own sex an "ideal companion" and a caretaker for the rest of her life (*Kathleen,* 187).

The Scrivens in *The Memorial* thus emerge as perhaps the first instance of Isherwood's lifelong project of re-visioning his family lineage and granting new significance to his odd, disowned, insane or even treacherous "Anti-Ancestors." This "anti-ancestry" includes female as well as male figures, his Aunt Mary alongside his Uncle Henry. It also includes such impressive personalities as Elizabeth Brubins, an eighteenth-century ancestor dispossessed of the family estate upon the death of the husband of her childless marriage, as well as the prominent John Bradshaw, who had been branded a traitor for signing the death warrant of King Charles I when all other judges had refused to do so (see *Kathleen,* 310–12, 292–97).

Kathleen and Frank records much of the information on these "Anti-Ancestors" in loving detail, yet Isherwood's careful construction of an entire "anti-ancestry," his act of seeking out queer kin in previous as well as in concurrent generations, is all but ignored in Paul Piazza's 1978 study *Christopher Isherwood: Myth and Anti-Myth.* Piazza offers the most extensive discussion of the role of family in Isherwood's novels, yet the headings of his first two chapters, both dealing with the early works—the first entitled "Mothers and Sons," the second "Fathers and Sons"—indicate Piazza's narrow focus on the nuclear family. His adherence to the Oedipal model of father-mother-son can be seen in his discussion of the dead war hero in *The Memorial,* of whom he writes: "Seen through the admiring eyes of Edward Blake or the love-beclouded eyes of Lily, Richard Vernon (Eric's father) is a cynosure of classical manhood" (56). This traditional but unconvincing division and assignment of identification and desire— Edward admires whereas Lily loves—is undermined by the language of the novel, for "admiration" is used to describe both Edward's attraction to Richard ("a deepening admiration"—130) and Eric's to Maurice ("whom [Eric] so painfully admired"—166), thereby taking on in its usage a meaning inseparable from desire and perhaps becoming a code term for homosexual attraction.

When Piazza does address the shared homosexual element in the relationship of Eric and Edward, the focus he has adopted leads him to proceed by means of a series of substitutions and displacements that, ultimately, replicates the conventional and heterosexual family unit (minus the mother) rather than explores alternative ways of viewing familial bonds and kinship. "Having lost a father in the war," Piazza explains, "Eric is in love with [Edward] Blake, a surrogate father . . . and though Eric and Blake do not yield to their mutual attraction, their truncated relationship satisfies a need in both: Blake assumes for Eric the role of Richard Vernon, Eric's father; and Eric, in turn, becomes Blake's son and idealized lover, a substitute also for Richard Vernon" (174). Viewing the relationship of Edward and Eric in terms other than a series of substitutions and a redirection of paternal-filial affection makes possible, however, a rereading of Richard Vernon himself, as it grants us two perspectives from which to view the absent father—through Edward Blake and through Eric. In one of the many flashbacks that further complicate the already disrupted chronology of *The Memorial,* Edward recalls the intimacy he shared with Richard Vernon before the latter's marriage to Lily: their friendship at school, Edward's frequent stays at the Vernon estate, an extended visit at the front, and a recurring suggestion—presented as "a standard joke of Richard's" (133)—that Edward should marry Richard's sister, Mary. Unable or unwilling to enter into a marriage that would cement the homosocial bond between these two men, Edward must content himself with being the best man at Richard and Lily's wedding, and he plays the role admirably even as he all but transforms the event into a farce. Lily's jealousy upon seeing Edward, Richard Vernon's "great friend" (99–100), at the memorial dedication likewise hints at a bond between the two men that was stronger than social conventions would suggest.

Even when there is no reference to the lost father and friend, Eric and

Edward continue to develop an increasingly close relationship in *The Memorial,* although this development is obscured by the rearranged chronology of the printed text; to see it requires both a chronological reordering of the narrative and speculation regarding critical but "tea-tabled" developments in their friendship. In the section bearing the earliest date (1920), they observe one another from a distance and without particular affection. At the dedication of the war memorial from which the book takes its title, Edward sees Eric as "the gawky boy getting into the carriage," and when we first see Edward through Eric's perspective, the portrait is even less flattering: "Quite apart from the jealousy" Eric feels when seeing Maurice enthused by Edward's presence, he "disliked him. Mistrusted him. . . . Eric couldn't imagine how his father could have been such friends with Edward Blake" (141, 158).

The conflict that soon develops between them over their attraction to Maurice, however, allows them to recognize their shared sexual desires and strengthens the bond between them. Eric confronts Edward about the gifts of money with which the latter has gained Maurice's attentions, points to a fear of scandal, and finally comes to realize in solitary reflection the extent of his own attraction toward his cousin. This rapprochement is drawn out through the 1925 and 1928 sections of the novel and more than likely culminates in some offstage confession of their similarities. Certainly, some sort of reconciliation is indicated in their mutual abandonment of Maurice and in the improved and regular communication between Eric and Edward in the later sections of the novel. By 1929, the date of the novel's last section, the two are in contact regularly: "Edward's the only one who sees him," Mary observes of Eric during a conversation with family and friends (244). The closeness of their relationship is underscored in the final scene of the novel, where Eric reveals in a letter to Edward his private plans to convert to Catholicism: "Perhaps this will surprise you. It would have very much more than surprised me a year ago. I don't know exactly when I shall make my first Communion, but it will be soon. Until that is over I shall say nothing to Mary or to my Mother, but I wanted you to know" (290–91).

Like the importance of Aunt Mary and Uncle Henry to the development of Isherwood's sense of self, the younger protagonist's conversion deserves a second look, for it, too, takes on new meanings and associations when read through Isherwood's autobiographical writings. A quick survey of critical pronouncements reveals that Eric's turning to Catholicism has been read again and again as a mark of failure:

Eric is in full flight back to authority, to exactly the force, now in intensified form, from which he has been fleeing and against which he has been revolting. (Wilde, 48)

Eric substitutes one mother figure for another—Mother Church, with her infallible authority, her cult of the Virgin, her celibate clergy. Having escaped from one mother, he is now tragically immured with another more tyrannical one. (Piazza, 41)

His social and political commitments are the products of his neurosis and it is therefore no surprise that he . . . ends up in the arms of the Roman Catholic Church, a mere substitute for his mother who was the source of most of his neurosis. (Finney, 97)

His flight to the Roman Catholic Church at the end of the novel is analogous to Philip Lindsay's reversion to childhood in *All the Conspirators,* a retreat into the arms of maternal authority. (Summers, 61)

Eric refuses any attempt to face himself and finds escape and solace first in left-wing politics and then in the Catholic Church, . . . an authoritarian institution. (Schwerdt, 44)

In these passages, Eric's conversion is read as an abandonment of the struggle for independence and as a return to the "maternal," "tyrannical," and even "infallible" authority of the Catholic Church. This critical position is unsatisfactory, oversimplifying the meaning of conversion and ignoring the personal associations that Roman Catholicism had for Isherwood.

For Isherwood, as for a number of other late nineteenth- and early twentieth-century authors, an embrace of Catholicism could in fact be part of an escape from rigid codes of behavior and thought, particularly part of an escape from what he was fond of calling the "heterosexual dictatorship." In a diary entry of October 27, 1979, perhaps the single most interesting section of *October,* Isherwood recalls: "When I was young, I liked the rich ritualistic Catholic smell of incense, because it represented religion of a forbidden and therefore attractive kind, frowned on by the Protestant members of our Family. My Catholic Uncle Henry used to burn incense in the fireplace of his sitting-room. He did this out of sensual pleasure in the smell, not as an adjunct to devotion, I am sure. . . . Because of Henry, incense became associated in my mind with homosexuality as well as with Catholicism—the two areas of intriguing mystery in his life" (75–76). This connection between Catholicism and homosexuality in Isherwood's private mythology can be traced back much further. In 1971, he records that his mother had held strong prejudices against Roman Catholics, thinking of them as "unscrupulous liars and agents of a foreign power. Worst of all, in her opinion, were Catholic converts; she called them 'perverts'" (*Kathleen,* 122) and thereby semantically linked the Catholic convert to the homosexual. Isherwood's Uncle Henry was both. And so, perhaps, was Aunt Mary; at any rate, she, too, converted to Catholicism in the early 1920s and thus provided the young Isherwood with yet another living "Anti-Ancestor" within his overwhelmingly Protestant family. And in an earlier diary entry, one dated July 12, 1940, Isherwood learns by cable from his mother that his uncle has been buried and writes that Henry "belonged to a ninetyish world of smart Catholicism—in which scandal was sniggered over at the end of dinner, and one's confessor was like a rich man's lawyer—paid to get you out of awkward spiritual jams" (*Diaries* 1:103). Scandal is thus reduced to the stuff of casual conversation, and the act of confession to the granting of permission and the allowance of all sorts of indulgences. The associations Catholicism had for Isherwood hardly seem to involve any renunciation at all.

A more recent critical statement on Eric's conversion likewise interprets it as a sign of failure, but here the critic faults the act for the secrecy in which it is shrouded: "In the ultimate histrionic gesture, at the conclusion where Eric writes to Edward about [Eric's] conversion to Catholicism, it is stressed that it is to be kept a secret from the family. Everywhere in society and the relationships of the novel there is duplicity, deceit and reserve, where people's lives are a trail of wreckage after the war" (Wade, 29). If one reads Eric's conversion as an analogue to his developing homosexual identity (and Isherwood's personal associations between the two warrant as much), Eric's plans for a "first Communion" take on sexual as well as spiritual meanings, and the desire to keep his conversion a secret between the two of them becomes more understandable. Insofar as the family of *The Memorial* is plagued by secrets (and Wade's claim seems overstated), perhaps the biggest secret of the novel—the homosexuality of Edward and Eric—is an open one. At the novel's end, Edward's friend Margaret relates a conversation she had with Mary in which things were said by being left unsaid: "I could think of no 'subtle' reason, so finally ended by telling Mary all, without disguise. It worked much better than I expected. In fact, I don't think she was at all seriously aggrieved. I remarked: You know what Edward is, and she agreed that we all knew what you were" (289). Today's reader, more accustomed to direct treatments of homosexuality, may view the "open secret" as yet another manifestation of the policing of desire, but indirect communication of this sort allows for knowledge to be conveyed that might otherwise not be transmitted at all. The young Isherwood himself might have benefited from this sort of veiled transmission. He writes much later, in 1979, that the "many half-disapproving, half-humorous hints dropped by my relatives" prepared him for the final discovery of Uncle Henry's homosexuality—a discovery, Isherwood hilariously recounts, that he made when happening upon his uncle and a younger male friend chasing one another around the gooseberry bushes in the garden at Marple Hall (*October*, 75–76).

In addition to demonstrating a degree of continuity in Isherwood's concerns regarding his family and sexuality, this reading of Isherwood's *The Memorial* as a queer "family portrait" highlights both the presence of homosexual bonds within extended family structures and the usefulness of queer "Anti-Ancestors" in strengthening both individual identities and family ties. Reading to understand how Isherwood went about revising his own lineage and uncovering new patterns of affiliation is itself an act of "re-vision," as Adrienne Rich has called it: "an act of looking back, of seeing with fresh eyes, of entering an old text from a new critical direction" (35). This sort of reading opens up interpretive possibilities, allowing new studies to be written to take their place alongside those already on the shelves.

Additonal Works Cited

Rich, Adrienne. "When We Dead Awaken: Writing as Re-Vision." In *On Lies, Secrets, and Silence: Selected Prose, 1966–1978*. New York: Norton, 1979.
Weston, Kath. *Families We Choose: Lesbians, Gays, Kinship*. New York: Columbia University Press, 1991.

15 *Antony Shuttleworth*

In a Populous City
Isherwood in the Thirties

Although the two novels collected as *The Berlin Stories* are usually acknowledged to be key texts of British writing in the thirties, it is hard to
miss a certain uneasiness, and a coolness, in their critical reception.[1] Set,
after all, in one of the most tumultuous periods of the twentieth century,
as a profoundly evil political regime gained power, it has never been entirely clear quite how, or whether, these reserved, somehow noncommittal
texts engage with their time. In what often seems like a collection of traveler's notes, a cast of crooks, gold-diggers, spent *artistes,* prostitutes, nervy
bourgeoisie, and would-be revolutionaries mingle in a world that seems
marked more by an ineffable sadness than by its developing history. The
novels seem to touch on big issues, but there is no very clear sense of
human drama or depth, no magisterial realist sweep, nor is there, by way
of alternative, any obvious formal innovation.[2]

Some years after their publication, Isherwood himself had misgivings
about the novels. Written in the tone of post-thirties recantation, Isherwood's prologue to Gerald Hamilton's *Mr Norris and I* (1956) presents
The Berlin Stories as callow, and callous, works. They show, he maintains,
the efforts of a young man who came to Germany in 1929 "twenty-four
years old and in many respects very immature for my age" (*Exhumations,*
86). In search of "the vilest place since Sodom," this young observer's
catchphrase is Iago's comment: "There's many a beast, then, in a populous

city, / And many a civil monster." But so keen was the young Isherwood to discover "civil monsters," we are told, that he invented them, oblivious to the human suffering behind his romanticizing daydreams: "What repels me now about *Mr Norris* is its heartlessness. It is a heartless fairy-story about a real city in which human beings were suffering the miseries of political violence and near-starvation. The 'wickedness' of Berlin's night-life was of a most pitiful kind; the kisses and embraces, as always, had price-tags attached to them. . . . As for the 'monsters,' they were quite or-dinary human beings prosaically engaged in getting their living by illegal methods. The only genuine monster was the young foreigner who passed gaily through these scenes of desolation, misinterpreting them to suit his childish fantasy" (86–87). Writing a prologue to a friend's book, Isher-wood had good reason to downplay the association between Hamilton and the morally suspect Norris, and to attribute the creation of Norris to a youthful hunger for glamorous, or easily condemnable, wickedness. But in doing so, he obscures what has been ignored in critical accounts of these novels, namely the attention within the novels themselves to the new role and power of fantasy, and of artifice, in European society of the thirties.

More recent accounts of the cultural and political circumstances of the novels make it clear that the young Isherwood was certainly not the only monster or artificer in Berlin between the wars. Nor, in fact, was the simple representation of suffering and cruelty the only, or even the most satisfac-tory, literary response to these monstrous times. The importance of *The Berlin Stories* stems from the fact that rather than voicing uncomprehend-ing liberal alarm at the horrors of the time, they delve into the possible causes of totalitarian politics, while also seeking to take account of their dangerous allure. The texts are disquieting in their suggestion that such politics should not be understood as a wholesale aberration from social conditions of the time but as a particular *instance* of circumstances and desires that were endemic to interwar European society. In place of the "proper" representation of suffering and human depth, the novels explore what conditions made possible new roles for artifice, and how artifice could give rise to suffering in the first place. Moreover, the texts are com-plicated by their suggestion that while politics can embody cultural forces that are catastrophically dangerous, these forces can, in very different ways, be productive.

Nazism, Aestheticism, Performance

One way of approaching Isherwood's treatment of these concerns is to consider how his work confirms, and anticipates, theories of Nazi politics that emphasize the Nazi reliance on spectacle, theatricality, and a certain form of performance. One of the better-known articulations of this feature of Nazism occurs in Walter Benjamin's "The Work of Art in the Age of Mechanical Reproduction." Benjamin saw in Nazism the result of humanity's "self-alienation," which had "reached such a degree that it can experience its own destruction as an aesthetic pleasure of the first order. This is the situation of politics which Fascism is rendering aesthetic" (242). Although Benjamin associates aestheticization with the representation of death, it is clear that such representation could only come about as a result of the role played by the aesthetic in the production of self-alienation in the first place. Nazism's aestheticizing of death is therefore an instance of a wider aestheticizing of politics, and of life itself, in the thirties.

Other commentators have offered descriptions of Nazism in these terms. Modris Eksteins, for example, has described the ways that, as "an instance of the avant-garde" that married "subjectivism with technicism," the power of Nazism came through the merging of the spheres of art and life (311). As a politics of "Will," Nazism was a particular transformation of German romanticism, which in its modern form produced "a realm of illusion which invented the outside world in its own image" (314). Within this realm, matters of life (violence, brutality) can be aesthetically pleasing, because art—in the form of myths of nation and race—has been merged with action. According to Eksteins, it was not the content of Hitler's "frantic neurotic tirades" that gave them force and excitement; it was rather the "style and the mood. It was above all the theater, the vulgar 'art,' the *grand guignol* productions of the beer halls and the street. It was the provocation, the excitement, the *frisson* that Nazism was able to provide, in the brawling, the sweating, the singing, the saluting. Nazism, whether one wore brass knuckles and carried a rubber hose or simply played along vicariously, beating up communists and Jews in one's mind, was action. Nazism was involvement. Nazism was not a party; Nazism was an event" (312). Under these conditions, a see-saw confusion of art and life exists where a political regime does not speak to a population so much as create it, and where a particular form of art finds its purpose in actions which are legitimated by nothing more than that art itself.

The Aesthete as Civil Monster: *Mr Norris*

Isherwood's first novel to deal with these conditions, *Mr Norris Changes Trains,* seeks to make connections between worlds where artifice is prominent: the worlds of the aesthete, of criminal intrigue, and of politics. The primary vehicle of exploration, the aging but newly politicized aesthete Arthur Norris, is quick to introduce Bradshaw, the narrator, to his guiding principles: "My generation was brought up to regard luxury from an aesthetic standpoint. Since the War, people don't seem to feel that any more. Too often they are merely gross. They take their pleasures coarsely, don't you find? At times, one feels guilty, oneself, with so much unemployment and distress everywhere" (22). As focus for the investigation of the power of art to change reality, Arthur is in love with created things, and Isherwood shows that this self-inventing figure's power to alter reality is intimately tied to his power to influence others. For the impoverished landlady Frl. Schroeder, for instance, Arthur is a means of reliving a lost time of elegance and grace, a time when she too exerted aesthetic power over coarseness. When he comes to tea she "would put on her black velvet dress . . . and her string of Woolworth pearls" (52). Arthur reciprocates with flattery and social games. As described, Arthur's world is artificial, but it need not be deceptive. He makes available a knowingly, and correctly, artificial world, the pleasures of which come about as a result of art's transformation, rather than deceptive simulation, of the real.

The dangers of this delicately balanced world, set against its pleasures, are signaled throughout the novel. The matter-of-factly "modern" Helen Pratt warns Bradshaw not to "trust [Arthur] an inch" (55), while the Berlin insider Fritz Wendel voices suspicion that "Norris is some kind of cheap crook" (57). For his part Bradshaw is quite aware that Arthur's dedication to the aesthete's world may be, at best, partial. Yet like Frl. Schroeder, Bradshaw creates an image of Arthur that reflects his own desires and longings, where Arthur is "a most amazing old crook," a "glorified being; audacious and self-reliant, reckless and calm. All of which, in reality, he only too painfully and obviously wasn't" (58–59). Bradshaw permits himself this antibourgeois fantasy because his image of Arthur is, he believes, tempered by a more accurate view. Arthur is a crook whose art deceives rather than transforms. Yet, because of his "weak nerves," Arthur seems a transparent and beleaguered figure whose small-time transgressions (constrained by incompetence) should not actually be dangerous, and whose feeble composure is in constant need of reassurance. In making this judgment Bradshaw trusts his own ability to determine when Arthur is lying, and his belief that Arthur can be trusted as a friend. As Bradshaw discovers to his cost, however, Arthur and the meanings of Arthur's actions will not be kept in place so easily. Although Arthur is not exactly the noble aesthete he claims to be in the early parts of the novel, he is also not the crook of Bradshaw's fantasies or of his sober consideration. The power of *Mr Norris* stems from Isherwood's ability to show how, in the particular way that he merges art with life, Arthur is more dangerous than any of these identities would suggest.

Ironically, we are given clues to Arthur's truly monstrous identity by his own descriptions of conscience, which confuse and intrigue Bradshaw. In

Arthur's work for the Communist Party he describes scruples which, although they *may* simply be the devices of a crook to advance his crimes, do not seem to be entirely so. Does Arthur lie when he says he believes he treated the unpaid Schmidt with the "utmost fairness" (154), that the earnest enthusiasm of workers "touched [him] very deeply" (173), troubling his tender social conscience? Bradshaw wonders whether it is possible that Arthur, after toasting "the world revolution," might have "undergone a sort of religious conversion." He adds that "it was difficult to believe" (83).

But while it is impossible not to be suspicious of Arthur's revolutionary principles, it is also very hard to disbelieve him entirely. After witnessing the euphoria of victorious workers, he entirely stumps Bradshaw by saying, "The simple enthusiasm of all those young people; it touched me very deeply. On such occasions, one feels oneself so unworthy. I suppose there are individuals who do not suffer from a conscience. But I am not one of them." To which the narrator comments, "The strangest thing about this odd outburst was that Arthur obviously meant what he said. It was a genuine fragment of a confession, but I could make nothing of it" (173). One might expect Bradshaw's confusion to be explained when the case against Arthur unravels: he is shown to be a spy against the Communist Party, the blackmailer of the unfortunate Von Pregnitz, and the betrayer of Bradshaw. It is hard to believe that Arthur has not been rehearsing his lines as "revolutionary" and "friend" since the start of the novel, just as he might have practiced his role as aesthete. The most startling thing about the narrative, however, is that when Arthur seems most obviously a plain deceiver, when he is stripped to his true colors, we come to realize that he is, in a particular and crucial sense, exactly what he has been claiming to be all along: an aesthete with a loyal sensitive nature, a tender heart, a conscience, and good intentions.

Instead of an aesthete unmasked as a crook, Arthur turns out to be a criminal unmasked as an aesthete. I mean to suggest not that despite wrongdoing Arthur has a "good" side but that, in a peculiar way, Arthur never lies when he describes his devotion to beauty, virtue, and sincerity. This odd brand of scruple is suggested after Bradshaw confronts Arthur with his crimes, and he fears Bradshaw (his friend) will turn him in to the police and collect a reward, presumably because in the same circumstances he would do just that (241). Yet Arthur at his most obviously criminal reveals the potency of his own brand of aestheticism when he returns from a moment of candor across the "delicate, almost invisible line which divided our two worlds" to his own world, and when his "orientally sensitive spirit" shrinks from "the rough, healthy, catch-as-catch-can of home-truths and confessions" of Bradshaw's rational temper (243–44).

The question of whether or not Arthur is capable of treachery and de-

ception turns not just on what he has done but also on what he himself
believes he has done. Critics who associate Arthur with amorality neglect
the importance of his constant insistence on his honor, loyalty, truth.[3] Arthur's retreat into what Bradshaw calls an "oriental" civility is not a retreat
into simple dishonesty. Arthur believes in his own devotion to virtue, since
belief, for Arthur, has become a facet of his own art, which allows him to
determine the meanings of these terms of judgment and to create an endlessly productive (and destructive) delusion. The delusion is, in Arthur's
terms, productive because it can be used to justify any course of action,
however monstrously wicked, and to describe this conduct as that of an
impeccably ethical and sincere agent. It is destructive for precisely the
same reason. Arthur implores Bradshaw to believe in his virtue, saying,
"This life is so very complex. If my behaviour hasn't always been quite
consistent, I can truly say that I am and always shall be loyal to the Party,
at heart. . . . Say you believe that, please?" Bradshaw's response is to consider Arthur "outrageous, grotesque, entirely without shame. But what
was I to answer? At that moment, had he demanded it, I'd have sworn that
two and two make five." And so he replies, "Yes Arthur, I do believe it"
(262). Bradshaw accedes here because, within Arthur's terms, belief is rendered meaningless, as meaningless as honor, loyalty, truth, and conscience.
Bradshaw speaks truthfully and not truthfully, because in Arthur's world
nothing is real or unreal. Arthur's unmasking is testimony not to the
power of truth to unmask deception but to the awful power of art to absorb and undermine any reality set against it, just as it can absorb ethical
restraints that would dissolve it. Arthur can in no way be loyal; but he
can, and presumably always is, "loyal," since it is always within his power
to arbitrarily set and manipulate the meanings that "loyalty" can have. In
Arthur's world the gesture, the performance, creates the reality, and not
the other way round.

It should come as no surprise, then, that Arthur is blind to his similarities to what he thinks he despises: Hitler and his Nazi regime. In this
blindness we recognize the full, and terrifying, topicality that Arthur's
power holds: "It is indeed tragic to see how, even in these days, a *clever*
and *unscrupulous liar* can deceive millions" (277). Arthur should know
that clever liars deceive millions because they can set the standards and
procedures of truth. He *should* know, but by virtue of what he is, or what
he has made himself, he cannot. Like Dr. Frankenstein, the great hero of
Romantic making, Arthur ends the novel locked in pursuit by, and in pursuit of, "the MONSTER" Schmidt (279). He is convinced until the last of
his own innocence, even though in his very fabrication of that innocence
we understand his monstrous freedom, and his monstrous guilt: "Tell me,
William, . . . *what* have I done to deserve all this?" (280).

Although Arthur comes to a sorry end, *Mr Norris* is an ambiguous work. Condemnation of Arthur's actions mingles with a recognition of the allure that his created world holds. The creator of his own reality, he is always in the right. Equally, the text acknowledges that set against Arthur's creation the claims and certainties of reason and truth can be rendered powerless. Arthur is invincible because he sets the terms of the game. Two other problems trouble the ending of the novel. Although Arthur's is a perverse, destructive use of the power of art to transform reality, plainly that power itself need not necessarily be destructive and may, as the Arthur of the early parts of the novel suggests, offer a valid means of liberation from the strictures of established reality. The text does not explore this possibility, but certainly the value of the aesthetic transformation of reality has to be felt as something that Arthur's actions destroy. Finally, there is the possibility that, in a novel about delusion, if Arthur's created world contains falsehoods to which he is blind, the reality he opposes might contain its own falsehoods and blindnesses, which warrant unmasking. These are the problems which Isherwood takes up in *Goodbye to Berlin*.

Resisting Performances: *Goodbye to Berlin*

Goodbye to Berlin casts its net wider than *Mr Norris* in its treatment of a society fallen under the spell of art, yet it begins with a narrow frame, a single Berlin street. Both novels begin with references to the faculty of sight, although in *Goodbye to Berlin* attention to appearances is set against a clear emphasis on objectivity and truth. The famous opening passage draws attention to appearance with mention of "top-heavy balconied facades" which hide "the tarnished valuables . . . of a bankrupt middle class" (13). The same emphasis is present in the passage which immediately follows, where private people preparing public faces are placed within a perspective that eschews such creations: "I am a camera with its shutter open, quite passive, recording, not thinking. Recording the man shaving at the window opposite and the woman in the kimono washing her hair. Some day, all this will have to be developed, carefully printed, fixed" (13). Critics have argued at some length over whether the narrator is or is not a camera, and what kind of camera (still, movie) he might be.[4] In fact he could be either kind. His shutter is open, and what is narrated are accumulated *instances* of observation made before the shutter closes, which might extend over time and space indefinitely. What matters is the mood of the narrator, his desire to observe in a certain way. He rejects comment and judgment and quite explicitly avoids the idea of objectivity as an overarching "view from nowhere." What we are offered instead is a situated objectivity ("from my window"), a small piece of the truth. More than anything else the narrator seeks, by receiving data like a camera, to be free of interpretation. It is not hard to see why, if we think of Norris's aestheticism as a kind of interpretation. It is also not hard to see that the narrator must fail to fulfill his wish, since although no camera selects data and interprets it, there is no human observation that does not select and interpret. Selection is itself an act of interpretation, and no camera can record that "signals echo down the *deep hollow* street, *lascivious* and *private* and *sad*" (14, emphasis added).

But critics have failed to notice the sense in which, precisely by failing to "observe" in the way that a camera—the actual piece of equipment— does, the narrator genuinely fulfills a cameralike role. For in offering a seemingly "objective" presentation of a Berlin street that turns out not to be objective, he actually mimics the cultural role that cameras can fulfill, though not the role they are commonly thought to fulfill. Cameras are used to provide images which are thought to be free of interpretation when they are not so, to provide what is thought to be the single truth but is not. The recognition of this false objectivity lends a considerable poignancy to the narrator's desire to rid himself of the dangerous activity of interpretation. His truth-telling status is compromised, and we begin the novel with the disconcerting idea that the "truth" that would undermine cultural appearances is, in its own particular way, a mythology that can offer its own deceptions.

If *Mr Norris* pursues the question of the aestheticizing of reality by looking at a particularly grand example, *Goodbye to Berlin* explores its smaller intensities, its infiltration of, and place within, everyday life. The latter is attentive both to the way life is transformed by its ritualization in art and to the way art hides within life, most particularly in ideas of authenticity. Such concern with the falsely authentic is a logical extension of the suspicion toward claims of objectivity. Yet if this suspicion implies a pessimism with regard to art's vertiginous colonization of life, the novel is not entirely desperate in its perspective. Against this usurpation of the real is a competing sense that although, say, Nazism may be a particularly dangerous form of aestheticism, the practice of aestheticism may be—in different forms—valuable and productive. It is through different ideas of *performance* that the novel suggests ways in which aestheticism may work to undermine both the strictures of bourgeois life and the totalitarian disappearance of the real.

A good example of the novel's consideration of these problems is the character of Sally Bowles. With her exaggeration, her theatricality, her self-invention, Sally is something of a counterpart to Arthur Norris: "'That's the man I slept with last night,' she announced. 'He makes love marvellously. He's an absolute genius at business and he's terribly rich'"

(46). Sally is dedicated not to the artificial in itself but to the naturally elemental, the authentic, the passionate. The importance and the pitfalls of this form of living theater are emphasized when Sally needles Christopher with claims of her sexual excess. In response to her question "Do I shock you?" he says: "When you talk like that it's really just nervousness. You're naturally rather shy with strangers, I think: so you've got into this trick of trying to bounce them into approving or disapproving of you, violently. . . . Only I wish you wouldn't try it on me because it doesn't work and it only makes me feel embarrassed. If you go to bed with every single man in Berlin and come and tell me about it each time, you still won't convince me that you're *La Dame aux Camélias*—because, really and truly, you know, you aren't" (60–61). The response is clearly very different in temper from those of the previous novel, and it is difficult to say why exactly. Why this new emphasis on authenticity? Why is it now important who Sally "really" is and isn't? Why is performance no longer valued for its own sake? How is Sally so very different from Norris?

Clearly both Sally and Norris claim that their presented identity is their whole identity. Yet apart from the differences in their degrees of composure, and in the role they assign to their audience—Norris's is participatory, Sally's is not—Norris and Sally differ in that Norris presents himself as a creation, whereas Sally claims that a created self is a natural one. Equally, whereas Norris *is* an aesthete who unsuccessfully disguises (so Bradshaw thinks) his role as a minor criminal, Sally only pretends to be a sexual adventurer, a pretense that unsuccessfully disguises her identity as a young middle-class woman, a significant identity which is, for the embarrassed Christopher, quite visible behind the assumed, and transparent, identity of sexual adventurer: "You're the daughter of Mr. and Mrs. Jackson-Bowles" (61). Furthermore, in her role as what Christopher calls *La Dame,* Sally implies that *La Dame*'s engagement with life is more tangible, more real, than that of others. In this respect her supposed transcendence of English middle-class values is in fact a covert confirmation of them: she replaces one "real" identity with another that is even more "real." *La Dame*'s sexual empiricism is therefore the logical outcome of Sally's deceptive attempt to erase her former identity and to claim, as the discourses of her class might well do, that a created identity can be natural.

Yet Christopher's attack on the authenticity of Sally's assumed "character" should not be read, as it has been, as an attack on her performance as a whole.[5] Indeed, he supports it, "as long as you're sure you're really enjoying yourself" (61). The implication is that although Sally is certainly a young English middle-class woman, she is not *only* a young English middle-class woman, which is precisely the reason it may be desirable to *perform* the role of *La Dame.* This performance can be, and often is, transgressive, parodic, transformative, liberatory. It calls into question the very "authenticity" it might suggest, while mocking the limitations of Sally's background.

The problem with this performative identity, however, is that it does not remain at a transgressively self-conscious level but rather falls into delusion. Sally and Christopher can fall about laughing at "a girl who sacrificed her stage career for the sake of a Great Love, Home and Children" (73), yet she too is very capable of mistaking fantasy for reality and succumbing to her myths of authenticity: "'He was so marvellously primitive: just like a faun. He made me feel like a most marvellous nymph, or something, miles away from anywhere, in the middle of the forest'" (69). Sally's ideas of love and career mimic Arthur's aesthetic delusions: "'If you're rich you can afford to stand out for a really good contract. . . . Of course, I'd be absolutely faithful to the man who kept me—' Sally said things like this very seriously and evidently believed she meant them" (76).

Just as Norris undermined Bradshaw's certainty in his power of judgment, Sally points out to Christopher the very failings he claims to identify in her. Her performance brings into the open that Christopher's identity as "the Novelist," guarantor of truth and rectitude, is a pose: "Wasn't I a bit of a sham anyway . . . with my arty talk to lady pupils and my newly-acquired parlour-socialism? Yes, I was" (105). Interestingly, Christopher castigates himself for being a sham, but also for not managing Sally's attacks in a properly "fatherly" way. Standards of authenticity and frankness—the hallmarks of the new generation—have obviously slipped, and Christopher is forced to recognize that his own undeceived world has hidden deceptions, and therefore a hidden contingency, of which he was unaware.

Yet Christopher is hardly alone in a city populated by appearances: "These people could be made to believe in anybody or anything" (293). Nazism gains its power by spreading mass delusion: the delusion arrived at by the imposition of aesthetic structures on experience, and by the individual experience of a fake authenticity. While having a clear validity, standards that are set against these delusions, such as objectivity, cannot be seen as entirely without artifice, especially when their false strictures are demonstrated by a figure like Sally. Yet Sally too becomes the victim of her own delusions. These are the conditions that lead Christopher, departing a city of which "Hitler is master," to think of Berlin as "a very good photograph" (316, 317). Photography is now seen not as a guarantee of truth but as a mark of artifice, mixing fact with fiction: "No. Even now I can't altogether believe that any of this has really happened" (317).

If any character seems to have understood these seemingly intractable problems, and how one might respond to them, it is the department-store owner Bernhard Landauer, who finds himself in a world disappearing before his eyes: "I have had an unpleasant feeling, such as one has in a dream, that I myself do not exist. . . . One evening, I was so much troubled by this hallucination of the non-existence of Landauers' that I picked up my telephone and had a long conversation with one of the night-watchmen" (276). Landauer witnesses his own disappearance from the aesthetic sanctuary of the flat over which he presides with "his over-civilized, prim, finely drawn, beaky profile [giving] him something of the air of a bird in a piece of Chinese embroidery" (240). Interrupted by phone calls from frantic associates, his sanctuary is far from perfect. Yet this tiny incongruity suggests something significant about Landauer and his world. Why have a telephone in a sanctuary? It is the very tenuousness of Landauer's world that grants it a validity. Unlike so many of the aesthetes in these novels, Landauer fully recognizes that the reality of his created world is contingent on other worlds, also created, about which he is "gently inquisitive, mildly satiric, poking his delicate beak-like nose into everything" (241). His world is doomed, yet its fragility is a particularly horrific confirmation of the fact that it was always tenuous, provisional, ironic—receptive to the relationship between self and world, and between worlds, that Nazism, like other aestheticisms, can erase. Landauer's death contributes so much to the sense of desperate sadness at the end of the novel not only because of his personal suffering but also because with it dies the delicate negotiation between art and life that he created. His art transforms, as one art among others, but it does not deceive. And a substantial part of its beauty resides in its recognition of its own contingency. Unable to withstand the chaos brought about by the totalitarian usurpation of life by art, Landauer's created world nevertheless shows that knowledge of art's possibilities, in creating worlds that recognize their own status as creations, can save us from art's dangers.

More than making monsters, therefore, the Berlin novels account for how monsters are made when history itself becomes monstrous. If the final sense of the texts is that the usurpation of life by art is disastrous, they are equally clear that the separation of art from life is impossible, and that the idea of an "artless" world, claiming authenticity or objectivity, is a delusion dangerous in itself. In going beyond the realist project of the thirties, Isherwood alerts his readers to the problems and limits inherent in that very project itself. Still, his Berlin is a city populated by real dangers, and by the sense that in order to properly attack these dangers for the suffering they cause, and the opportunities they destroy, they must first be properly understood. Isherwood's fiction of the thirties thus gains its importance not merely by presenting the perils of the times but by showing that art can most readily engage with them by revealing its own role in their creation.

Notes

1. *The Berlin Stories* collects *The Last of Mr. Norris* (1935) and *Goodbye to Berlin* (1939). The title of the U.K. edition of *The Last of Mr. Norris* is *Mr Norris Changes Trains.*
2. Samuel Hynes, for example, notes in *The Auden Generation* that in *Goodbye to Berlin* "there are no public figures . . . and no great events: Hitler never appears, and the political struggles of the time are virtually ignored" (354). In "a city without connections . . . the representative Berliner is the narrator, an isolated foreigner without real human contacts" (355–57).
3. Richard Johnstone, for instance, speaks of Norris as "delightfully amoral" (111).
4. See, for example, Schwerdt, 81.
5. See Mizejewski, 84. Mizejewski argues that Christopher's disapproval of Sally's theatricality reveals a suspicion of its links to Nazi performance and to female power. But Nazi aestheticism is not necessarily synonymous with performance, and Christopher's criticism of Sally's authenticity is echoed when authenticity is asserted in the discourse of Nazism and by Christopher himself.

Additonal Works Cited

Benjamin, Walter. *Illuminations.* Ed. Hannah Arendt. Trans. Harry Zohn. New York: Schocken, 1968.

Eksteins, Modris. *Rites of Spring: The Great War and the Birth of the Modern Age.* New York: Doubleday, 1990.

Johnstone, Richard. *The Will to Believe: Novelists of the Nineteen-Thirties.* Oxford: Oxford University Press, 1984.

The Dog beneath the Schoolboy's Skin
Isherwood, Auden, and Fascism

If a literary collaboration can begin before pen is put to paper, then the collaboration between Christopher Isherwood and W. H. Auden began not in a Berlin cabaret or a London flat in the 1920s but on a prep school cricket field in Surrey in 1917 or 1918. As a mutual friend, Harold Llewellyn Smith, recalls the occasion, Isherwood and Auden planned a Gothic historical novel "surreptitiously" while they "should at least have been going through the motions of playing cricket" (Spender, *Auden,* 36). While the boys of St. Edmund's did not finish their story, they nevertheless had made a start of sorts.

After Isherwood left St. Edmund's in 1918, he and Auden did not meet again until 1925, when Auden was a student at Oxford and Isherwood, who was two and a half years older, was working in London. At this meeting, the two quickly renewed their friendship. Within a few years, they had become close friends, sometime lovers, traveling companions, and literary collaborators. Their first mature literary collaboration began in 1929 with a play entitled *The Enemies of a Bishop,* which evolved from a play by Auden called "The Reformatory." Their characterization of the play's hero, Bishop Law, shows the young Isherwood and Auden to have ambivalent attitudes toward fascism and fascist leader-worship—attitudes they would continue to confront throughout the 1930s. Law emerges as the very picture of a fascist leader: he wears "a police hat and medals" and issues commands in militaristic language to a schoolboy "Flying Squad" decked out in "gym-shoes, shorts and zephyrs marked with a scarlet F" (*Plays,* 74).

In the political parlance of the time, flying squads were located decisively on the fascist side of the political spectrum. The blue-shirted British Fascists, for example, divided their ranks into flying squads and reserves (Benewick, 27, 30). The flying squads were made up of young, unmarried men who could be called to go anywhere at short notice, while the reserves were comprised of older men. Thus the Bishop appears to be a fantasy figure for both authors—a character who realizes his own vision of personal and social redemption through acts of heroic individualism that also win him the adoration of young male followers.

As they matured, Isherwood and Auden became increasingly conscious of these personal tendencies toward fascist-like daydreams of heroism and leadership. In his 1938 autobiographical work *Lions and Shadows,* Isherwood ascribed these hero-fantasies to what he called "homosexual romanticism" (78). For Isherwood this romanticism was experienced most intensely during his time at Cambridge in the early 1920s. It involved, he wrote, a "cult of the public-school system" based on "the daydream of an heroic school career." These daydreams centered on himself as a leader who passes something called "The Test" (76) and proves himself a man. "The Test" refers to his generation's "shame that we hadn't been old enough to take part in the European war" and their resulting desire to encounter a similar event that will prove their manhood (74). Isherwood considered how this psychological complex made him and those like him prey to fascist rhetoric: "The rulers of Fascist states . . . profoundly understand and make use of just these phantasies and longings. I wonder how, at this period, I should have reacted to the preachings of an English Fascist leader clever enough to serve up his 'message' in a suitably disguised and palatable form? He would have converted me, I think, inside half an hour" (78–79).

Although Isherwood was never "converted" by such a leader, he did come into indirect contact with one in 1931: Sir Oswald Mosley, who would eventually become the most influential fascist leader in Britain. Mosley, a Labour M.P., used the economic crisis of 1930–31 as an opportunity to break from his party and form a new organization called, appropriately, the New Party. Espousing a blend of protectionism, nationalism, and Keynesian economics to address the financial crisis, he attracted support among the middle classes with his call for an emergency response to the nation's economic problems. He also attracted active support from social circles closely linked to Isherwood and Auden. These ranged from Oxford students who served as Mosley's bodyguards at rallies to the writer Harold Nicolson. Nicolson, in fact, recruited various people to write for *Action,* the New Party weekly, including Gerald Heard, Osbert Sitwell, Vita Sackville-West (Nicolson's wife), and Isherwood. In 1931, Isherwood contributed an article to *Action* entitled "The Youth Movement in the New Germany," in which he describes the absorption of the early twentieth-century German *Wandervogel* youth movement by the Communist Party and National Socialist youth groups. His tone favors neither political party; instead, it simply celebrates youth's victory over bourgeois repression. "German boys and girls," Isherwood wrote in a hearty tone, "will grow up to be real men and women, whatever their party. . . . They will live to become brave and worthy citizens of their country. It is to be hoped that we can say as much for our own younger generation" (18).

Although Mosley initially denied any connections with continental fascism, evidence of the New Party's increasingly fascistic tendencies mounted throughout 1931. Soon national newspapers regularly portrayed Mosley as nothing less than an "English Hitler" and carried stories of the New Party's formation of a youth movement similar to that of the Nazis. On May 18, 1931, the *Daily Express,* for example, carried an article with the headline "Sir Oswald and a 'Hitler Plan': Flying Squads to Be Formed." The party's "soldiers," the story said, were to be trained in gymnasiums and taught boxing and other manly arts. By 1932, Mosley had disbanded the New Party and formed the British Union of Fascists, the most powerful fascist party in Britain between the wars. Before this happened, however, Nicolson and many others had already abandoned the movement.

While Isherwood's political ambivalence found expression in his essay on German youth, Auden struggled with his own mixed feelings regarding politics. In particular, he sought to explore those feelings in *The Orators: An English Study,* a work he wrote in 1931. The book's obscure plot concerns a group of young "initiates" and their leader, the "Airman," whose relationship seems homoerotic. After completing the book, Auden commented disappointedly: "It is meant to be a critique of the fascist outlook, but from its reception among some of my contemporaries, and on rereading it myself, I see that it can, most of it, be interpreted as a favourable exposition" (Mendelson, 104). In a summer 1933 letter to Stephen Spender, Auden attributed such sentiments partly to his position teaching at the Downs School, Colwall, which apparently only encouraged the continuation of schoolboy complexes: "I entirely agree with you about my tendency to National Socialism in Germany, and its dangers. It is difficult to be otherwise when one's surroundings and emotional symbols are of necessity national symbols" (Bucknell, 62).

Isherwood and Auden, of course, did not become Nazis. By late 1934, when they began to work on a new play, *The Dog beneath the Skin,* they had instead become active opponents of fascism and even flirted with its ideological opposition, communism. Their work on the play would mark another step in their growing awareness of how English culture had formed them and how it had predisposed its middle classes to adopt a reactionary political position. Isherwood's years in Germany, 1929 to 1933, served as a political awakening as he witnessed firsthand the rise of National Socialism. This direct historical experience proved to be a crucial element shaping the Isherwood-Auden plays into successful political satire.

Before Isherwood rejoined Auden as a dramatic collaborator in the mid-1930s, he completed *Mr Norris Changes Trains,* a novel that interrogates many of its author's attitudes regarding politics. Finished in August 1934, several months before Isherwood and Auden began *The Dog beneath the Skin, Mr Norris* weaves into its plot events relating to the growing power of fascism in Germany.

The novel's semiautobiographical narrator, William Bradshaw, may be viewed as a version of Isherwood's more naive earlier self, the schoolboy who could have been "converted" by a fascist leader "inside half an hour." Bradshaw is "converted" by the novel's other main character, Arthur Norris, into a follower, eventually becoming involved in a scheme that funnels Communist Party secrets to the French secret police. As Claude Summers has argued, Norris may be viewed as an analogue to Hitler; he is a figure with the charm to induce others to become involved in his exploits—exploits that aid the forces of reaction rather than revolution (28).

Bradshaw has opportunities to join the forces that oppose fascism, but his mixed feelings regarding politics keep him from doing so. When he attends a Communist Party rally, he feels that he remains "outside" the "passion" and "strength of purpose" of those around him (*Berlin Stories,* 48). Instead he can only sit and watch, "half-hearted," while any sympathy he may have with the Communists is "muddled" by his English middle-class past, "by slogans from the confirmation service, by the tunes the band played when my father's regiment marched to the railway station, seventeen years ago" (48). Still dominated by the loss of his father in the Great War, still muddled by romantic notions of "The Test," this young Englishman cannot take decisive action.

If *Mr Norris* shows Isherwood to be fully conscious of his original political ambivalence, his next fictional creation, *The Dog beneath the Skin,* shows him experimenting with political commitment rather than political passivity. As will be seen, however, this creation was fraught with its own difficulties, including a vision and model of political action that were still imbued with the schoolboy's daydreams of individual heroism.

While Isherwood remained on the Continent through the early 1930s, Auden looked on enviously from England. They remained in close contact, however, and in November 1934, when Auden had difficulty completing a play called *The Chase,* he enlisted Isherwood's help. In letters written in November and December of that year, Isherwood suggested eliminating two subplots and concentrating instead on a plot involving an English village's search for a missing heir. In this new version, the play would be more explicitly political. Isherwood proposed, for example, that the main character, Alan Norman, return from the search for the heir to find a nascent "religious-fascist organisation" in the village consisting of the Vicar leading a brigade of smartly uniformed boys (*Plays,* 563). His scenario also suggested that the majority of the play's action occur on the Continent. With Isherwood's help, therefore, the revised version of *The Chase*—which would soon receive the title *The Dog beneath the Skin*—became a tour of the entire European political landscape. No less important, Isherwood's suggestions made *Dogskin* a viable drama in a way that *The Chase* had not been.

As a result of Isherwood's influence, *Dogskin* is as much about contemporary Europe as it is about contemporary England. Isherwood's changes locate the play's English village in a larger political and cultural context, and the play becomes a vehicle for instructing the English about their shared destiny with Europeans. With its continental connections, the *Dogskin* reshaped by Isherwood also led to a crucial change in Auden's writing: from an exclusive concern with English settings and subjects, he now broadened his perspective to include Europe. As Michael J. Sidnell has described the Isherwood-Auden collaboration on *Dogskin,* "Isherwood was pulling in the direction of Europe, Brecht and political didacticism; Auden towards England, melodrama and psycho-social diagnosis" (159).

Although Isherwood pulled *Dogskin* in the direction of the Continent, the play is still very much about England. The village of Pressan Ambo emerges as a symbol of the nation and its backward-looking ways. Throughout the play, and even in its Continental scenes, the chorus—whose lines were written by Auden—addresses an English audience directly and asks it to compare the events of the play to those occurring in England.

Isherwood's simplified plot begins in Pressan Ambo with the selection by lottery of a young man to search for the missing heir of the local landed gentry, "the ancient family of Crewe" (198). The late Sir Bingham Crewe has pledged half the family land, while his daughter, Iris, has promised her hand in marriage, to the man who can find Francis. Alan Norman wins the lottery and, accompanied by a stray dog from the village, travels to the Continent, where he has adventures in the monarchist state of Ostnia and the fascist state of Westland. Unsuccessful in his attempts to find Francis, Alan finally returns to Pressan Ambo, only to find out that Francis has been with him all along in the guise of the dog.

Isherwood and Auden altered the play's ending several times,[1] but in all of their versions the town fails to live up to its promise of rewarding Alan for returning Francis. Indeed, rather than welcoming home the two native sons, the village greets them with scorn and ignores their message. And by ignoring the message of these two returning prophets, Pressan Ambo chooses to turn in on itself and be deaf to outside viewpoints. In a world in which the international news is becoming ever more alarming, the village attempts to prepare for the future by looking to the past, remaining insular and static, ultimately putting its hope in political and spiritual reaction.

In fact the motivating premise of the play—the search for a missing heir—is a function of the village's reactionary outlook. In their quest for "the Master's son," the people of Pressan Ambo seek continuity, or an unbroken line of inheritance into a past they consider to be more secure than the present, a feudal era when each village was ruled by a lord. In that search they also seek to reinforce their idea of themselves as an extended family—an element of fascist ideology intended to foster a sense of nationalism. "He was our brother and our son," one of them sings (199). And when Francis and Alan ultimately renounce their ties to the village, they are also renouncing their ties to the family that it once embodied for them.

When Alan and Francis first leave Pressan Ambo to tour Europe, they discover a world very different from their pastoral home. This new world includes a variety of contemporary political and social horrors. In the continental cities especially—those places "whose loyalties are not those of the family" (218)—they learn how small and protected the world of Pressan Ambo truly is. In autocratic Ostnia, for example, they witness summary executions of political prisoners, and in Westland they encounter a fascist state with a "Leader" whose face is represented by a loudspeaker and whose nationalistic speeches echo Hitler and Mussolini.

When Alan and Francis return home in the last scene, they arrive with a very different view of the historical moment—and they soon learn that Pressan Ambo, though isolated, is not immune to the social forces shaping the Continent. In the published version of the scene—written mostly by Isherwood—Pressan Ambo has become a miniature, proto-fascist state. Alan and Francis, Isherwood wrote in a letter planning the scene, return to the village and find a "Patriotic Meeting" in progress: "I think that the

Patriotic Meeting is definitely a ceremony to initiate a kind of Lad's Brigade in the village, a religious-fascist organisation designed vaguely to help England in an 'emergency' and to carry out the 'ideals of the church.' The boys would have a very fetching uniform specially designed by the Vicar" (563). Such a scenario clearly draws on existing fascist organizations, not only the Nazis in Germany but also groups such as Mosley's British Union of Fascists.

Accordingly, Isherwood created a final scene in which Alan arrives home to find the vicarage garden now occupied by the paraphernalia of fascist oratory: a platform draped with the Union Jack and other national flags of the British Empire, along with a banner reading, "The Lads of Pressan teach Britain a lesson" (573). Upon surveying this scene, one of the two journalists in the play comments that Pressan is "moving with the times"; he also summarizes the Mosley-like creed of the Boy's Brigade, which has been founded by the Vicar and General Hotham: "Standing outside all political parties and factions, for Church, King and State, against communism, terrorism, pacifism and other forms of international anarchy, to protect Religion and succour England in times of national crisis" (574). Shortly thereafter, the Vicar expounds this ideology to the uniformed lads in his dramatic sermon, the topic of which, the Curate has commented, is "Bolshevism and the Devil." The stage directions tell us that as he speaks he becomes a veritable picture of the political orator. He works himself into "an hysterical frenzy," foaming at the mouth with tears streaming down his cheeks (575).

Alan and Francis watch the proceedings in hiding but reveal themselves when they learn that the village has betrayed its promises to Alan and has arranged for Iris to marry Mr. Rudolf Trunnion-James, a "well-known munitions manufacturer" (580). In what constitutes the climax of this version of the play, Francis then makes a didactic speech denouncing the village and proclaiming his intention to oppose it and all it stands for. Then five of the villagers, including a young man and one of the Lads of Pressan, respond to Francis's call for volunteers, and they, along with Alan, come down from the stage and exit as a group through the audience. The play concludes with a choral epilogue asking that the audience "choose . . . that you may recover" and construct "another country"—a country better than the one they have seen on the stage (585).

So ends the first version of *Dogskin*, which was published by Faber on May 30, 1935—after Auden was forced to scramble to make sure that Isherwood would receive credit as co-author. The Group Theatre production of the play was delayed, however, and preparations did not begin until December 1935. During rehearsals, Auden and Rupert Doone, director of the Group Theatre, agreed that the final scene was difficult to stage, and in December 1935 Auden asked Isherwood for assistance in rewriting it (586). Isherwood promptly submitted a revised outline for the scene, and Auden used it as he composed the final version.

The result of these changes is a scene in which Pressan, and therefore England as well, seems much less like a miniature fascist society. The authors dropped the patriotic meeting, the uniformed Lad's Brigade, and the Vicar's sermon. Mr. Trunnion-James, meanwhile, who is to marry Iris, is not identified as a munitions manufacturer but as an M.P. for something called the "National Independent" Party (283). Auden and Isherwood debated how to deal with the marriage. Isherwood argued successfully to save it. By having Iris marry an establishment figure and then having the journalists cover the marriage rather than the fate of Francis, he explained in a letter, a vital theme would be preserved: "the [effect] of the hideous social lie and the death of truth" (587). The villagers, as a result, ignore the protestations of Iris, who expresses a desire to be with Alan and fulfill the promise originally made, and instead congratulate themselves on marrying off a member of their "family" to a moneyed man. In doing so, this apparently quaint village is implicated in the larger corruptions of English society.

The most important divergence from the earlier version of the final scene, however, is in the character of Francis. Although Isherwood contributed ideas to this revision of the final scene, most of the rewriting was left to Auden. According to Edward Mendelson, in this version Auden "made Francis into an Audenesque instructor in history and choice," removing Isherwood's reference to "the army of the other side" as well as Francis's triumphant exit (278). So Francis makes a different denunciatory speech to the villagers, one emphasizing the importance of choice: "For choice is what you are all afraid of. . . . That is what terrifies you. 'Anything,' you cry, 'anything for the old feeling of security and harmony; if nature won't give it, give us a dictator, an authority who will take the responsibility of thinking and planning off our shoulders'" (285–86). Above all else, this version of *Dogskin* tells us, it is fear of responsibility that causes the people of Pressan Ambo to wish for a return to a time of supposed "security and harmony."

Predictably, Francis's message is not welcomed in Pressan Ambo, and in this version he is killed by Mildred Luce, a disturbed woman who is haunted by the Great War and consumed by hatred of the German nation. The journalists proceed to remove all traces of his existence by sewing him up into his dogskin. Alan Norman, meanwhile, the other truth-teller in the play, exits silently through the audience, pursuing his new course in life alone, not as a leader in any organized opposition.

If the people of this final version of Pressan Ambo are any indication, the English seem unlikely to take the kind of action requested by the play. The village's annual contest to search for Francis turns out to be only a means of legitimizing their complacency with an air of tradition, allowing them to believe they are carrying on in the ways of their ancestors. Like other Europeans seduced by the speeches of fascistic leaders, the villagers are caught between a rapidly changing modernity and their own mis-guided desire to return to outmoded ways of life. Rather than choose to live freely in modernity, they have taken refuge in a number of different means of escape, as the chorus tells us:

> Some turn to the time-honoured solutions of sickness and crime: some to the
> latest model of aeroplane or the sport of the moment . . .
> Some have adopted an irrefragable system of beliefs or a political
> programme, others have escaped to the ascetic mountains
> Or taken refuge in the family circle, among the boys on the bar-stools, on the
> small uncritical islands. (280)

Only Alan and Francis are able to leave the "family circle" of Pressan Ambo and its political escapism, and their different fates point to the dangers of doing so. Francis ultimately pays with his life for his renunciation of the village family, while Alan chooses exile—a choice that Isherwood had already made and that Auden would soon make as well.

Two questions concerning the last scene remain: why did Isherwood and Auden alter Francis's fate from a heroic exit to a tragic death, and why did they drop the representation of Pressan Ambo as a proto-fascist community complete with uniforms, banners, and youth brigades? Judging by Isherwood's correspondence, the answer to the first question appears to lie in the authors' continuing realization of their own tendencies toward the romantic, fascistic pose of heroic leadership. Isherwood wrote in his outline to Auden that "the appeal for volunteers" in the earlier version seemed "horribly quisb" (*Plays*, 587–88)—a word he and Edward Upward used for "disgustingly sham" expressions (*Lions and Shadows*, 80–81). Like his "homosexual romanticism," such "quisb" expressions had their origins in a schoolboyish mindset. Francis's leadership of a team of young male recruits was too tainted with adolescent daydreams and sham emo-tions for a play that sought to maturely assess the European political scene. It was also too tainted with the methods of fascism itself.

As for why the authors eliminated the Lads of Pressan, the banners, and other fascist trappings, it is more difficult to say. The change may represent their choice to present a conclusion less characterized by political ex-tremes, less dominated by a polarization of society between Communism and Fascism, Right and Wrong. This is most apparent in the alterations to Francis's closing speeches. Though he still utters the communist call for revolution—as, for example, when he asks Mildred Luce to help "destroy" the "social system" (287)—his dying words to Alan, who is about to leave home, adopt a different rhetoric: "Long may you live / Your powers to give / In every season / For justice and for reason." While the play remains doubtful about England's capacity for social change, it is hopeful regarding the individual's capacity to create "justice" and "reason" elsewhere.

Thus, with Isherwood's help, *The Dog beneath the Skin* grew from a strictly English setting to a Candide-like tour of the entire European political scene, eventually maturing into a didactic play intended to warn England of the perils of fascism and inform the country of its unavoidable connections with the rest of Europe. As for the play's portrait of England, it is a pessimistic one. England, as it is depicted through the village of Pressan Ambo, is characterized by provincial insularity, nationalistic fervor, political demagoguery and corruption, obsession with an idealized past, and denial of a troubled present—all traits that it shares with the fascist dictatorships on the Continent. England also appears to be beyond the hope of revolutionary politics, even communism. In this way, *The Dog beneath the Skin* anticipates its authors' eventual disaffection from radical politics and their departure for America.

Note

1. For a discussion of Auden and Isherwood's different contributions to the final scene, see *Plays*, 553–97, and Mendelson, 278.

Additional Works Cited

Benewick, Robert. *The Fascist Movement in Britain.* London: Allen Lane, Penguin, 1972.

Bucknell, Katherine, and Nicholas Jenkins, eds. *W. H. Auden: "The Map of All My Youth." Auden Studies 1.* Oxford: Oxford University Press, 1990.

Isherwood, Christopher. "The Youth Movement in the New Germany." *Action* 10 (December 1931): 18.

Mendelson, Edward. *Early Auden.* London: Faber, 1981.

Sidnell, Michael J. *Dances of Death: The Group Theatre of London in the Thirties.* London: Faber, 1984.

Spender, Stephen, ed. *W. H. Auden: A Tribute.* New York: Macmillan, 1975.

17 *Marsha Bryant*

Documentary Dilemmas
Shifting Fronts in *Journey to a War*

By the late 1930s, documentary had become inflected with the tough masculinity of George Orwell's *The Road to Wigan Pier* and Ernest Hemingway's dispatches from the Spanish Civil War. Christopher Isherwood reflected the anxiety of measuring up to Spain's "star literary observers" by asking, "How could one compete with Hemingway and Malraux?" He and Auden confronted dominant documentary practice in their texts about the Sino-Japanese War—three collaborative essays and the co-authored book *Journey to a War* (1939). According to *Christopher and His Kind,* Auden declared upon their departure that "we'll have a war all of our very own" (289).

Ostensibly, *Journey to a War* depicts Auden and Isherwood trying to reach the front of the Sino-Japanese War so they can understand and represent this international conflict. Finding the front would also validate them as "documentary men," but this literal journey is constantly thwarted. For in seeking a focal point for the war, these gay Englishmen must negotiate competing models of masculinity and mediating signs of European colonialism. On the one hand, encounters with seasoned journalists, combat photographer Robert Capa, and especially the resourceful Peter Fleming make it difficult for Auden and Isherwood to sustain their manly performance. On the other hand, European embassies, businesses, and missions make it difficult for them to mark with certainty what is

172

"Chinese." The resulting self-consciousness and self-parody disrupt their travelogue with a camp sensibility that exposes the "fronts" of documentary discourse. *Journey to a War* reveals the lack of self-reflection in thirties documentary practice, most notably the failure of British documentary to confront its own heterosexist and colonialist genealogy.

In the text of *Journey to a War,* Auden and Isherwood's position as gay Englishmen is unsettled, as is the ostensible object of their study, wartime China. Because it did not meet his expectations of war reportage, Randall Swingler issued this prediction in his review: "Many people will, I think, be annoyed by this book" (291). Several contemporary and later readers of *Journey to a War* found its discontinuous form a vexing issue. No table of contents or list of illustrations prepares the reader for the book's shifting formats; instead, title pages divide *Journey to a War* into four sections: "London to Hongkong," "Travel-Diary," "Picture Commentary," and "In Time of War." The 226-page "Travel-Diary," composed by Isherwood from both writers' notes, covers the journey from Hong Kong to Shanghai and constitutes the longest part of the book. Auden took all but one of the sixty-one photographs in the "Picture Commentary," and the book ends with his sonnet sequence, "In Time of War." Auden and Isherwood's text is, to use Samuel Hynes's characterization, "a discontinuous collection of parts in different forms" (342).

An Elusive Front

As Auden and Isherwood try to gain access to the Sino-Japanese front, Auden asks in exasperation, "How long . . . to the nearest fighting?" (206). Although the book's title evokes the dangers of frontline combat, the bulk of the "Travel-Diary" recounts, as reviewer Evelyn Waugh pointed out, "sleeping-cars, mission stations, consulates and universities" (289). Yet paradoxically, the same imperialist legacy that allows Auden and Isherwood such mobility also thwarts their access to the war itself. Their lack of success in the conventional sense, however, enables *Journey to a War* to provide important insights into thirties culture.

Cut off from the "nearest fighting," Auden and Isherwood faced not only the problem of meeting their readers' expectations but also the dilemma of validating their status as documentary men. By the time Auden and Isherwood construct the text of *Journey to a War,* they face the additional problem of having no combat photos for their book—even though a large section of the "Picture Commentary" is labeled "War Zone." Consider, for example, Auden's long shot titled "Japanese Front Line," taken in the daytime when no fighting took place (on page 174). Evoking nothing of the war, this flat image of buildings across the Grand Canal clashes

Japanese Front Line. Photograph by W. H. Auden. Copyright © by the estate of W. H. Auden. Used by permission.

with its arresting caption; reviewer William Plomer wrote that Auden and Isherwood "made their way to the front, or perhaps we had better say the scene of military operations" (292). Such thwarted encounters with the elusive "front" yield tension-ridden representations, triggering the authors' scrutiny of their own expectations and motives. They challenge the validity that their culture assigned to war reportage, a subgenre of documentary that had gained popularity with the Spanish Civil War.

Auden and Isherwood made two attempts to reach "the front"—first in the north and then in the southeast. *Journey to a War*'s images of these expeditions both conceal and confess the authors' lack of contact with the nearest fighting. In the process, their self-deflation also punctures the aura of male heroism that readers expected from the decade's war correspondents. Almost half of Auden's photographs are grouped in the "War Zone" section, seemingly echoing his insistence to military officers that "a journalist has his duty, like a soldier. It is sometimes necessary for him to go into danger" (112). The soldier analogy evokes the writer-fighter image popular in documentary texts of the Spanish Civil War, but *Journey to a War* quickly undermines this impression when we learn that Auden and Isherwood hired private rickshaws for transportation to the front. Their "Chinese Diary" dispatch (published before the book) includes a breezy aside recommending rickshaw travel "to anybody wishing to visit a battle area whose location and extent are vague"; this touristy tone shifts toward manly reportage when the authors point out that "if enemy planes come over, a single bound will land you safely in the ditch" (95). Auden and Isherwood did, in fact, face Japanese planes during their visit to the northern front, an encounter represented in Auden's photograph "Enemy Planes Overhead" and in "Travel-Diary." The tensions between the text and the photograph reflect *Journey to a War*'s schizophrenic figuration of "front-line" experience.

Auden's photograph of Isherwood and a Chinese soldier clashes with its swaggering caption and its related portion of the diary. The soldier is one of their escorts from Li Kwo Yi to the Grand Canal front, where Auden and Isherwood managed, after several attempts, to gain military passes to the first-line trenches. While inspecting this portion of the "War Zone," the party is "interrupted by three tremendous detonations" (114) from Chinese guns, and the escorts hurry their English visitors away from the front line in anticipation of counterattack from Japanese bombers. Isherwood recounts their departure through the bare fields: "From the north came the drone of approaching planes. The Japanese were out looking for the Chinese guns. They circled the sky several times, passing quite low above us. Whenever they came over, the soldier signalled to us to lie down. It was an unpleasant feeling lying there exposed in the naked field: one couldn't help remembering the many anecdotes of aviators' caprice— how a pilot will take a sudden dislike to some solitary figure moving beneath him, and waste round after round of ammunition until he has annihilated it, like an irritating fly" (115).

This description suggests two types of dramatic shots—a tight close-up of Isherwood and the soldier conveying their tense situation, or a long shot in which the planes appear as a visible threat. But Auden's snapshot, taken from a middle distance, makes their situation appear absurd (on page 176). Both Isherwood and the soldier gaze toward the right, which could indicate either that the planes are approaching or that they have already passed. Because the soldier in the foreground almost smiles, the latter scenario is more likely. Isherwood points out that the soldier grinned "delightedly" after each Chinese shell exploded, obviously amused at his inexperienced companions. Although Isherwood writes that "Auden seized the opportunity of catching the two of us unawares with his camera" (115), the soldier's posture—back straight, forward-clasped hands, torso turned toward camera—certainly looks like a pose. If Auden had the time to take this photograph, just how much danger was at hand? According to Carol Shloss, photographers and writers depicting war "either shared the threat of death at the hands of a common enemy, or else their very safety forced them to confront their unarguable position as outsiders

Enemy Planes Overhead. Photograph by W. H. Auden. Copyright © by the estate of W. H. Auden. Used by permission.

to the action they sought to represent" (20). Here Auden and Isherwood present another possibility by blurring these positions through image and text. Simultaneously in *and* out of the scene, the authors of *Journey to a War* represent staple images of war reportage—soldiers and trenches— in ways that call into question the manly heroics of documentary realism.

Isherwood comes to understand that what he and Auden consider their journalists' "duty" is really a selfish imposition on those they supposedly aid. This growing awareness is most clearly shown in the account of the journey toward the southeast front, which Auden and Isherwood under- take in the company of popular travel writer and *Times* correspondent Peter Fleming. As the travelers enter the rain-soaked streets of the town of Meiki, a group of citizens greets them with a WELCOME banner. But when the beleaguered divisional commander meets with the whole party and informs them that the town will soon fall to the Japanese, all illusions of self-importance vanish: "Although very polite he couldn't conceal his dismay at our presence. We were tiresomely notorious foreigners, who might add to his responsibilities by getting killed. Our proper place was on a platform in London—not here, amongst exhausted and overworked officers and officials. We might have to leave, he warned us, in the middle of the night. . . . Touched, and rather ashamed of myself, I thought of those men and women who had wasted their last precious hours of safety, waiting to welcome us with their banner in the rain" (222).

Becoming part of the story did not make them heroic documentary men but a danger to others. This is one point Swingler missed in his blistering review, which claims that one goes to a war-stricken country "to find out what is really happening and to report it or to participate" (291) and then faults Auden and Isherwood for doing neither. "Finding out" *is* participation, and counterproductive participation at that.

The "Travel-Diary" ends with the confession that "one doesn't know where to start" (253). Where was the war? After their final journey toward the front, Auden and Isherwood are disabused of the belief that war has clear focal points and dividing lines. As Auden came to understand on the road to Meiki, "War is bombing an already disused arsenal, missing it, and killing a few old women. War is lying in a stable with a gangrenous leg. War is drinking hot water in a barn and worrying about one's wife. War is a handful of lost and terrified men in the mountains, shooting at something moving in the undergrowth. War is waiting for days with nothing to do; shouting down a dead telephone; going without sleep, or sex, or a wash. War is untidy, inefficient, obscure, and largely a matter of chance" (202). In other words, war is a decentered experience devoid of the man-making feats that structure linear plots—whether in novels, travel books, commercial films, or documentary texts. Once Auden, Isherwood, and their readers are disabused of frontline illusions, they can perceive how Western masculinity and imperialism interpose themselves between the authors and China.

Performing Masculinity

While the failure to produce an orderly march to "the front" has motivated rebukes of *Journey to a War,* I see an equally determining factor at work in the criticism—Auden and Isherwood's refusal to sustain a seamless performance as documentary (i.e., straight) men in their text. Theatrical tropes permeate unfavorable commentary on this book, ranging from Waugh's accusation of "pantomime" to Paul Fussell's more recent complaint that "uncertainty and frustration compromise the travel performance of Auden and Isherwood" (222). Swingler expended more energy berating Auden and Isherwood's textual theatrics: "It is impossible to escape the impression that the authors are playing: playing at being war correspondents, at being Englishmen, at being poets" (291). In other words, Swingler finds a lack of *authenticity* in *Journey to a War* because Auden and Isherwood forthrightly acknowledge that they perform not only their profession but even their gender and nationality.

Given the Anglo-American tendency to characterize gay men with such terms as "theatrical" and "stagey," I cannot help but wonder if the underlying issue for *Journey to a War*'s staunchest detractors is the authors' supposed failure to measure up as "real" men. The unreality these critics find in Auden and Isherwood's textual performance assumes a heterosexual "authenticity" behind war reportage and travel writing that has been travestied. As Judith Butler has argued, "Compulsory heterosexuality sets itself up as the original, the true, the authentic; the norm that determines the real implies that 'being' lesbian [or gay] is always a kind of miming, a vain effort to participate in the phantasmatic plenitude of naturalized heterosexuality which will always and only fail" (20–21). When the heterosexism of thirties documentary discourse is factored in—where "realness" means not only documentary's subject matter but also its dominant constructions of masculinity—we can see that gender is very much at stake for *Journey to a War*'s readers and authors.

Part of Auden and Isherwood's difficulties in representing the Sino-Japanese War arose from their position as gay men writing within an established documentary framework. This position was markedly different from their earlier collaborations within the gay circle of the Group Theatre. We know from *Christopher and His Kind* that Isherwood and Auden had been occasionally sleeping together for a decade by the time they embarked for China. As Isherwood puts it, "They couldn't think of themselves as lovers, yet sex had given friendship an extra dimension" (264). Given the inevitable self-representation in *Journey to a War,* and the possibility of readers' finding signs that the authors do not conform as "real" men, Auden and Isherwood risked being perceived as unreliable narrators of social reality. In response to this documentary dilemma, *Journey to a War* becomes—as Harold Nicolson's dust-jacket blurb for the American edition astutely noted—"the carefully gay account of their adventures." (Nicolson, a politician and historian, was also a gay man.) Critics who question Auden and Isherwood's political "commitment" in their account of China fail to consider the gender and sexual politics that the authors confront throughout the book. *Journey to a War,* in fact, provides a triple *coverage:* Auden and Isherwood cover (report) the war, cover (conceal) their sexual orientation, and cover (re-perform) prior acts by straight men.

Journey to a War's double coverage of maleness succeeds in exposing traditional Western masculinity as a documentary "front," employing four performative strategies. First, Auden and Isherwood at times perform what Butler calls the "necessary drag" of passing for straight. We can best see this strategy by considering what they omit from *Journey to a War* and by reading the book's signs of gay coding. Second, Auden and Isherwood often respond to their position as gay documentarians in China by camping traditional masculinity, which we see in their self-representation. With these methods of strategic concealment, the book's status as a gay text is sufficiently "covered" while still allowing space for critique of the norm; this interrogation occurs in Auden and Isherwood's third and fourth performative strategies, which reproduce images of patriarchal masculinity. In their third strategy, the authors highlight the constructed nature of masculinity by portraying documentary men they encounter—especially the theatrical Fleming. By depicting the consummate war reporter as consummate performer, Auden and Isherwood anticipate Butler's performative theory of heterosexuality and begin the work of what Lee Edelman calls *homographesis*—creating a text that both writes and unwrites compulsory heterosexuality. Finally, Auden's "Commentary" to the sonnet sequence rewrites history by critiquing the "great men" theory of Western civilization. These textual-sexual strategies work with and against each other to disrupt *Journey to a War*'s reportage of the conflict, the male heterosexual framework of thirties documentary discourse, and Western masculinity itself.

Journey to a War conceals overt references to homosexuality while at the same time providing coded references to it. Isherwood and Auden wrote more freely about homosexuality in pieces that were not included in *Journey to a War*. Auden's poem "Passenger Shanty" was completed in 1938 and published in *The English Auden* (1977), and Isherwood published his reminiscences of China in *Christopher and His Kind* (1976). Each of these telling omissions glosses the coded references to the authors' homosexuality in the "Travel-Diary."

The diary reflects anxiety that others might detect the authors' homosexuality. For example, their first appearance at a Hankow press conference draws "inquisitively hostile eyes" from the seasoned correspondents (53). Ostensibly, Auden and Isherwood feel out of place because they are journalist-poseurs—they confess that they "were not real journalists, but mere trippers"—yet the "hearty, square-shouldered, military-looking man" who acts as sentry alerts them, and the attentive reader, to the possible dangers of passing (53). Later, Auden and Isherwood encounter Dr. McClure at the American Mission Hospital; this "stalwart" Canadian Scot wears "a leather blouse, riding breeches and knee-boots with straps" (77). Intimidated by McClure's "dynamic presence," Auden and Isherwood find themselves "uneasily suspecting" that he thinks them "slightly sissy" (79). *Journey to a War*'s tightrope walk between covering and disclosing the authors' sexuality reflects the twofold dilemma Esther Newton sees in the gay man's compulsory social performance: "First, he must conceal the fact that he sleeps with men. But concealing this *fact* is far less difficult than his second problem, which is controlling the *halo effect* or signals that would announce that he sleeps with men. The covert homosexual must in fact impersonate a *man,* that is, he must *appear* to the 'straight' world to be fulfilling (or not violating) all the requisites of the male role as defined by the 'straight' world" (48–49). Auden and Isherwood must rely on the straight world of press men, doctors, missionaries, ambassadors, and military and government officials to aid their passage through China. In order to succeed at gathering the information necessary to their documentary book, they must first pass inspection.

Necessary Drag

Isherwood's omissions and codings participate in the necessary drag of *Journey to a War. Christopher and His Kind* offers a direct rendering of their erotic adventures when Isherwood recounts "afternoon holidays from their social consciences" in Shanghai. This post-text fills in *Journey to a War*'s missing information about "a bathhouse where you were erotically soaped and massaged by young men." We also learn that "you could pick your attendants, and many of them were beautiful" (308). Although *Christopher and His Kind* is quite open about these "pleasingly exotic" encounters, it echoes *Journey to a War*'s anxieties about passing. Immediately after making his bathhouse disclosure, for example, Isherwood discusses his and Auden's act of concealing their sexual excursions from their Shanghai host, the British ambassador Sir Archibald Clark-Kerr: "Archie accepted their lies without comment, but a certain gleam in his eye made them wonder if he was playing a game with them" (309). By contrast, the only mention of Shanghai bathhouses in the "Travel-Diary" divorces them from the authors' own experience and—more telling— frames them in the distancing, drag voice of "establishment" masculinity that characterizes British travel books: "Nevertheless the tired or lustful business man will find here everything to gratify his desires. You can buy an electric razor, or a French dinner, or a well-cut suit. . . . You can attend race-meetings, baseball games, football matches. You can see the latest American films. If you want girls, or boys, you can have them, at all prices, in the bath-houses and the brothels" (237). Here the available "boys" are presented almost as an afterthought, sequestered by commas in a passage that otherwise presents the commodities "appropriate" to the well-traveled British businessman. The necessary drag of the "Travel-Diary" even goes so far as to point out an incident at a train station in which a Chinese boy nudged Isherwood "in a sensitive place" and offered to procure a "nice girl" (123).

Like its accounts of hostile eyes, the diary's account of Chinese boys allows the reader an occasional peek beneath the authors' drag costumes.

Auden and Isherwood's stay at Journey's End—a mountain resort staffed by shorts-clad houseboys—is easily *Journey to a War*'s most diversionary episode. Significantly, William Plomer, whose life and writing were closeted, singled out this episode as the book's high point, finding it one of the "two passages . . . where Mr. Isherwood gets a chance to be completely himself" (293). Although reviewers focus on the novelesque treatment of the hotel's eccentric proprietor, Mr. Charleton, it is the houseboys, whose "beautiful legs" Charleton praises (178), who give the episode much of its energy. In addition to the accommodating staff, each guest has, as Charleton puts it, "a boy attached to him" (179). Isherwood closes his account of Journey's End by describing the farewell tipping of the boys, who "giggled shamefacedly—as Europeans giggle over Sex—and asked for a little, a very little, just a trifle more" (183). Like Isherwood's remark about available Shanghai boys, this one linking boys, money, and sex serves as a textual wink at readers who can see through the authors' drag performance. Such "double talk," to use Wayne Koestenbaum's term, opens a gap in *Journey to a War,* providing working space for Auden and Isherwood to call into question traditional masculinity. Their next strategy—camp—marks a transitional maneuver between concealing their own sexuality and critiquing the institution of Western male heterosexuality.

Whereas Fussell and Valentine Cunningham find the book's campiness inappropriate, I find it one of *Journey to a War*'s most productive methods of confronting the politics of gender. Isherwood would go on to become one of the first commentators on camp in his 1954 novel *The World in the Evening,* so it is not surprising to find its energies shaping his work of the late thirties. The necessary drag of passing can, according to Jack Babuscio, "lead to a heightened awareness and appreciation for disguise, impersonation, the projection of personality" (25). In *Journey to a War,* this theatrical aspect of camp is most apparent in the authors' self-representation, their strategy of exposing the "front" of masculinity in documentary discourse. While their canon-breaking position as gay documentarians necessitates strategic camping, the elegant artifice they see in Chinese culture makes it easier.

To these English travelers, China blurs Western boundaries between the theatrical and the non-theatrical in ways similar to camp sensibility in gay culture. For example, the "Travel-Diary" devotes an entire entry to the Chinese opera *Lady Precious Stream,* a "highly artificial and ritualistic" affair with lavish robes and headpieces (62). The singers unsettle Western notions of stage boundaries by accepting tea from assistants after their more difficult songs—in full view of the audience. Gender boundaries also prove unstable at the opera; men perform the female roles with "faces transformed by make-up into pink and white masks" (62). Edward Said asserts that such theatrical renderings of China replicate Orientalist constructions of the East "as spectacle, or *tableau vivant*," yet they also provide the gay writer a protective covering in which to present himself to his predominantly heterosexual audience (158).

Once *Journey to a War* establishes theatricality as a norm, Isherwood and Auden can stage their self-representation in ways that challenge traditional masculinity while maintaining their pose as documentary men. The incongruous image of Isherwood in "Enemy Planes Overhead" camps conventional combat photography while capturing the surrealism of Auden and Isherwood's search for the front. *Journey to a War*'s only photograph of Auden, captioned "In the Trenches," pulls off its documentary posing with more success—but the attuned eye can still detect camp elements (on page 183). Posing side by side with a Chinese soldier from the Grand Canal front, Auden appears on the scene of his reporterly duties. The soldier seems to cast Auden an admiring gaze beneath the brim of his cap, while the Englishman calmly regards the camera with a self-assured, close-lipped smile. Other soldiers, apparently unaware of the camera, go about their tasks in the background, further inflecting the photograph with documentary veracity. Yet the relation of background to foreground also gives this photograph a certain campiness: Auden's Western-cut, lighter-colored clothing and more brightly lit face make him appear out of place, as if he were matted into the shot. We return to his cryptic smile again, which now seems to indicate his awareness of this discrepancy; he is *acting* the part.

We often see the incongruity and humor of camp in accounts of the authors' train travel. For example, the Englishmen's presence on the Hankow–Chengchow train prompts many curious stares and smiles from the car boys, which prompts in turn a comical self-staging: "But perhaps we were not unimposing figures, with our superbly developed chests—padded out several inches by thick wads of Hankow dollar-bills stuffed into every available inner pocket" (73). By humorously donning the big-chested disguise only to expose its artificiality, this self-representation deflates the authors and, more seriously, ridicules the he-man image of Western heterosexual masculinity. As Babuscio asserts, "Camp, by focusing on the outward appearances of role, implies that roles, and, in particular, sex roles, are superficial—a matter of style" (24). In *Journey to a War*'s strategic camp, Auden and Isherwood don the garb of straight masculinity to challenge the equation of "straight" with "real."

They are not the only ones who perform masculinity in *Journey to a War*. Their extended portrait of Peter Fleming serves as another strategy of interrogating traditional masculinity; it, too, involves a theatrical un-

In the Trenches. Copyright © by the estate of W. H. Auden. Used by permission.

derstanding of maleness. In fact, Fleming upstages Auden and Isherwood whenever he enters the scene. As it does throughout the "Travel-Diary," Fleming's presence points up Auden and Isherwood's comparative lack of finesse while at the same time making his appearance of consummate manliness seem ridiculous. We can see the comic absurdity in Auden's photograph of Fleming, captioned "Special Correspondent, Peter Fleming" (on page 184). Clearly conscious of his performance, Fleming fingers his

Special Correspondent, Peter Fleming. Photograph by W. H. Auden. Copyright © by the estate of W. H. Auden. Used by permission.

pipe and gazes off in pseudo-reflection, all the while maintaining a flattering profile posture. Ironically, the "real" war reporter looks much less authentic here than Auden camping in the trenches.

By showing that the heterosexual Fleming is just as theatrical in his resourceful masculinity as they are in their documentary drag, Auden and Isherwood also reveal the same "inevitable exchange of meanings in the prefixes 'homo' and 'hetero'" that Edelman finds in the practice of homographesis—a productive tension in which compulsory heterosexuality is "*in*scribed" and "*de*-scribed" (14, emphasis added). Auden and Isherwood exemplify this dynamic by presenting Fleming as the alpha male they fall short of *and* the absurdly correct figure they can see through. A "double operation," homographesis both codifies and resists "the ideological purposes of a conservative social order" (10); it provides the gay writer a means of subverting the dominant culture from within its disciplinary frameworks.

In the self-reflective text of *Journey to a War,* Auden and Isherwood scrutinize their own culture, revealing the ways that gender politics—specifically, Western constructions of masculinity—distort their "firsthand experience" of China. Joseph Allen Boone has shown that for male French and British writers, Egypt and the Near East "put into crisis assumptions about male sexual desire, masculinity, and heterosexuality that are specific to Western culture" (90)—the same dynamic that Auden and Isherwood confronted in China. It is impossible for them—or any European male traveler—to enter the East without preconceptions of what they will see. The gnawing question "Are you really a Man?" governs the travelers' voyage East, which becomes a testing ground that challenges the English authors' understanding of masculinity in three ways. First, the Sino-Japanese War becomes a last chance for them to at least see the front against fascism, if not fight there. In addition, China unsettles Western masculinity by prompting Auden and Isherwood to stage it in new dresses. Finally, the East bears signs of European imperialist conquest, signs which also mark the passages of earlier exploring men. Intersecting with the conquest narratives of Western patriarchy, imperialism shaped thirties documentary discourse in ways that worked against its aims to reveal "other" cultures' reality and to advocate on "their" behalf.

Auden and Isherwood prompt us to examine more closely John Grierson's characterization of the British documentary film movement in the 1930s. The rhetoric of male imperial conquest erupts sporadically in his publications, justifying "the documentary men's" goals and defending them from their detractors. In "The Course of Realism," he describes documentary films as ground-staking "flags of vitality . . . flown over the British cinemas" (210). Grierson's most blatantly imperialist defense of documentary filmmaking occurs in this essay: "We have taken our cameras to the more difficult *territory*. We have set up our tripods among the *Yahoos* themselves, and schools have gathered round us" (203, emphasis added). Giving his documentary men the conquering vision of imperial eyes, Grierson likens them to swaggering explorers who conquer "hostile" countries by attacking "new materials and [bringing] them into visual focus on the screen" (215). To what extent can documentary bear effective witness to some social inequalities while participating in others? For Auden and Isherwood, gay men writing against the grain of dominant documentary practice, this contradiction became insurmountable by the end of the thirties.

Additional Works Cited

Auden, W. H. *The English Auden: Poems, Essays and Dramatic Writings, 1927–1939*. Ed. Edward Mendelson. New York: Random, 1977.

Babuscio, Jack. "Camp and the Gay Sensibility." In *Camp Grounds: Style and Homosexuality*, ed. David Bergman. Amherst: University of Massachusetts Press, 1993.

Boone, Joseph A. "Vacation Cruises; or, The Homoerotics of Orientalism." *PMLA* 110 (1995): 89–107.

Butler, Judith. "Imitation and Gender Insubordination." In *Inside/Out: Lesbian Theories, Gay Theories*, ed. Diana Fuss. New York: Routledge, 1991.

Cunningham, Valentine. *British Writers of the Thirties*. Oxford: Oxford University Press, 1989.

Edelman, Lee. *Homographesis: Essays in Gay Literary and Cultural Theory*. New York: Routledge, 1994.

Fussell, Paul. *Abroad: British Literary Traveling between the Wars*. Oxford: Oxford University Press, 1980.

Grierson, John. *Grierson on Documentary*. Ed. Forsyth Hardy. Rev. ed. Berkeley: University of California Press, 1966.

Koestenbaum, Wayne. *Double Talk: The Erotics of Male Literary Collaboration*. New York: Routledge, 1989.

Newton, Esther. "Role Models." In *Camp Grounds: Style and Homosexuality*, ed. David Bergman. Amherst: University of Massachusetts Press, 1993.

Plomer, William. Review of *Journey to a War*, by W. H. Auden and Christopher Isherwood. In *W. H. Auden: The Critical Heritage*, ed. John Haffenden. London: Routledge & Kegan Paul, 1983.

Said, Edward. *Orientalism*. New York: Vintage, 1979.

Shloss, Carol. *In Visible Light: Photography and the American Writer, 1840–1940*. New York: Oxford University Press, 1987.

Swingler, Randall. "On Being Uninvolved, Two Intellectuals in China." Review of *Journey to a War*, by W. H. Auden and Christopher Isherwood. In *W. H. Auden: The Critical Heritage*, ed. John Haffenden. London: Routledge & Kegan Paul, 1983.

18 *Stephen da Silva*

Strategically Minor
Isherwood's Revision of Forster's Mythology

Fictions of the Immature Homosexual

Several strains of sexological theory, drawing on the language of evolution, represent same-sex desire as a form of atavistic regression (Williams, 726–27). The Nazi-sympathizing doctor in Isherwood's "On Ruegen Island" implicitly draws on that sexological equation in viewing Otto, the teenage German lover of an English homosexual, Peter, as a regressive scientific curiosity. He tells the narrator, "This type of boy always reverts. From a scientific point of view, I find him exceedingly interesting" (*Goodbye*, 142–43). But this equation also influenced antihomophobic sexologists. Thus, we learn from *Christopher and His Kind* that the homosexual sexologist Magnus Hirschfeld complacently classified Isherwood's strain of homosexuality as "infantile" (27). In differentiating between "mature" and "immature" strains of homosexuality, Hirschfeld was replicating the generational terms used to divide heterosexuality from homosexuality within sexological discourse.

While psychoanalysis ostensibly rejects the biologism of sexology, it too often represents homosexuality as a developmental failure. One common psychoanalytic account of male homosexuality, for instance, holds that the gay man is excessively attached to his mother and so cannot successfully negotiate the trajectory to adulthood and a mature (read heterosexual) object choice (Lewes, 36–37). This etiological narrative is rehearsed in Isherwood's *Prater Violet* by Friedrich Bergmann, the film director and surrogate father figure to the narrator: in an accusatory tone, Bergmann says to Isherwood, the young first-person narrator, "You are not married. . . . You are a typical mother's son. It is the English tragedy. . . . [Englishmen] marry their mothers" (39–40). That this national inability to resolve the Oedipal complex results in homosexuality, latent or overt, is suggested by Bergmann's pointed question to the narrator later in the novel, "Is it Mr. W. H. you seek, or the Dark Lady of the Sonnets?" (50).

Unfortunately, the persistent ideological association between homosexuality and immaturity seen in psychoanalytic and sexological discourse also insidiously inflects critical accounts of gay writers. Thus, both Isherwood's and E. M. Forster's works are often dismissed as "minor" with the double sense of insignificant and immature. G. H. Bantock, for instance, challenges the estimation of Isherwood as "a major figure" and instead assesses the writer as being "a comparatively negligible [one], negligible, that is to say, by any reasonably mature standards" (46). Isherwood's aesthetic immaturity/insignificance manifests itself in his inability to create major characters. The critic illustrates this weakness by comparing Isherwood's characters to those of Shakespeare: we are told, for instance, that Philip, the protagonist of *All the Conspirators,* is "a minor Hamlet, a crashing bore" (50). Bantock's idioms of phallic size and tumescence imply that Isherwood's inability to create Shakespearean characters is connected with his diminished or compromised masculinity. He suggests that "Mr. Norris is Isherwood's version of Falstaff" (54), who fails to "measure up" (47): "How deflated a version of that Falstaff theme Norris appears to be. . . . The physical shrinkage has been paralleled by a psychic one" (54). Further, Bantock links Isherwood's interest in the "more sordid type of eroticism" to his refusal in texts like *Lions and Shadows* to address the "normal adolescent difficulties of growth" (48, 53–54).

Similar evaluative comments which equate homosexuality with aesthetic immaturity can be drawn from critical responses to Forster's work. F. R. Leavis, for instance, dismisses Forster's works as "unmistakably minor," "disconcertingly inexperienced," and "immature" (264, 268). Although he does not explicitly mention Forster's homosexuality, he continually feminizes the writer, implicitly invoking the link between homosexuality and gender inversion. Leavis writes of Forster's "light rather spinsterly poise" (262), his "spinsterish inadequacy" (263), and "his lack of force or robustness of intelligence" (267). Other critics like Barbara Rosecrance attempt to quarantine Forster's mature, universally appealing work from his "immature" texts which explicitly thematize homoeroticism. Rosecrance's solution to this contradiction is to characterize the homoerotic texts as "a byway opened in *Maurice*" that should not distract our attention from the mature strain of Forster's art with its aesthetic "culmination in *A Passage to India*" (150).

Paradoxically, the same generational tropes that are used to denigrate homosexuality can and have been used in constructing an antihomophobic discourse as well. In *The History of Sexuality,* Michel Foucault points out that the same sexological and psychoanalytical discourses that have been used to discipline deviant sexualities provided a lexicon for articulating a "reverse discourse of male homosexuality" (101). Consonant with Foucault's insight, Thomas Yingling suggests that rather than challenging the "minor," immature status of homosexuality, gay writers may be able to use and partially revalue this denigratory designation: "Considerable effort has been spent . . . to erase from homosexuality the stigma of personal and cultural immaturity. . . . But perhaps the paradigm of non-adult sexuality . . . is our most subversive stance. . . . What happens if we think of gay and lesbian literature as minor?" (110–11). Both Forster and Isherwood deploy versions of the subversive strategy articulated by Yingling, illustrating its uses and limitations.

Using Forster's Minor Mythology

Forster challenged the developmental norm by reinscribing and inverting it. He repeatedly associates sex between men with the crossing of racial and class boundaries. Since he also represents working-class and non-Western men, such as the eponymous object of desire in the story "Ansell" or Vithobai in "The Life to Come," as belonging to a primitive state of innocence, homosexual relations in his work become associated with youthfulness or its recovery. In many of his texts, a movement back in time or a movement to non-Western spaces that he associates with an earlier period of history generates homosexual possibilities. For instance, Harold in "Albergo Empedocle" evades the marriage plot by slipping into the Classical world, and in "The Other Boat" Lionel is able to return to his childhood intimacy with Cocoanut, which becomes more intense as Lionel's ship moves eastward.

Isherwood draws on this Forsterian mythology and uses it to particular effect when he writes about Forster, stressing Forster's youthful appearance and spirit. In *Down There on a Visit,* he celebrates Forster's "light, gay, blue baby eyes" (162), and in *Christopher and His Kind,* he writes, "[Forster] never ceased to be babylike. His light blue eyes behind his spectacles were like those of a baby. . . . He had a baby's vulnerability, which is also the invulnerability of a creature whom one dare not harm" (106). In his 1957 anthology *Great English Short Stories,* Isherwood describes

Forster's personality as "perennially boyish" (173). Further, the Forster
story that he chooses to anthologize foregrounds Forster's idealization of
Mediterranean primitivism. In "The Story of the Siren," an Italian boatman is described as "a *child* of nature" (174, emphasis added), a phrase
from the story that Isherwood cites in his introductory summary of the
tale. The boatman understands nature's wonderful and sometimes sinister
mysteries that are denied to the excessively cerebral English narrator.

One can even see Isherwood's reliance on the Forsterian reversal of developmental logic in his reactions to his mentor's embarrassment about
the datedness of *Maurice.* When Forster asked Isherwood, "Does it date?"
Isherwood responded, "Why *shouldn't* it date?" (*Kind,* 126). Just as heterosexist culture is only able to see homosexuality as an immature stage that
must be left behind on the way to adult heterosexuality, a homophobic
critical establishment tends to devalue *Maurice* for its anachronistic, pastoral nostalgia and to regard it as a work that does not deserve to be
ranked with Forster's "timeless" major masterpieces, like *A Passage to India.* By contrast, Isherwood celebrates *Maurice* as a work that must be
valued, even though, or perhaps because, it bears the mark of temporal
contingency.

Isherwood's inversion of traditional generational values further manifests itself in the opposition he repeatedly draws between the modest and
youthful heroism of Forster and the false heroics of patriarchal authority.
In *Down There on a Visit,* Isherwood compares the "antiheroic hero" Forster, "entirely human and deeply loveable," to national political icons like
Chamberlain: "The newspapers are moved to tears by the spectacle of a
gentleman [Chamberlain] standing his ground against a non-gentleman
[Hitler], so they call him 'England.' . . . Well *my* 'England' is E.M.; the
antiheroic hero" (162). In addition to the explicit opposition that he establishes between Forster and Chamberlain in this text, Isherwood implicitly
draws a comparison between Mr. Lancaster's father, a Victorian patriarch,
and Forster. The narrator tells us that Mr. Lancaster, a distant relative
living in Germany, has a photograph of his father "showing a vigorous,
bearded old man of perhaps seventy-five. What a beard! . . . It roared in
torrents from his finely arched nostrils and his big lobed ears, foamed over
his cheeks in two tidal waves that collided over his chin to form boiling
rapids" (23). The comically hyperbolic description of the Victorian father's
beard associates him with almost manic energy and excess. By contrast,
the description of Forster foregrounds his modesty and endearing odd-
ness: "My England is E.M. . . . with his straggly straw mustache, his light,
gay, blue baby eyes and his elderly stoop. Instead of a folded umbrella or
a brown uniform, his emblems are his tweed cap (which is too small for
him) and the odd-shaped brown paper parcels in which he carries his be-

longings" (162). Isherwood's witty description of the Victorian patriarch's beard challenges the developmental stereotype of immature homosexual narcissism: the old man is described as being "a beard-conscious old beauty—tilting his head up to be admired with an air of self-indulged caprice" (23). This campy description suggests that patriarchy, rather than the supposedly immature homosexual, is hopelessly narcissistic.

In *Kathleen and Frank,* Richard eloquently articulates the oppressive role that the heroic father, killed in the First World War, occupies in his son's mythology: "I did so hate being everlastingly reminded of him, when I was young. Everybody kept saying how perfect he was, such a hero and so good at everything. He was always held up as someone you could never hope to be worthy of, and whenever I did anything wrong, I was told I was a disgrace to him. . . . I used to simply loathe him" (57). The deadly role that this oppressive father figure can play becomes evident when we learn at the end of "Mr. Lancaster" that the title character commits suicide, as though unable to measure up to the heroic role he has assigned to his dead father. By contrast, gaily childlike Forster is associated in *Down There on a Visit* with vitality and hope: "While the others tell their followers to be ready to die, he advises us to live as if we were immortal" (162).

Revising Forster's Mythology

While Isherwood depends on a romantic inversion of developmental logic in his representation of Forster, he draws on different strategies in challenging that mythology in other parts of his work. Early in *Down There on a Visit,* for instance, the narrator clearly endorses the view that his older self has access to greater knowledge than the youthful self from whom he feels a great gulf, telling us that his former self "embarrasses me often, and so I'm tempted to sneer at him." However, the narrator refuses to dismiss this former self, declaring, "I will never sneer at him. I will never apologize for him. I am proud to be his father and his son" (14, 15). Unlike Forster, Isherwood here does not valorize immaturity; his embarrassment seems in part to validate the cultural norm's rejection of the youthful self. But in refusing to repudiate his immature self, Isherwood embraces that persona as part of his identity.

The father-son connection for Isherwood is inherently homoerotic. In *Kathleen and Frank,* for example, Isherwood describes how his father "exercised every morning in his dressing room, naked except for his undershorts. He let Christopher come in and watch him. Christopher can remember taking a pleasure which was definitely erotic in the sight of his father's muscles tensing and bulging within his well-knit body and in the virile smell of his sweat. . . . Sometimes [Frank] would fly into rages with

Christopher and shake him till his teeth rattled. Christopher may have been frightened a little, but this too is a sensual memory for him: his surrender to the exciting strength of the big angry man" (349–50). Isherwood also repeatedly frames his relations with younger lovers in father-son terms. In his diary, for instance, responding to his brother's maudlin declaration of fraternal love, Isherwood writes, "I have had a hundred brothers already and a thousand sons" (*Diaries* 1:572). In an exchange with Stephen Spender, Isherwood makes clear he thinks of his lovers in primarily filial terms: "Sons! My God, my life seems surrounded by sons! I've had more of them than anything else. Seventy at least" (Spender, *Journals,* 312). Further, commenting on his relationship with his longtime lover, Don Bachardy, Isherwood writes, "I am very happy in my father relationship with Don" (*Diaries* 1:458).

The way in which the encounter between the narrator and his younger self is dramatized provides another justification for seeing their relationship as homoerotic. The narrator remembers his earlier self by recalling gazing at his earlier persona in a mirror: "I know how I looked and felt as I stared into that restaurant mirror. I see my twenty-three-year-old face regarding me with large, reproachful eyes from beneath a cowlick of streaky blond hair. A thin, strained face, so touchingly pretty" (*Down There,* 27). This mirror scene can be read as the narrator's homoerotic meditation on his earlier self, regardless of the father-son terms he employs. In these terms, then, one can see the narrator's plea to respect the otherness of his youthful self as a demand to acknowledge the otherness of immature homosexuality, refusing to apologize for homosexuality in the face of heterosexist ideology.

Minor Mythologies?

For Yingling and other commentators on "minor" literatures, mature canonical values are informed by certain complacent assumptions about identity: "The presence of a literary canon has been imagined as an indicator of national . . . maturity," which implies a "fetishized valuation of identity. To be mature in our culture means to have reached a developmental point of self-possession" (Yingling, 109, 110). The subversive potential of "minor" and marginalized writers lies in the challenge they pose to this arrogant conception of the self.

In Yingling's terms Forster and Isherwood can be thought of as "minor writers." In their work, homosexuality is often associated with an ironic distance from humanist conceptions of the self. In Forster's "The Other Boat," for instance, Lionel March starts out with a rigid conception of identity, but Cocoanut, his primitive, racially and culturally hybrid lover, destabilizes all of Lionel's certainties. The double life that Lionel leads in the closeted space of his cabin and on deck with his compatriots denies him any easy sense of self-possession. Indeed, the story ends with Lionel ecstatically merging with Cocoanut in a moment of deadly sadomasochistic intensity. Likewise Isherwood undermines faith in a unified self and often associates that subversion with homosexuality. In *A Single Man,* for instance, George is acutely aware of the constructed nature of identity: "Never once has he seen his passport stamped at a frontier, his driver's license accepted by a post-office clerk as evidence of identity, without whispering gleefully to himself, *Idiots—fooled them again!*" (33). Ironically, the oppressive nature of the closet gives the "minor" homosexual a unique perspective on the fictions of identity that sustain the Anglo-American cultural majority.

However, the intimate connection between ethnic and national hybridity and the term "minor literature" makes it problematic to describe Forster and Isherwood as "minor" writers. Yingling takes the term "minor literature" from Deleuze and Guttari, who theorize it in the context of discussing Kafka, a Czech Jew who wrote in German: "A minor literature doesn't come from a minor language; it is that rather which a minority constructs within a major language. . . . Kafka marks the impasse that bars access to writing for the Jews of Prague and turns their literature into something impossible, the impossibility of not writing, the impossibility of writing in German, the impossibility of writing otherwise" (16).

Moving from ethnicity and nationality to sexuality poses certain problems. As gay men in a homophobic culture, Isherwood and Forster are "minor"; however, because of their national and class origins, they are not "minor" in relation to the objects of their desire—whether they be men of color from Britain's colonies or working-class German "boys." Although they were both critical of colonialism, the antihomophobic narratives they created are complicit with the primitivist fictions that undergirded the civilizing mission of British imperialism. The same writers who appear "minor" on one discursive register simultaneously occupy another position in another discursive realm.

Isherwood's representation of his relationship with Swami Prabhavananda suggests that Britain's changing imperial status might inform his simultaneous reliance on and ironic distance from the Forsterian primitivist idiom. The youthfulness, babyishness, and diminutiveness that Isherwood stresses in describing Swami Prabhavananda recall his descriptions of Forster: "Prabhavananda, though nearly forty-six, was still aware of his boyish appearance. . . . He was considerably shorter than I was. This made me able to love him in a special, protective way, as I loved little Annie Avis, my childhood nanny. . . . His smallness sometimes seemed babylike"

(*Guru,* 38–39). The swami is deeply enmeshed in Britain's colonial history. Isherwood tells us that the guru had been a nationalist rebel, and he speculates that the guru's revolutionary past was bound to affect his attitudes toward British disciples like Isherwood. Unlike the unselfconscious primitive of racist mythology, then, Isherwood's swami self-consciously negotiates ambivalence in his relationship with the writer. Like Prabhavananda, Isherwood cannot escape colonial history and, at several places in the text, explains the effect that being "an heir to Britain's guilt in her dealings with India" exerted on his relationship with the swami (36).

In describing the guru's past as a nationalist fighter, Isherwood stresses the role that the swami's youthful appearance played in those activities: "Because [Prabhavananda] looked so boyish and innocent, his comrades entrusted him with some revolvers which had been stolen from a British storehouse; he hid them in his room" (32). His boyishness is not some essential non-Western quality; rather, it is a strategic pose that he adopts for political ends, and in that sense, he occupies a position very similar to that of his Western acolyte, Isherwood, who likewise manipulates developmental stereotypes for antihomophobic purposes.

In differentiating between Forster and Isherwood's antidevelopmental fictions, my intent is not to award Isherwood a "higher grade" than Forster. Rather I suggest that Isherwood's ironic distance from Forsterian primitivist mythology is connected to their different historical situations. While *The Life to Come* includes stories that were written throughout Forster's career, the ethos of the stories is primarily Edwardian. Though deeply critical of colonialism, Forster falls back on its primitivist terms, projecting a youthful, eroticized innocence onto non-Western men. Situated at a later moment in Britain's colonial history—when the process of decolonization had already been set into motion—Isherwood could not rely on the idiom of primitivism. Instead, he simultaneously uses and debunks this mythology, and his ironic equivocation is not immature; minor, perhaps, but certainly not immature.

Additional Works Cited

Bantock, G. H. "The Novels of Christopher Isherwood." In *The Novelist as Thinker,* ed. Balachandra Rajan. London: Dennis Dobson, 1947.

Forster, E. M. *The Life to Come.* New York and London: Norton, 1972.

Forster, E. M. *Maurice.* New York: Norton, 1971.

Foucault, Michel. *The History of Sexuality: Volume 1.* Trans. Robert Hurley. New York: Vintage Press, 1980.

Leavis, F. R. "E. M. Forster." In *The Common Pursuit.* New York: George W. Stewart, 1952.

Lewes, Kenneth. *The Psychoanalytic Theory of Male Homosexuality.* New York: Simon and Schuster, 1988.

Rosecrance, Barbara. *Forster's Narrative Vision.* Ithaca: Cornell University Press, 1982.

Spender, Stephen. *Journals, 1939–1983.* London and Boston: Faber and Faber, 1985.

Williams, Sherwood. "The Rise of the New Degeneration: Decadence and Atavism in Vandover the Brute." *ELH* 57, no. 3 (fall 1990): 107–36.

Yingling, Thomas. "Wittgenstein's Tumour: AIDS and the National Body." *Textual Practice* 8, no. 1: 97–113.

A Single Man, Then and Now

If I were to make a list of the books that have mattered most to me, Christopher Isherwood's *A Single Man* would figure near the top. When I first read the novel many years ago, its influence on me was enormous because of the matter-of-fact, positive presentation of the main character's homosexuality. More recently, I read it from a new perspective, one created by the passage of many years of life experience. This time I found it to be equally powerful but for quite different reasons.

As a young man during the Eisenhower and Kennedy years, I began to come to terms with my sexuality and to acknowledge to myself that the attraction I had always felt for other boys and older men was not going to go away. But, except for these sometimes confused inner feelings, most of what I knew about being gay I learned from the novels I read. Although I was a good student, I was shy and introverted and insecure about many things. I spent a lot of time alone with books.

Mary Renault's novels, especially the first of her books about the ancient world, *The Last of the Wine,* were important to me, as was Gore Vidal's *The City and the Pillar,* which I discovered when I was in high school. Later, in the early sixties, I read *Last Exit to Brooklyn,* by Hubert Selby Jr., and John Rechy's *City of Night.* Both these novels I found fascinating but at the same time depressing because of the sordid and unhappy lives of the gay characters. *Another Country* also made a lasting impression, although I have to say that my clearest memory of that book is of being confused by James Baldwin's intense but carefully obfuscated sex scenes: What exactly was happening? Who was doing what to whom? Maybe it was just my own inexperience.

I was finishing a master's program in English at Columbia in 1965, and it was during this period that I first read Isherwood's short novel *A Single Man,* which had been published the year before. I had been out as a gay man in certain social contexts for a couple of years. It had taken me no time at all after arriving fresh from college in 1963 to discover that New York was the place to be. I took full advantage of the gay scene—the bars, the baths, the beaches on Fire Island, and the inevitable weekend parties at friends' houses. At the same time, I was careful to maintain a "straight" facade at school and at my various part-time jobs.

As I look back on those pre-Stonewall years in New York, I realize that my life was indeed compartmentalized and difficult in terms of the juggling that I had to do to maintain my two identities. I had my straight friends and my mostly weekend crowd of gay friends. I went to straight social events or to gay parties. If I went to the beach, it was either to family-friendly Jones Beach with school friends or to the Pines or Cherry Grove on Fire Island with my weekend party crowd.

This kind of double life was much more the norm than the exception for most young gay men in Manhattan in those days, at least those in my particular world, and I suppose we didn't really question the subterfuge. "Gay" in those days, by the way, was not the universally operative word, and it did not roll easily off my tongue. At the same time, "queer" was beginning to have a pejorative connotation—*their* name for us—and "homosexual" was somewhat clinical and clumsy.

Even in strictly gay social activities, there was a certain apprehensiveness that one learned to live with. At night I went happily to the bars, but not without some concern that I would be caught in a raid and arrested. I was in fact present at raids of several bars, usually in Greenwich Village, but I never experienced more than the indignity of exiting the premises through a kind of gauntlet of uniformed police leading from inside the bar to the curb outside. There was actually a certain excitement in the air when these raids occurred; we were still several years away from the kind of anger to which Stonewall finally gave meaning and purpose.

So it was during this period and in this social milieu that I first came upon *A Single Man.* I was already familiar with Isherwood, having read *The Berlin Stories, Down There on a Visit,* and a couple of other novels, and it was clear to me from the uniquely personal perspective Isherwood typically used in these books that he was gay. I suppose I assumed that the writers of other novels with gay themes were gay as well, but Isherwood

was somehow different. I was intrigued by a point of view that seemed
to reveal the personality of the writer as much as it informed us of the
fictional narrator.

A *Single Man* was a real revelation to me, however, because here was a
book—unlike the earlier Isherwood novels I had read—where the main
character was quite clearly depicted as gay right from the beginning of the
narrative. The reviews and blurbs on the book's cover and inside pages
also emphasized the homosexual theme of the novel. A *Single Man* takes
place in one day as it recounts the actions and thoughts of George, a
middle-aged English professor at a California college grieving for Jim, his
lover, who has died. The novel begins with George's waking in the morning, takes us through an event-filled but not extraordinary day of teaching
and socializing, and ends with George's going to sleep—and possibly dying—alone, as we first met him.

From that reading of A *Single Man,* more than thirty years ago, here is
what I remembered most clearly: the intimate yet dispassionate description of George's waking moments, a scene that establishes the complex
point of view that both involves and distances the reader; the little bridge
that separates George's house from the road, creating, in my memory, a
warm and safe haven; George's naked midnight swim with the student
Kenny, along with the sexual tension of their meeting; and the "supposi-
tional" death of George at the end of the novel, an event I did not want
to believe had really occurred.

What I remembered more than anything about A *Single Man,* however,
was that Isherwood had created in this novel an intelligent character
whose homosexuality was presented in a natural and life-affirming way. I
had never read a book quite like A *Single Man.* George's sexual orientation
is a given. It is not sensationalized, nor is it the pivotal fact in George's
story. By the end of the book, indeed, George is meant to be seen as a kind
of Everyman, a character whose closely observed life reflects the human
condition. And yet George is gay.

To read about a gay man presented in this way was of great significance
for me, especially because the novel was written by a famous and distinguished novelist. I admired Isherwood as courageous and visionary and,
because of the apparent transparency of the narrator/creator, as a kind of
role model. It was a great thrill for me to meet him in the early 1970s, after
a staging of his play A *Meeting by the River* in New York. We had a brief
conversation, and I was able to tell him how much A *Single Man* had
meant to me.

Not long ago, an announcement about the recently published first volume of Isherwood's diaries got me to thinking about A *Single Man* again.
I went to an overflow bookcase in my basement and found my origi-

nal paperback, carefully arranged between similarly preserved copies of Isherwood's *Prater Violet* and *The World in the Evening*. What I own is a 1965 Lancer Books edition of *A Single Man* that sold for fifty cents. The pages are yellowed around the borders and no longer pass the standard library "brittle book test" (the paper snaps in two with a couple of folds), but the cover is in good shape. A black-and-white drawing depicts a pensive middle-aged man; behind him, in shades of pink and purple, are two other drawings. In one the same man, solitary and sad, is standing at a bar; the other shows him looking equally unhappy and alone in front of a small house. There are two blurbs on the cover, one from Graham Greene ("This is the Isherwood we have been waiting for. It seems to me his best novel."), the other, interestingly, by James Colton from the early gay magazine *One* ("The most honest book ever written about a homosexual . . . about life, death, love, sex . . . it would be difficult to overpraise it.").

I began rereading *A Single Man*. I found I could not put the book down, and I finished it in one long sitting. I realized once again why Isherwood's novel had been so important to me and why I've carried such a strong memory of it all these years. How could this pioneering book, moving and intimate and frank, *not* have spoken to me? Additionally, however—and this was the surprise—I found that I was affected this time in a completely new and different way. With this reading I felt more empathy with the main character, George, and with Isherwood.

Thirty-some years later, I have found additional levels of meaning in the book. Not only are George and I now the same age, but there are parallel circumstances in our lives that make my empathy with him even greater: the loss of a partner; the working environment of an academic community and daily contact with much younger students; and general feelings of aloneness that come at a point in life when one had truly not expected to be leading a solitary existence. Times are different now, of course, and George's reticence about revealing his sexual orientation and his distance from the gay community are circumstances he and I do not share. Suffice it to say, though, that my reading of *A Single Man* this time was a very different personal experience, and I felt a "shock of recognition" many times.

I was also very much struck by how little dated the book seems. A few anomalies stand out. For example, it would be quite unusual now for George, a seemingly affable man working in an academic community, to be without any other gay acquaintances, as we are led to assume in the novel. While this may lock the book squarely in pre-Stonewall gay America, however, it does work to Isherwood's advantage in one respect. Claude Summers, in his perceptive study *Christopher Isherwood*, writes: "The absence of a viable gay community in the days before the Stonewall riots and the gay activist movements . . . may be one of the most significant factors in

Isherwood's use of homosexuality as a metaphor for the alienation endemic to the general human condition" (114).

Jim's death, in an auto accident while out of town, would also probably not be kept a secret from George's neighbors in a similar novel today (although, I dare say, the death of a partner from AIDS might occasion a parallel hiding of the truth in a contemporary setting). Finally, some aspects of George's encounter with Kenny now appear a bit coy. George's own sexuality would probably be more "out," given the intense nature of their conversation, though this fact would by no means diminish the sexual tension of the incident or Kenny's somewhat provocative behavior toward George.

I also admire Isherwood's perceptive remarks about what we now call homophobia, a term coined in 1972 by George Weinberg in his landmark *Society and the Healthy Homosexual*. Talking about his neighbors, George thinks: "They are afraid of what they know is somewhere in the darkness around them, of what may at any moment emerge into the undeniable light of their flashlamps, nevermore to be ignored, explained away. . . . Among many other kinds of monster . . . they are afraid of little me" (22). This passage remarkably presages Weinberg and his pioneering work, a study that reversed the traditional focus of analysis by examining irrational fears within the heterosexual community and affirming homosexual identity. Weinberg describes a second kind of homophobia, experienced by a gay person as "self-loathing." Self-deprecating though he may be about his deteriorating physical appearance, among other things, George has a generally healthy ego, another testimony to Isherwood's forward-thinking presentation of a gay personality.

Having examined *A Single Man* from a nineties perspective, I was curious to read some contemporary reviews of the book. The novel was extensively reviewed—as A. A. Gross wrote in *The Christian Century,* "A new book by Christopher Isherwood is always a Literary Event"—yet I was struck by the wide range of opinions about it. I was shocked but not surprised at the lack of serious attention paid to the frank and affirming depiction of George's homosexuality. Reviews of *A Single Man* ranged from patently homophobic and obtuse to reasonably astute.[1] For example, Phoebe Adams in the *Atlantic* cited "George's battle with the *normal* world," stating further that he is a "prisoner of his *perverse physical appetites*" (italics mine). On the other hand, in a perceptive essay in the *New Republic,* Stanley Kauffmann wrote: "The book holds us because it runs parallel with the truth of our lives, but like any parallel, it keeps a certain distance."

There is no positive mention of the front-and-center depiction of George's sexuality in any mainstream review, certainly nothing to compare to Colton's cover blurb from *One*. Aside from using the adjective "homosexual" to describe George, reviewers tended to ignore this groundbreaking aspect of the book. Respected for his earlier novels, where gay themes are somewhat veiled or of peripheral importance, Isherwood in *A Single Man* may have ventured into territory too uncomfortable for most critics to explore.

While disregarding what is clearly one of Isherwood's intentions in the book—the depiction of George as a homosexual man—many reviewers did elevate George to the status of a virtual Everyman. In the most perceptive critiques of *A Single Man,* there was at least agreement that Isherwood had successfully represented a universal aspect of the human condition. Perhaps it was prudent in 1964 for reviewers to take that express route as a way of praising the book, conveniently bypassing the particular details of George's sexual life along the way.

George as a kind of Everyman is, I believe, a valid interpretation of Isherwood's thematic intention. Significantly, too, George is an Everyman who embraces life, who tries to live in the now, who still cares, and who has, for the most part, lived life as he chose. But even the most perceptive of the sixties reviewers tended to emphasize the more somber aspects of the book. Elizabeth Hardwick, writing in the *New York Review of Books,* commented: "It is a sad book, with a biological melancholy running through it, a sense of relentless reduction, daily diminishment." That view accurately reflects the universality of the situation Isherwood is examining, but it does not acknowledge the life force that makes George a vital and passionate being.

Recent critics, on the other hand, do not ignore the dark truths of *A Single Man* but have tended to focus in a more positive way on the significance of the novel within the pantheon of modern gay literature. Mark Lilly, who devotes a chapter of his critical study *Gay Men's Literature in the Twentieth Century* to *A Single Man,* writes: "It deserves attention because, however tame it might now appear, it is one of the very earliest novels to give an emphatically positive face to the gay experience. The tradition of social realism [in] coming out novels . . . is indebted to the work of Isherwood" (189).

I now embrace passages that I suspect did not hold much meaning for me a generation ago. At one point in the novel, George is driving down a holiday-bedecked boulevard: "*I am alive,* he says to himself, *I am alive!* And life-energy surges hotly through him, and delight, and appetite. How good to be in a body—even this old beat-up carcass—that still has warm blood and live semen and rich marrow and wholesome flesh! . . . He wants to rejoice in his own body—the tough triumphant old body of a survivor" (104). I'm reminded here of Thoreau's statement in *Walden* describing his journey into the woods: "I went . . . because I wished to see if I could not learn what life had to teach . . . and not, when I came to die, discover that I had not lived"

(66). If, like most men, George leads what Thoreau called a "life of quiet desperation," he has the advantage of self-awareness and the willingness and ability to go on learning what the journey has to teach.

How satisfying to realize a book that spoke to you in your youth can still have profound meaning many years later. And how brave and visionary of Isherwood to have written in 1964 a novel about the gay experience that has as much social and philosophical relevance today as it did back then, when such matters were not often discussed. That *A Single Man* predated the clamorous wave of the gay liberation movement by several years testifies all the more to the power and clarity of its subtle truths.

In an interview in 1973 with Winston Leyland, Isherwood remarked that he regretted not having been more open about homosexuality in his earlier works, in particular *The Berlin Stories*. "I'm often asked if I regret that I didn't say outright . . . that I was homosexual. Yes, I wish I had" (192). Later in the interview, however, he states, "I feel *A Single Man* is the best thing I have ever written. This was the only time when I succeeded, very nearly, in saying exactly what I wanted to say" (198).

Isherwood got it right in *A Single Man*. What he says in this novel about being gay—about being human—will endure.

Notes

1. In addition to those essays cited in the text, see the following reviews of *A Single Man:* David Daiches, "Life without Jim," *New York Times Book Review* (August 30, 1964): 5; and "George and Jim," *TLS* (September 10, 1964): 837.

Additional Works Cited

Adams, Phoebe. "Prisoner of the Perverse." *Atlantic* 214 (September 1964): 122–123.
Gross, A. A. "An Ineluctable Fact." *Christian Century* 81 (September 30, 1964): 1214.
Hardwick, Elizabeth. "Sex and the Single Man." *New York Review of Books* 2 (August 20, 1964): 4.
Kauffmann, Stanley. "Death in Venice, Cal." *New Republic* 151 (September 5, 1964): 23–24.
Leyland, Winston. "Winston Leyland Interviews Christopher Isherwood." *Gay Sunshine Interviews.* Volume 1. Ed. Winston Leyland. San Francisco: Gay Sunshine Press, 1978.
Thoreau, Henry David. *Walden, or Life in the Woods.* New York: New American Library (Signet Classics), 1962.
Weinberg, George. *Society and the Healthy Homosexual.* New York: St. Martin's Press, 1972.

20 *David Bergman*

Isherwood and the Violet Quill

For the generation of gay writers who developed in the wake of Stonewall, the first generation of openly gay writers, Christopher Isherwood was a persistent, pervasive, and profound influence both artistically and personally, not that such a distinction was easy to make. In contrast to such tormented and self-destructive American gay writers as Truman Capote or Tennessee Williams, Isherwood provided a calm, sane, and productive counterexample whose work was imaginatively rich, stylistically challenging, and politically and spiritually engaged. More than any other writer, Isherwood gave direction to the gay literary movement. This is not to say that these later writers were merely branches off Isherwood, but rather that Isherwood planted the roots for what has become a luxuriant grove.

One indication of Isherwood's importance to this generation of gay writers is the prominence his work took in an early symposium on the gay novel organized by writer George Whitmore. In 1980, Whitmore put together a panel to discuss the gay novel. Among the discussants were novelist Edmund White; Seymour Kleinberg, a professor at Long Island University and the editor of an important early anthology of lesbian and gay writing, *The Other Persuasion* (1977); Byrne Fone, a teacher at City College; and Scott Tucker, a writer and activist. At the symposium, each of the panelists read a work of his choice by a "pre-Stonewall gay voice" and discussed "how the novel represented a tradition." White read from

Jean Genet's *Our Lady of the Flowers,* Kleinberg from Hubert Selby Jr.'s *Last Exit to Brooklyn,* Fone from a variety of nineteenth-century texts, and Tucker from Isherwood's *A Single Man* (*VQR,* 53).

This symposium was not a minor event at the time. The hall was filled with what attendee Felice Picano called in his journal "a glittering company," including Arthur Bell, a columnist for the *Village Voice;* Richard Goldstein of the *Advocate;* and writer Larry Kramer (*VQR,* 53). It was a formative event for the group that soon would call itself the Violet Quill, perhaps the most important coterie of gay writers to emerge in the late seventies and early eighties. Three of the men involved in the symposium—Whitmore, White, and Andrew Holleran (who was scheduled to appear on the panel)—went on to become members of the Violet Quill. The other members were Christopher Cox, Robert Ferro, Michael Grumley, and Picano. The occasion helped these writers map out a genealogy for their work and provide a public forum for their evolving sense of the kind of writing they wished to do.

The writers' choices of texts are interesting. *A Single Man* and *Last Exit to Brooklyn* are both novels of the sixties, and *Our Lady of the Flowers,* although originally published in 1943 and translated into English in 1949, was not readily available until Grove Press issued a revised translation in 1963. For all intents and purposes, *Our Lady of the Flowers* is a sixties work. Clearly, for the panelists, the living tradition of the gay novel was barely twenty years old at the time of the symposium.

We can gain some perspective on Isherwood's influence by comparing it to Genet's. Genet is the more flamboyant writer, and *Our Lady of the Flowers* the more dramatic work, its style more easily recognizable, if not so easily imitated. Nevertheless, most of Genet's major accomplishments were not particularly useful to White or the rest of the Violet Quill. A debt to Genet's style may be found in the opening of *Nocturnes for the King of Naples,* in which White sacramentalizes the profane environment of the piers off West Street. Yet these stylistic influences are very limited. Furthermore, Genet's greatest limitation as a model for the Violet Quill was not stylistic but social. His homosexual world is entirely circumscribed by the criminal and lower classes, and although for the most part the Violet Quill rejected bourgeois life, they also rejected what had become a homophobic trope of equating homosexuality with the criminal classes. As White comments, Genet (along with William Burroughs and John Rechy) "rendered gay life as exotic, marginal, even monstrous" (*BL,* 275). The Violet Quill were children of the upper middle class. Prep school was the closest some ever came to a penal institution. To be sure, they opted for the particularly American bohemian existence of being social workers, waiters, night copyeditors in law firms, freelance ghost writers, and shop clerks, jobs that did not bring in much money but left them time to write. They did not, however, equate homosexuality with the outlaw world of prostitutes, pimps, petty thieves, and drug addicts. By and large they felt that gay American fiction needed stories of middle-class men who identified as gay and who attempted to live their lives not in the closet but as openly gay men. In this project Genet was no help.

Isherwood offered more fertile literary ground. In his lecture "Gay Literature Today," Robert Ferro placed Isherwood on a list of the "eight or ten great homosexual writers" who were "literary forebears" and whose works should be taught "in every college curriculum in the country." He cited *A Single Man* as a work "steeped in literary and moral bravery" (*VQR*, 392). Similarly, Edmund White has called *A Single Man* "one of the first and best novels of the modern gay liberation movement" (*BL*, 347). To the question of whether *The Beauty of Men* was a rewriting of *A Single Man*, Andrew Holleran unhesitatingly answered me, "Of course."

Isherwood's work relies neither on extreme stylistic clashes nor on a narrow social milieu. His plain style and middle-class characters fit more closely the direction the Violet Quill writers were to explore. More significantly, he provided a useful example of autobiographical fiction. Isherwood's novels *Goodbye to Berlin* and *Prater Violet* trade on autobiographical experience, and his memoir, *Lions and Shadows,* reads like a novel. Long before David Leavitt attracted attention by naming a character in a novella "David Leavitt," Isherwood had used the same device in *Down There on a Visit.* Starting in the seventies, Isherwood published a series of autobiographies including *Kathleen and Frank,* a memoir of his parents, *Christopher and His Kind,* and *My Guru and His Disciple.* Only the last of these is written in the first person. In the others, Isherwood speaks of himself as a different and separate person. Thus, although these books try, in Isherwood's words, to be as "frank and factual" as he could make them, still they have the feel of novels. Conversely, his novel *A Single Man* reads like an autobiography and contains many autobiographical elements. It is about a middle-aged Englishman, a longtime resident of California, who teaches English at a California college. Isherwood was all these things. The Englishman's crush on a college student draws, at least in part, from Isherwood's relationship with Don Bachardy, whom he met in 1953 when Bachardy was an eighteen-year-old college student and Isherwood was in his late forties. By crossing and recrossing the boundaries of genre, Isherwood gave the Violet Quill lessons in creating autobiographical fiction and fictional autobiographies.

Robert Ferro, for one, thinks that the autobiographical novel is the great contribution that gay writers have made to postwar fiction. He sees gay fiction standing against canonical taste, which has chosen to view autobiographical fiction as "the recourse of a limited imagination" (*VQR,* 389). Ferro suggests that gay novelists are vitalized by their mission: first, "the removal from fiction of various negative and stereotypical myths" about gay people; second, the invention of "new myths, new themes" (*VQR,* 389). How do gay novelists escape homophobic myths? Not by recirculating the homophobic representation available from past writing; but, Ferro insists, by "telling their own stories" and mining their own lives they can create something different (*VQR,* 390). Gay writers are not alone in feeling the vitalizing energy of "telling their own stories." According to Ferro, "Blacks, certain women writers, Jews—in fact, the return of the narrator has been effected by those with a story to tell, and for whom the particularized devices of realism are again useful" (*VQR,* 391). Following Isherwood's example, Ferro believes that only through the particulars of autobiographical fiction can gay writers create new myths for the larger society, and only by stressing the singularity of their lives can they exert a force strong enough to countervail the weight of homophobic myths.

Isherwood revises the received notions of gay people, and *A Single Man* stands in marked contrast to the two reigning images of the homosexual in the sixties: the denizen of the demimonde and the beautiful ephebe. *A Single Man* is a novel not only about an unmarried man, a gay widower, but also about a *singular* man who defies the stereotypes so often forced on homosexuals. Likewise, the novel escapes those stereotypes because, Ferro would argue, it draws so heavily from Isherwood's own experience.

George, the central figure of the novel, is as far apart from the underworld figures of Genet as possible; moreover, he is not the golden young man of so many other gay novels. Yet Isherwood does not reject these as possible modes of representation. For example, he had explored the world of prostitutes in *Goodbye to Berlin,* and in Kenny, one of George's students, he affirms the attractiveness of youth. In fact, George's relationship to Kenny recalls the Greek model of *erastes* and *eromenos,* older man and adolescent. Yet even as Isherwood invokes this model, he alters it, describing George's conversation with Kenny as a dialogue, "but not a Platonic dialogue" (154). Later in the scene, after George and Kenny go skinny-dipping in the Pacific, they exchange roles. Kenny becomes the authority while George becomes the child under his control, only now the Greek allusion is abandoned and replaced by the metaphor of nanny and infant-charge. Like some grotesque Mary Poppins blown up to the size of a Macy's Thanksgiving Day balloon, Kenny looms over the shrinking George. But Isherwood is not finished with this Swiftian reversal of perspective; this nanny in the last moment becomes something of a Tom of Finland as "everything about [Kenny] is larger than life: the white teeth of his grin, the wide dripping shoulders, the tall slim torso with its heavy-hung sex" (164). This constant shifting of perspective—an essential part of Isherwood's moral and spiritual project—breaks down any established model into which one might try to fit George.

Isherwood's playfulness with the conventions of the "serious" gay novel are evident in the conclusion. The "serious realistic" gay novel of the sixties was required to end in degradation and death. To be sure, George has drunk a little too much for his own good, but his behavior is not necessarily a sign of alcoholism, nor is George falling apart physically. He exercises at a gym, where, on the particular day of the novel, he does eighty sit-ups. He goes to bed happy, falling asleep with a smile on his face. Nothing is amiss; his heart "works on and on, needing no rest. . . . Everything seems set for a routine run from here to morning. The odds are enormously against any kind of accident" (184–85). If readers were insurance actuaries, they would find that "the safety record of this vehicle is outstanding." How then to effect the death that is required of the serious gay novel of the sixties? Isherwood's answer is to ask, "Just let us suppose, however. . . ." In this hypothetical mood the novel ends, ironically giving the homophobic reader the required "tragic" ending while undercutting it with the hypothetical language. Isherwood comically throws into the conventional readers' faces their need to see the gay character die in the end. For even if we suppose that George does die, his death is not the wages of sin, a penalty paid for being gay. Instead it is a quiet, gentle, painless death—the "good death" we believe granted only to the virtuous, and the biological death that all mortals must eventually suffer. In this remarkable ending, Isherwood plays deftly with the requirements of the gay novel, simultaneously recognizing and rejecting them.

Not only does Isherwood defy the received structure of the gay novel and turn stereotypes on their head, but he also uses "the particularized devices of realism" that Ferro thinks are the tools most important to the gay novelist. As Claude J. Summers has pointed out, in *A Single Man* Isherwood "captures the fullness of an individual life in a particular place at a specific time," yet in doing so, George becomes "an emblem of the human condition in any place at any time" (121). This particularization is not opposed to a universalizing strategy; but rather it is the very means of connecting George to a larger consciousness.

Isherwood is careful to indicate George's social and economic position, as a member of the upper middle class. Unlike the characters in Rechy, Genet, or Burroughs, George is no "sexual outlaw," and his rebellions are contained by his personal circumstances. His "little private income" and his English origins protect him from an otherwise hostile environment (86). Yet he does not identify with the power structure, and, despite a certain license for eccentricity given to the English, he never uses it to win favor with Americans. Thus the figure of George, while less exotic than the standard underworld homosexuals of sixties gay fiction, is in many ways more iconoclastic.

Isherwood strives to make George worth following for a day, not because he does anything heroic and not because he is "dirty, degenerate and dangerous" (85), but merely because he is a single man, and, as Isherwood might argue, any one person is worthy of our attention. As White points out, George expresses feelings that "everyone knows—the suffering that arises from the death of loved ones, the numbing of routine, the fear of loneliness" (*BL,* 275). In the only sustained apologetics in the novel, George defends Aldous Huxley's *After Many a Summer Dies the Swan* against charges of anti-Semitism. His long explanation of Huxley's position is a defense that minorities are not deserving of rights because they are particularly worthy people, or because they are the same as the majority, but because no matter how different they may be or how much they may give cause to hate them, no one has a right to deny anyone else his or her full humanity. George taunts his class—which contains Asian, African, and Jewish Americans—saying that minorities are probably more unpleasant than the majority: "A minority has its own kind of aggression. It absolutely dares the majority to attack it. It hates the majority—not without a cause, I grant you. It even hates the other minorities, because all minorities are in competition: each one proclaims that its sufferings are the worst and its wrongs are the blackest. And the more they all hate, and the more they're all persecuted, the nastier they become! Do you think it makes people nasty to be loved? You know it doesn't! Then why should it make them nice to be loathed?" (72). If the gay writer is to create "new myths," as Ferro says he must, it cannot be done by turning gays into flawless superheroes, paragons of sweetness and light. To the contrary, the responsibility of the gay writer in telling his story is to represent gay people as the kind of flawed humans they actually are. Isherwood frames George as neither angel nor devil.

While Isherwood insists on his character's singularity, George must also be regarded as a representative of gay men in general. One of the most often quoted passages of Isherwood, which White repeats in his memorial essay, develops the central conceit of the rock pool:

Up the coast a few miles north, in a lava reef under the cliffs, there are a lot of rock pools. . . . Each pool is separate and different, and you can, if you are fanciful, give them names, such as George, Charlotte, Kenny. . . . You may think of the rock pool as an entity; though, of course, it is not. The waters of its consciousness—so to speak—are swarming with hunted anxieties, grim-jawed greeds, dartingly vivid intuitions, old crusty-shelled rock-gripping obstinacies, deep-down sparkling undiscovered secrets, ominous protean organisms motioning mysteriously, perhaps warningly, toward the surface light. How can such a variety of creatures coexist at all? Because they have to. The rocks of the pool hold their world together. And, throughout the day of the ebb tide, they know no other.

But the long day ends at last; yields to the night-time of the flood. And, just as the waters of the ocean come flooding, darkening over the pools, so over George and the others in sleep come the waters of that other ocean—that consciousness which is no one in particular but which contains everyone and everything. . . . Some of the creatures are lifted from their pools to drift far out over the deep waters. . . . Can they tell us, in any manner, about their journey? Is there, indeed, anything for them to tell—except that the waters of the ocean are not really other than the waters of the pool? (183–84)

On the one hand, the individual must be recognized in all her or his specificity, although Isherwood is careful not to make the individual a unified or unitary entity; rather, the individual is first and foremost a contained fluid in which there circulates "protean organisms," ever-changing components. Thus, the individual, for Isherwood, is not a solid but instead a dynamic and complex amalgam of not entirely coherent or harmonized elements batched rather accidentally together. Yet on the other hand, this very individuality which he honors in all its specificity is an illusion of the moment. Not that we are all the same—Isherwood clearly repudiates that notion—but that all individuals come out of the same dynamic and complex amalgam of incoherent and inharmonious elements. One is both an individual and a synecdochal sample of the whole, but since the whole is not homogenized, no sample can give a precise measure of the whole, or necessarily contains all the same ingredients as the whole. Still, by rendering the individual in all her or his specificity we can gain a notion of the whole. This is the final pun of Isherwood's title.

For White, Isherwood is not alone in exploring the relationship between the isolated individual and a common spiritual existence. The same tension can be found in late Genet as well, although Genet, according to White, began with the notion that "saintliness is singular" and cuts the saint off from the rest of humanity. Yet in *Prisoner of Love,* Genet's last book, he came to reconcile "the tension between the romantic cult of the unique individual and the Christian faith in spiritual equality" (*BL,* 306). This transformation in Genet's attitude occurred one day when he was riding a train "opposite a dirty, ugly little man." As White retells it, Genet suddenly "felt a strange exchange of personality with this stranger. Genet flowed into the man's body at the same time as the man flowed into Genet's body," and Genet "realized that everyone is of the same value" (306).

But Isherwood goes further than Genet because Isherwood is less involved in Christian formulations of the problem. White, in his foreword to *The Faber Book of Gay Short Fiction,* quotes Isherwood: "*What* I am has refashioned itself throughout the days and years, and until now almost all that remains constant is the mere awareness of being conscious. And that consciousness belongs to everybody; it isn't a particular person" (x). As a Vedantist, Isherwood has gone much further than any of the writers in the Violet Quill in emphasizing adherence to "the mere awareness of being conscious," yet this sense of constant refashioning—the destabilizing of a sense of self even as it is being created—is something that the Violet Quill develops as an important part of its aesthetic. For example, Felice Picano's *A House on the Ocean, a House on the Bay* is yet another formulation of autobiographical fiction. In the novel, Picano consults *The Tibetan Book of the Dead* for "hints and ideas about how I could change myself from the middle-class postgrad with little work experience into an entirely new person: totally individual and never before seen on earth" (14). Picano does not imagine a constant reformation as Isherwood does, but he sees selfhood as plastic, as something constructed by class, education, and work and, therefore, capable of reconstruction. Picano's aim is not the egolessness that is Isherwood's; rather it is an individuality that is open to everyone, provided they subject themselves to the discipline of critical self-reflection.

One of Isherwood's achievements is telling a story of a gay man in his fifties, the point at which popular belief and gay social patterns have determined active homoeroticism should end. By general consensus, a fifty-year-old man still wanting sex is a "dirty old man." In most gay fiction he is simply unrepresented; the few times he does appear, he is a reptilian letch. Isherwood's motivation for representing the middle-aged man is in part that he was George's age when he wrote *A Single Man,* but more important that he wished to resist the belief that self-construction ends at biological maturity. For Isherwood, the imperative for self-transformation cannot stop. However difficult it was for Isherwood to represent the middle-aged man in perpetual reconstruction, it may be even more challenging in the nineties. During the sixties, when *A Single Man* was published, gay culture was less stratified by age. The current age stratification has come about in part because AIDS has reduced the size of an entire generation and in part because the body culture that has developed in post-AIDS gay society largely excludes older men from participation. According to White, a rift of experience has opened between AIDS survivors and younger gay men. In a 1997 interview in the *Advocate,* White said, "I think there will be people over 30 now who have survived and who will feel themselves becoming more and more marginalized by younger people who aren't as aware of the whole battle [over AIDS]. That's going to be painful in a very different way. It's one thing to think, *We all went through this together and survived, and here's my story of what I went through*. It's going to be another thing to have nobody want to read those stories" (62). Because those who can testify to the experience of gay culture of the seventies are relatively few in number, there is less understanding, more misinformation, and less sympathy with them.

Andrew Holleran's *The Beauty of Men* is a retelling of *A Single Man* within the context of the post-AIDS realities. The similarities between the two novels are striking, especially since they were written thirty years apart and are distanced by Stonewall and AIDS. Yet they both concern men who are isolated by death, George by the sudden death of his lover, Jim, and Mr. Lark by all his friends who have died of AIDS. They are men whose sexuality has isolated them from the communities in which they live. George has seen the bohemian community along Camphor Tree Lane die off and be replaced by veterans and "their just-married wives, in search of new and better breeding grounds." He bitterly reflects on how "one by one, the cottages which used to reek of bathtub gin and reverberate with the poetry of Hart Crane have fallen to the occupying army of Coke-drinking television watchers" (18). Lark is even more bitter about the changes he has witnessed in Florida: "When Lark comes to a stop at the red light on Orange Heights, he watches the station wagons go flying past . . . hell-bent for the Magic Kingdom, and he thinks, *That's right! Keep going!* How nice of Disney to build a park with artificial rivers, man-made lakes, trucked-in beaches; it drains off the hordes who otherwise might visit the real thing. Leaving untouched for at least a few more years the rural patchwork of farm, field, pecan grove, Baptist church. . . . He wants to send away for a T-shirt he saw advertised in *Out* magazine: CAN'T FEED 'EM, DON'T BREED 'EM" (19). Isherwood and Holleran see the downfall of their communities resulting from overpopulation and the habit of heterosexuals to reproduce without concern for the quality of life.

There are a number of small parallels between George and Lark. They are torn between two places—George between England and California, Lark between New York and Florida. Both make regular visits to the hospital—George to see his friend Doris, who is dying; Lark to take care of his quadriplegic mother. And there are major differences too. George seems to have no contact with a gay community. He and Jim have lived as a couple removed from any larger gay network. Lark is in touch not only with gay friends in New York and the few gay men in his little community but also with wider gay culture. What most forcefully unites these two works is the insistence that gay men—even in middle age—have the need for love that we automatically expect the young to have, and a sexual desire, if somewhat diminished, which does not disappear with age. George and Lark have very different attitudes toward the search. George is hopeful ("he believes he will find another Jim. . . . He believes he will because he must" [82]), but Lark is in despair. With the death of his mother and the end of his obsession with Becker (the object of his pursuit), Lark returns to the boat ramp, the local cruising spot, to see if he can meet "the security guard from the prison north of Starke," who he has heard is very handsome. But although Lark goes to the boat ramp, approaching the possibility of love, he erects barriers to it. He tints the windows of the car so that no one can see him and "sits in his car till dark, without once getting out; while other people wonder who it is and finally drive off, tired of waiting" (272). Lark is too traumatized by age, death, and displacement to seize whatever love he might find. No doubt the differences in personality between Isherwood and Holleran mostly account for the very different attitudes their protagonists have to the likelihood of finding that love, but surely the cultural shifts between the sixties and nineties affect these endings as well. George has lived through World War II, but Lark lives in the aftermath of AIDS, blown far from the ground zero of an epidemic that continues. His rural Florida in the shadow of tourism is, to use Yeats's phrase, "no country for old men." The despair of the novel is not just Holleran's personal depression but also cultural depression.

Although Holleran's novel is closely related to Isherwood's masterpiece, Edmund White is perhaps the Violet Quill writer most indebted to Isherwood. They met in the late seventies and continued as friends until Isherwood's death. White credits the simplifying of his style to Isherwood's influence. In *A Boy's Own Story* White adopts a style that is considerably less baroque than the one he used in *Nocturnes for the King of Naples*. Indeed, it is in *A Boy's Own Story* that White followed Isherwood's practice of suggesting the collective by attending to the very particularities of the individual.

White has often commented on the odd relationship between autobiography and fiction. He argues that fiction is better than memory for rendering things in all their particularity and individuality. Perceptions blur people into categories. What is possible in fiction is to reinstate the specificity and individuality memory loses from experience while suggesting the larger groupings and relationships that give experience its coherence and meaning. For White, as for Isherwood, the writer's job is to present gay people not merely as they now are but also in the process of their own reconstruction. "If gays tell each other—or the hostile world around them—the stories of their lives," writes White in the foreword to the *Faber Book of Gay Short Fiction*, "they're not just reporting the past but also shaping the future, forging an identity as much as revealing it" (ix). Or, as Frank Bidart puts it in "The Second Hour of the Night": *"We fill pre-existing forms, and when I we fill them, change them and are changed"* (56). Moreover, gay writers in the very act of representation undermine the invisibility society imposes on gay people. These representations make gay people visible to themselves and perhaps more significantly insist that gay lives are important enough to write about.

White is aware of the dialectic between representation and society. He described in a lecture he gave at CUNY how he tries to depict gay characters free from the homophobia that he had himself internalized: "My greatest invention was that I let my queers think about everything except the one subject that obsessed them: how they came to be that way, how they could evince the world's compassion rather than hate, and how they could be cured of their malady. I knew I didn't have the equilibrium or self-acceptance of my characters, but I thought by pretending *as if*. . . this utopia already existed I could authenticate my gay readers if not myself" (*BL,* 371). For White, the consciousness of gay people, their sense of identity, is not static. It is affected not only by the outside forces of a hostile world but also by the internal resistance which benefits not the resistors but those who might come after. White traces this sense of the dialectics of identity to Isherwood and to Isherwood's sense of a constantly refashioning consciousness.

Finally, one of Isherwood's gifts to gay writers is placing himself in a line of gay fiction that is also spiritual or religious. The gay writer's exploration of such spiritual issues as life and death is not achieved, George Whitmore argued in "The Gay Novel Now," by taking the conventional moralistic line but by moving through specifics that others might consider "trivial, degenerate, or at least ephemeral." Whitmore sees the possibility of transcendence in the campy, and White follows a similar line. His *Nocturnes for the King of Naples* was described on the dust jacket of the first edition as the reinvention of "devotional literature" by Mary Gordon, the staunchly Catholic novelist. White regards *Nocturnes* as a work that "blends the carnal with the spiritual, a tradition that includes Saint John of the Cross, the Sufi poet Rumi and Baroque poets such as John Donne" (*BL,* 370). The act of coming out and telling about it have their spiritual dimensions for White, and indeed are essentially spiritual exercises: "'Coming out' is the rite that marks the passage from homosexual desire to gay identity, and this transition begins and ends in avowal [which is based] on Christian confession and assuming . . . that sexual identity is profound, hidden, constitutive, more a matter of being than doing" (*Faber,* ix).

There is a spiritual aspect to Holleran's work as well, for Lark is obsessed with the quotation of St. John that his roommate has attached by a magnet to the refrigerator door before committing suicide: "In the twilight of Life, there is only Love" (246). How does one interpret this message: as the ironic denunciation of the most saccharine of platitudes, or as a heroic assertion at the very moment of despair? In a passage that recalls similar incidents in *A Single Man,* where Isherwood invests the most abject bodily moments with metaphysical significance, Lark wakes at night to urinate. "Where's God?" he wonders: "God is not in heaven, or in the sea, or in the clouds or sky, or in the tabernacle or the cathedral in which mass is being celebrated. He is in the bathroom at three in the morning. That's where He is. In the middle of the night. When you stand above the toilet bowl, face-to-face with Reality" (242). God is in the unmediated awareness of the present. It is where, as Isherwood would say, we possess "the mere awareness of being conscious. And that consciousness belongs to everybody; it isn't a particular person" (*Faber,* x).

Isherwood provided the Violet Quill writers with a precedent they would find useful. He became a model of a gay writer who is out because he refuses to be cut off from the freedom to create whatever representations he chooses. Another precedent that Isherwood set was presenting his gayness both in his fiction and his life with utter matter-of-factness. This matter-of-factness derived not from a desire to maintain British understatement but from inner equipoise. He had many contemporaries from England who never managed to gain the same balance of unselfconsciousness and awareness. Indeed, I think the members of the Violet Quill—in part because they came to write at a time when sexuality was more highly politicized—never found the same assured perspective that organizes *A Single Man.* More than any other work published before the formation of the Violet Quill, *A Single Man* discusses a gay man's experience without apologetics or sexual titillation, as though the reader will regard this life as any other life, that is, not as something merely unique in itself, nor as part of a class of similar lives, but as life connected to all life. George is neither a freak nor a blank, a gargoyle nor an idealized figure. He is a representation of gay men not because he is typical but because he is individual. Finally, Isherwood provided an example to the Violet Quill for how to write a "gay" novel which is also a "spiritual" novel. Now that it is fashionable to flog the fiction of the seventies and eighties for being only about sex, examining Isherwood's relationship to the Violet Quill can draw our attention to the fact that their work is about the complex and often ambivalent ways gay men deal with spirituality. For Isherwood was the best example of how one could combine both spiritual and sexual concerns.

Additional Works Cited

Bergman, David, ed. *The Violet Quill Reader: The Emergence of Gay Writing after Stonewall.* New York: St. Martin's, 1994. Cited as *VQR.*
Bidart, Frank. *Desire.* New York: Farrar, Straus & Giroux, 1997.

Ferro, Robert. "Gay Literature Today." In Bergman, *VQR.*
Holleran, Andrew. *The Beauty of Men.* New York: Morrow, 1996.
Holleran, Andrew. *Dancer from the Dance.* New York: Morrow, 1978.
Picano, Felice. *A House on the Ocean, a House on the Bay.* Boston: Faber, 1997.
White, Edmund. *The Burning Library.* Ed. David Bergman. New York: Knopf, 1994. Cited as *BL.*
White, Edmund, ed. *The Faber Book of Gay Short Fiction.* Boston: Faber, 1991. Cited as *Faber.*
White, Edmund, and Sarah Schulman. "The White Party." *Advocate* (September 16, 1997): 61.
Whitmore, George. "The Gay Novel Now." *Gaysweek* (October 9, 1978): 11–12.

PART IV
FINDING A PATH

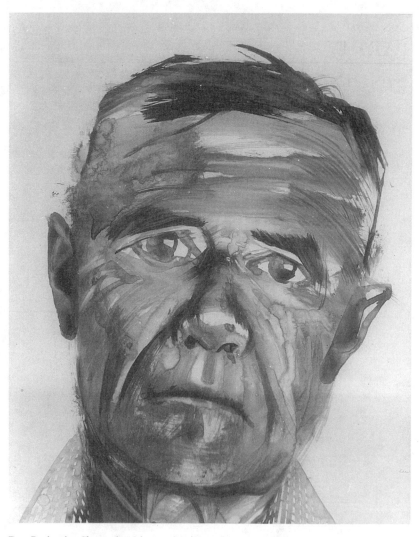

Don Bachardy: *Christopher Isherwood, August 14, 1980.* Acrylic on paper. 24″ × 40″. Copyright © Don Bachardy. Used by permission.

If God exists at all, there can be only one question: how can I get to see Him
and know Him? . . . Either you are moving nearer to God, or you are not.
                                                              (*Diaries* 1:283)

A significant portion of Christopher Isherwood's life was taken up with the
study of Vedanta, that branch of Hinduism based on the ancient teachings of
the Vedas and focused on the nineteenth-century avatar, Ramakrishna. As Isherwood wrote in his diary in August 1949, "Prayer, meditation, thought, creation are the *only* refuge and stronghold. Without them, I am nothing. Without
them, life is really an agony" (414). Clearly, for Isherwood the spiritual life was
crucial to his daily life and influenced every aspect of it. He developed a regi-
men of meditation, study, prayer, and regular attendance at his temple. His
relationship with Swami Prabhavananda, in particular, was the central fact of
his belief. He saw the swami as a saint.

This section contains material related to Isherwood's study of Vedanta, his
relationship with the Vedanta Society of Southern California, and the influence
of Vedanta on Isherwood's work. The essays come from a variety of points of
view and both from people who seek to understand Isherwood's beliefs and
people who share them.

In "Christopher under the Wishing Tree," Peter Shneidre provides an overview of Vedanta and Isherwood's relationship to it. As a devotee of Vedanta, a
friend of Isherwood's, and an editor for the Vedanta Press, Shneidre has a
unique perspective on Isherwood and his faith. He provides a glimpse into the
contradictions and conflicts in Isherwood's attempts to "renounce the world,"
including his own literary fame and the social demands of life in Hollywood, in
favor of the "active search for awareness."

A sense of Isherwood's spirituality, as it comes through his work, provides
the framework for David Garrett Izzo's essay, "Christopher Isherwood in Jail."
Izzo has taught Isherwood's work to inmates in a corrections facility in North
Carolina. As he explains in the essay, Izzo wanted to share Isherwood's
strength and example, which he sees coming from Vedantism, with his students. Reading and discussing Isherwood's work had a strong impact on many
of the students in the class and was life-changing for one student in particular.

The essays by John McFarland and Mario Faraone discuss the significance
of Vedanta to Isherwood's fiction. In "'Always Dance': Sex and Salvation in
Isherwood's Vedantism," McFarland traces how Isherwood came to Vedanta in

219

the 1940s and the spiritual struggles that followed. He pays particular attention to *The World in the Evening* and *A Single Man* as indicators of Isherwood's continued attempts to balance a life of the body and a life of the spirit. Faraone's "The Path That Leads to Safety: Spiritual Renewal and Autobiographical Narrative" uses the Bhagavad Gita as a point of reference for Isherwood's personal journey to religious and poetic belief. Faraone traces the figures of the "four men of the Gita" in Isherwood's final four novels, culminating with his coming to terms with the two sides of himself in the brother relationship in *A Meeting by the River*.

The volume closes with Isherwood speaking for himself in a previously unpublished interview conducted by Carola M. Kaplan in 1973. Kaplan was working on her dissertation at the time and describes her approach to Isherwood, his hospitality and openness to her, and the effect of this meeting on her work. The interview is far-ranging and shows Isherwood to be charming, witty, thoughtful, and incisive about his own work, his collaborations with Don Bachardy, his relationship with E. M. Forster, and his spiritual beliefs. The conversation ends with Isherwood emphasizing the possibility of reaching spiritual peace by multiple paths. It is a reassuring gesture, similar to the experience Carolyn Heilbrun recounts in "My Isherwood, My Bachardy," which appears in Part I. Like Heilbrun, Kaplan feels that Isherwood was intending to help her in her own quest without being intrusive or proselytizing.

As Isherwood explained in his diary in September 1957, his belief gives him faith that others will also be saved: "I believe that there is something called (for convenience) God, and that this something can be experienced (don't ask me how) and that a man I know (Swami) has had this experience, partially, at any rate. All this I believe because my instinct, as a novelist and connoisseur of people, assures me, after long, long observation, that it is true in Swami's case.... Believing this is also my guarantee that somehow in the end everything will come out all right for me and everyone. Because if God *is* there, then we needn't be afraid" (*Diaries* 1:728–29).

Christopher under the Wishing Tree

I am trying to hatch out into something different.
Diaries 1:366

In the summer of 1943 a celebrated English novelist, as famous for his freewheeling lifestyle and liberal politics as for his powers of observation and the beauty of his prose, entered an obscure monastery in the small town of Hollywood, California. There, he considered spending the rest of his life practicing a version of poverty, chastity, and obedience, translating scripture and assisting the abbot, a swami from Bengal. But if Christopher Isherwood wanted to renounce the world, the feeling wasn't mutual. His art, his friendships, and his politics had already been scrutinized the world over. His role in life hadn't been anything like the minor character he played in his autobiographical novels. Before he was out of his thirties, he'd inscribed his life across literary skies. He'd been praised by E. M. Forster and published by Virginia Woolf. He'd created at least one character, Sally Bowles, who would long outlive any children and grandchildren he might have had. His relationships with fellow writers, notably W. H. Auden and Stephen Spender, his sojourns in foreign lands, his journey of emigration to America, and his refusal to join in his country's war effort were the stuff of public comment. His arrival in New York with Auden on the eve of war had been especially newsworthy to a generation waiting to see what this charismatic group of friends was going to do next. "That young man," said Somerset Maugham to Woolf, "holds the future of the English novel in his hands" (*Kind*, 325).

221

In California, Isherwood not only wrote novels but movies too, pic-
nicked with Greta Garbo and Charlie Chaplin, and studied Vedanta, an
ancient creed more commonly but less accurately known as Hinduism. By
the end of his days, this writer who had posed as a camera, watching
everyone and everything with dispassion, was himself posing on his deathbed for his postmonastic companion of more than thirty years, an artist
who didn't stop painting even when the subject stopped living. And ten
years later, the first nine hundred or so pages of Isherwood's private diaries have been published, selling well and producing a clamor for future
installments.

Although the quotidian world didn't renounce Isherwood, it would
never be completely satisfied with him again. He was criticized as a coward
for abandoning his homeland in its time of need; his pacifism was seen as
an adventitious dodge that only made matters worse. His spiritual aspirations, even in an era of celebrity conversion by the likes of Auden and T. S.
Eliot, were derided as California faddishness, something to do between
parties while sitting out a war. He spent some of his most vigorous literary
years doing routine and sometimes inconsequential screenwriting work
for Hollywood studios as well as translating scripture and doing literary
odd jobs for his small Hindu church. Literary critics and at least one
movie auteur informed him that he had betrayed his talent, insinuating
that his brain had gone to mush in the overrated California sun. Even
fellow American Vedantists were uncomfortable with his unapologetic attitude toward sex, and one can still find Sanskritists upset with the poetic
license he took with Hindu scripture.

But most unforgivable of all was his quiet entry into another paradigm.
For in fact, the concerns of others stopped concerning him around 1939,
when he met Swami Prabhavananda and, in striking contrast to his lifelong contempt for God and religion, began to practice prayer and meditation under the monk's guidance. A few of Isherwood's London acquaintances—including novelist Aldous Huxley and Gerald Heard, an elfin
Irishman who was a popular lecturer on evolutionary science—had already joined the swami's two dozen or so followers in the foothills of
Hollywood, and they welcomed Isherwood into the group. Prabhavananda
was a member of the monastic order founded by Swami Vivekananda,
who, around the turn of the century, had been the first Hindu missionary
to the United States. Together they were all engaged in an exploration of
contemplative disciplines, having come to the conclusion that there was no
other way for either individuals or the world to stop their self-destructive
downward spiral.

Mysticism—the idea that one can access God or the eternal through a widening of the aperture of one's own individual consciousness and that one might thereby stumble upon a sense of "self" so awesomely pervasive as to make one's former strivings and fears seem like laughable delusions—was the ongoing subject of their discussion and the goal of their practice. It is, as Huxley demonstrated convincingly in *The Perennial Philosophy,* a message that barely changes from messenger to messenger as it is rediscovered in turn by the major figures of every religion, from Buddha to Jesus to Ramakrishna and beyond. Islam has its Sufi sects, Judaism its kabbalah. In Prabhavananda, a man of roughly their own age, Huxley and Heard had found someone they considered to be an adept at this mode of knowing whose own tradition happened to be Hindu. Huxley, Heard, and Isherwood helped the swami to render his intimate approach to God ("There is no failure in the search for God. Every step you take is a positive advance." [*Diaries* 1:44]) more accessible to Westerners; they edited the magazine *Vedanta and the West* and wrote reviews and essays for it; Isherwood began a collaboration with the swami translating key Hindu texts, notably a version of the Bhagavad Gita that after fifty years is still continually reprinted and is regarded as one of the most poetically inspired and readily comprehensible English versions of this essential scripture ever produced. Isherwood later wrote a biography of the Bengali saint Ramakrishna.

The world followed Isherwood into the little stucco temple, but it never quite picked up the trail again. In a change of life worthy of an Auden sonnet, he was now no longer a leftist intellectual or even primarily an artist but an incipient lover of the Absolute, a lifelong spiritual seeker committed to the introspection of yoga, or union with God. "'This,' I said to myself, 'is what religion is really all about. Religion isn't a course of passive indoctrination; it is an active search for awareness'" (*Wishing Tree,* 57).

Isherwood opened himself up to this new influence to a disarming degree. His inner struggles now had as much to do with trying to see the infinite behind everyday appearances—and pursuing the unglamorous task of trying to curb the ego's veiling of it—as with seeking sex or writing. Having had practice at being unpopular, as both a homosexual and a quasi-Marxist, he now plunged into one of the least popular acts a human can commit: the implicit repudiation of most of what the world holds dear.

We went to the Club Gala on the Strip. My farewell visit to the End of the Night. I haven't been to a place of this sort in ages, and it was so nostalgically reminiscent of all the other times—the baroque decorations and the cozy red velvet corners,

the sharp-faced peroxide pianist with tender memories and tongue like an adder,
the grizzled tomcat tenor, the bitch with the heart of gold, the lame celebrity, the
bar mimosa, the public lovers, the amazed millionaire tourist, the garlanded cow,
the plumed serpent and the daydream sailor. . . . I have loved them all very much
and learnt something from each of them. I owe them many of my vividest moments of awareness. But enough is enough. And here we say goodbye.

Or do we? Isn't this entirely the wrong spirit in which to enter Ivar Avenue [i.e.,
the Vedanta monastery]? I am not going there to forget such places, or any other
part of life. No—if this training really succeeds, I shall be able to return to the
Gala, or any other scene of the past, with the kind of understanding which sees
what it is really all about. (*Diaries* 1:265–66)

What is the kind of understanding which "sees what it is really all
about" really all about? What were its points of intersection with Isherwood's rebelliousness, his sense of isolation from the common stream of
life, his restless search for a home and companionship? Why did it attract
him? How did it change him? The questions that are typically asked in
regard to a religious conversion arise from a paradigm of psychological determinism that Isherwood, like most spiritual aspirants before him,
was quickly abandoning. *X* seems to have caused *Y*. But what if *Y* was
about to happen anyway, and *X* was simply prefiguring or announcing it?
Then it is as true to say that *Y* caused *X* as that *X* caused *Y*. Thus, did
Isherwood's hearing about Vedanta from his friends turn him into a Vedantist? Or was he someone who already felt that there must be more to
life than aiming the camera of his awareness in new directions outside
of himself, a crypto-Vedantist already subliminally seeking the company of
others experimenting with a more effective and comprehensive way
of encountering reality? In that case, his need to know had led to his
interest in a group of people inquiring along similar lines. To say that
Isherwood had found in Vedanta a religion free from the oppressive constraints of his late Victorian upbringing, or that in the Hindu goddess Kali
he found a way to acknowledge and accept the terrible femininity of the
world, or that in the ecstatic Ramakrishna he had found a witty and campy
avatar tailor-made for gay worship, would be condescension, tantamount
to explaining his love for boys by saying that they were substitutes for girls.
To explain anything from the point of view of a paradigm that holds one
thing as normal and all else as a substitute for it chiefly serves to demon-
strate the stranglehold of the paradigm itself.

Vedanta is not the same as Hinduism; each is both less and more than the
other.[1] While on the one hand the Hindu tradition is an all-embracing
octopus of spirituality whose arms include Hare Krishna chanting and the
astringent nondualism of Krishnamurti, both of which would seem to

reach beyond Isherwood's concerns, Vedantists such as Huxley and Heard traced their particular quest and practice back just as confidently through other traditions as well, to hardcore mystics of every tradition who, in their utter isolation, seem to be functioning simultaneously at the molten core of some sui generis religion. These are the seers who feel that within one's own subjective field of experience are all the clues one needs to find God, mystics such as the Englishman Richard Rolle and the anonymous author of *The Cloud of Unknowing,* Catholics who in turn traced themselves back through Dionysius the Areopagite, who followed the neo-Platonists who, in many accounts of this lineage, were linked by Plato to Socrates himself, who was said to be an adept. Though they recognized kindred spirits in Ramakrishna and other mystics of India including the authors of the Upanishads, the southern California Vedantists didn't restrict themselves to Indian thoughts. Swami Prabhavananda happened to be a Hindu; Isherwood remarked that had his teacher been an inspired rabbi who spoke as one having authority, he would have undoubtedly become a Jew. Thus Vedanta might better be seen as the thread upon which the religions of the world are strung, rather than a particular bead upon it. It wasn't a Hindu truth Isherwood discovered in himself, but rather an evolutionary extension of his I-am-a-camera credo. Religion helped him to find who was pointing the camera and deciding what to shoot, and how best to develop the film. "Meditation filled me with an excitement which I have seldom felt since. It was most exciting to sit on the floor in a corner of the room, in the darkness of early morning or evening, and feel that one was face to face with the unknown that was oneself. This was a sort of flirtation with the unconscious—made exciting, like all flirtations, by the eventual possibility of 'doing something about it'" (*Wishing Tree,* 18).

Isherwood's symbolic renunciation of the world as he knew it in the pursuit of knowledge with an Eastern accent was a gesture that was soon to become emblematic and a recognizable paradigm of its own with the publication, in 1944, of Somerset Maugham's *Razor's Edge.* Though this fictional account of a man who cannot settle for ordinary life and seeks self-knowledge instead was published a year after the Isherwood diary passage quoted above, the passage could serve as a study note for Maugham's novel. With the passage of time, it's clearer that Isherwood might as well have been the model for Larry Darrell, as was reported by *Time* to the annoyance of Isherwood, who fired back this response: "I am not, as you have twice stated in your columns, the original, or part-original, of Larry in Maugham's *Razor's Edge.* I can stand a good deal of kidding from my friends, but this rumor has poisoned my life for the past six months, and I wish it would die as quickly as possible" (see *Guru,*

181–84). In some ways the comparison was not very apt: Larry is an American war veteran without a career who visits a holy man in India and comes back to drive a taxi; Isherwood was an internationally celebrated British writer who moved to America and met a Hindu monk in Hollywood. But in its spiritual dimension the parallel is apt. Maugham had visited the sage Ramana Maharshi in India as well as Isherwood in Hollywood, and by the end of Maugham's novel Larry Darrell becomes a sort of Isherwood minor character, a deliberately anonymous working-class saint, an unpretentious Isherwoodian Everyman.

What Isherwood rebelled against most in Christianity was the priests, and although Vedanta, an unorganized religion, doesn't have priests per se, in many ways Isherwood was to become a latter-day *rishi.* There's no evidence in his diaries that he regarded himself as such, but in some ways he resembles the brahmins he described in *Ramakrishna and His Disciples:*

The brahmin is much more than just a priest. According to the Gita, he must be the seer of the community; the man through whom its contact with the life of the spirit is maintained. In India, the religious ideal has always been to obtain knowledge of the Atman, the divine nature within man, through direct experience; revelation has never been the property of a Church, as in the West. It is not towards any religious body but towards the individual seer, the knower of the Atman, that the community looks for an example to sustain it in its own struggles to gain enlightenment. That this enlightenment can actually be obtained by any individual is the fundamental proposition of the Hindu religion. . . . How can the Atman be known? By meditation, and by self-disciplines which open the eye of the spirit. Therefore the brahmin must be chaste, austere, scrupulously truthful, compassionate towards all living creatures. His faith in the Atman must be based on direct self-knowledge, not credulity. He may be a scholar and interpreter of the sacred books; but his interpretations must be drawn from his own experience, not merely from academic knowledge of former commentators. (7–8)

> Life isn't "about" air raids, swamis, love affairs, places, deeds done or undone—those are only the shapes of the letters in which the message is written. To read the message, that's all that matters.
>
> *Diaries* 1:369

Literature creates, preserves, and destroys meaning on the basis of shared assumptions about how the world works. A story that depends upon coincidences or a God to advance its plot seems weak, even though most of us can recall major turning points in our lives that seem to be the result of serendipity or grace more than well-wrought planning. For the moral of a story to cohere and bring catharsis, we demand an inexorable chain of cause and effect that relates to the world we know. But the thesis of

Indian religion is that the world we know is the creation of our own unen-
lightened minds. Knowledge gained through the senses or intellection is
distorted by our desires, fears, and presuppositions. Thus the devotee
comes to yoga or spiritual practice, the supposed systematic reduction of
subjective error, in the search for a truth whole and undistorted that goes
beyond our desires.

Fiction and biography suffer the same fate as our thinking: they cannot
with impunity cut themselves off from the natural laws of the world from
which they grow. Thus religion, practiced in faith, will quickly take a human soul to where literature, even religious literature, cannot follow. For
the laws of literary gravity will be broken by a reality they do not contain.
It's why saints, according to Isherwood, "unfortunately, are not in the
habit of writing novels" (*Wishing Tree,* 168). They do not write novels
because they don't wish to fabricate. In order not to lie, they'd have to
make their fiction reflect a universe of grace and miracle the world would
not recognize. And, as a diary entry from 1954 notes, "Why invent—when
Life is so prodigious?" (*Diaries* 1:455).

In a fable written in 1943, Christopher Isherwood tells of a tree that will
grant anyone's wish and of a boy who, overwhelmed with the beauty of
the tree itself, forgets to wish for anything. We will sadly bid Isherwood
farewell as he stands forever under the wishing tree. Was his a noble mind
overthrown, or had he nobly overthrown the hold our minds have on us
all and become a saint? We cannot say, but the questions the world must
ask about him have now become, for better or worse, the same ones it
has always asked of St. Teresa, Meister Eckhart, St. Augustine, Rumi,
Ramakrishna. It is doubtful that the answers will come any easier now,
but there is still plenty of room under the wishing tree for anyone who
wants to try.

Note

1. I am obliged to John Schlenck, editor of the quarterly *American Vedantist,*
for clarifying this point in a recent editorial.

Christopher Isherwood in Jail

Now it can be told: Christopher Isherwood was in jail with me in the summer of 1995.

That summer, Isherwood came with me as a teaching assistant in my capacity as coordinator of college and adult continuing education and English instructor at Butner Federal Corrections Complex. The course was called "Aldous Huxley, Christopher Isherwood and W. H. Auden: The Way to Reality." The course title might make one think that I was actually an inmate from the prison's psychiatric wing, and Butner does have one. In fact, when a psychologist feels one of his in-patients is ready to try some out-patienting, the shrink thinks, "I'll tell him to go take one of Izzo's classes."

Butner is the leading corrections facility in the federal system for rehab, recovery, counseling, and education. Each inmate here is a first-time convict and deemed a good candidate for future successful release; hence, he is not sent to a hard-time prison, from which he might come out even more deranged. Butner looks like a college campus—other than the barbed-wire fences—and the inmates are housed in dorm-style buildings, not cells. There are only non-violent felons here—criminals of the brain. Butner is also the "joint" where certain minorities are placed: former law enforcement officers, Native Americans, spies, and homosexuals. Of course, inmates and ex-cons are themselves a growing minority. Over all, Butner's not bad . . . for a prison. Nonetheless, in five years there, I never forgot that I could go home after class and that my students couldn't.

All inmates are encouraged to take classes, whether they already have degrees or not. The idea is to keep their idle hands busy, something Isherwood would have related to when, in the early 1940s, he was think-ing about becoming a monk. In this particular class, six of the eighteen students were gay inmates. One was Kevin Martinelli, who took the class having no previous clue who Isherwood was except that one of the other guys told him he was a gay writer. *Herr Issyvoo* would ring Kevin's bell and not only start a platonic love match, but turn Kevin into a gay activist.

I had chosen Huxley, Isherwood, and Auden with the intent of empha-sizing the metaphysical aspects of their work because a prison can be a very spiritual place—this one can, anyway. Prison is a form of enforced monasticism with lots of time for introspection. I also chose these three authors because I am a fan of their work. At first, I was drawn to Huxley and Isherwood not as artists but as Vedantists; then, when I got to Auden, I found him to be a spiritualist too.

Before this class began, I had driven to work listening to tapes of the trio lecturing or reciting: Huxley, stentorian, and so very British; Auden, dry and crackling, like his aged face; and Isherwood, whose almost silly, high-pitched voice, child-like even at age sixty-eight in 1972, sounded like the enthusiastic upperclassman who had deliberately "camped" his final exams at Cambridge as a rebellious lark. His voice bubbled infectiously toward a college audience in California, sounding almost American. By the time he did this lecture, he had long been under the calming influence of his Vedantism, which was enhanced by the contentment of his relation-ship with Don Bachardy. This happiness could be heard on the tape com-ing through his delightful voice, which, by some accounts, sounded similar to the also child-like voice of Sri Ramakrishna, the nineteenth-century namesake of Isherwood's Vedantic order. I played this tape for my students, who listened raptly to Isherwood's enthusiasm. On tape, Isherwood's sense of awakening to his inner child was well developed. The inmates them-selves, through counseling, were not unfamiliar with judiciously manifest-ing their own inner children and recovering some youthful wonder.

As for Isherwood's Vedantism, I first read his essays in the posthumous compilation *The Wishing Tree.* Now an admirer of Isherwood the philoso-pher, I wanted to know more about his life and art. I read Brian Finney's biography and then Isherwood's fiction. I was amazed to discover that this philosopher had been, in his early years, far from the wise sage he became. Was I then disappointed that the man of the essays had not always been a barometer of worldly wisdom? Not at all. I was actually encouraged that this person, like any other person who had lived a typically angst-filled twentieth-century life, had not only survived but thrived. Here was a role model for myself and for my students, all of us recovering from something.

At that time, I realized that Isherwood the novelist was a "mentor" to a peer group of angry young men in the 1930s who later became icons for new generations of angry young men. What I also learned was that Isherwood's evolution from frantic to Vedantic in his life and in his fiction was the foreshadowing of today's *sensitive* man. The consideration of this conversion became the basis for teaching Isherwood.

As for the guru-disciple relationship, teaching on its good days can emulate that. A teacher should be able to learn from his students, and I have learned a lot at Butner. The students here, ranging in age from twenty-one to sixty, are bright, motivated, and disciplined and have a perspective that traditional young undergraduates do not. The theme I would emphasize for these students would be the one created by Isherwood and Edward Upward, Isherwood's lifelong friend and sounding board, a theme then disseminated to Auden, Stephen Spender, and the rest of the "Auden Generation." The Isherwood-Upward theme, which Isherwood subsequently developed throughout his art, was the dichotomy of the Truly Strong and Truly Weak Man.

Prior to 1938, Isherwood's novels implicitly portray the Truly Strong/ Weak theme. Then, in his autobiographical *Lions and Shadows,* he explicitly traces "an education in the twenties" (the book's subtitle) shared by many of his peers who endured the guilt of *not* having been in the First World War, which meant they had been unable to prove themselves as men as had the "noble dead." These were the husbands, fathers (including Isherwood's), brothers, uncles, sons, cousins, and friends who were eulogized endlessly and who were a constant source of guilt by comparison. This insecurity-inducing contrast was magnified by the oppressively large number of widowed, possessive mothers dominating and antagonizing their sons. Isherwood and Upward gestated these conflicts into their *Mortmere* fantasies, composed during their undergraduate years at Cambridge from 1925 to 1928. They intended the stories to be psychodramas about "us" against "them"—the "poshocracy" of "old men" who had caused the war in order to protect their bourgeois world. The twenties generation was left facing "The Test," which required young men to assuage their frail egos by acts of attention-getting foolhardiness. For example, Isherwood bought a motorcycle so he could ride fast like T. E. Lawrence. My students would find echoes here of some of the motivation for their own behavior. Similar pseudo-heroic posturing by Isherwood and his peers was soon to be trivialized by the harsh realities of the 1930s: the Depression, fascism, Stalinism, the Spanish Civil War—a world of deals and double-crosses.

The Truly Weak Man, exemplified by Colonel Lawrence, suffered from a compulsive need to prove himself by seeking, confronting, and passing tests of rebellious derring-do. Conversely, the Truly Strong Man is, according to Auden, "pure-in-heart." Isherwood, in *Lions and Shadows,* defines the Truly Strong Man in the terms offered by the German psychologist Bleuler: "The signs of the truly strong are repose and good-will. . . . The strong individuals are those who without any fuss do their duty. These have neither the time nor the occasion to throw themselves into a pose and try to be something great." Isherwood added, "In other words, the Test exists only for the Truly Weak Man: no matter whether he passes it or whether he fails, he cannot alter his essential nature" (207). In effect, he can pass tests but never truly be satisfied, at least not until he understands the underlying insecurities that have driven him. The best that the angst-filled, obsessive-compulsive Truly Weak Man can hope for is to comprehend then overcome his subliminally formulated motivations and aspire to be truly strong instead. In the interim, his bifurcated self struggles to reconcile these conflicting urges, resulting in a confusion of his public/private, inner/outer, and real/fantasy worlds.

When I decided to teach this theme, I knew Butner was the right place to do it. The psychological implications were desperately relevant to these student-inmates, who were all in counseling in order to deal with these very same issues. Greed was not their primary motivation to commit crimes; their compulsive need for approval, based on their insecurities, was. I am not excusing them; I am, however, trying to understand them, knowing that the only difference between these students and many people on the outside is that they got caught. Another motivation for me was to teach Isherwood and Auden to the gay students, but not just for them. I wanted the other students to learn that "gay" and "straight" are just words applied to corporeal contingencies which, from a Vedantic standpoint, make no difference. People are people, period, with the same joys and heartaches. The physical component of sex is, metaphysically speaking, one of the least important distinctions among them. As for the student-inmates, I believed that they would be open-minded, as I'd seen that prison was a common denominator that leveled the field for all of them. It's hard to cop attitude in jail—this microcosm city-state equalizes the diverse population very quickly.

In any class, teachers have favorites. Kevin Martinelli was one of mine. At forty-three, he looks and sounds like the singer-songwriter Tom Waits, who doesn't sing so much as croak in a whiskey-seared, cigarette-scarred voice. Kevin's voice is like that, but worse, a gargly basso, with each word emerging very s-l-o-w-l-y. Martinelli is not his original last name but the name he legally adopted to honor a companion who had passed away. He chain-smokes and, like many of his fellow inmates, is a recovering alcoholic and drug addict. His ascetically thin frame fits this image. He has tattoos and sticks his cigarettes into a rolled-up T-shirt sleeve. It seemed school was a good influence on him. After he took public speaking, the super-introvert joined the prison chapter of Toastmasters. When I first met Kevin as a college freshman who had just gotten his GED, I realized that as streetwise as he was, he seemed to have missed most of his formal education, requiring him to be a regular visitor to my office for extra help. Later, when he didn't need the extra help anymore, he was still a regular for conversation. Over three years, Kevin changed from a semi-literate, uncultured individual into a well-read student. His writing had gone from abysmal to utilitarian to college-level to fluid and, finally, creative. And, due to Isherwood's influence, Kevin became a gay activist.

I taught Huxley first, using short stories and novel excerpts to set up the class with his fictional accounts of the postwar 1920s. This prepared the way for Isherwood, who I knew would be accessible to the students. His work is engaging to read and, more important, has readily identifiable psychological implications for this audience. I emphasized Isherwood's transition from the anxious, conflicted homosexual of the 1920s and 1930s to the spiritual, liberated homosexual of the 1960s, 1970s, and 1980s. I also explained to them that being gay then was much harder than it is now, as gay men were subject not only to discrimination but also to arrest. This they could understand. We related the gay minority to minorities in general who are disenfranchised and disempowered. The students were living examples and could grasp this also.

We read excerpts from *The Memorial* first, to establish the Truly Strong/ Weak theme, then moved on to *Mr Norris Changes Trains*. Arthur Norris is an over-the-top, nefariously amoral portrait defining the paranoia of the 1930s. I knew Norris would go over well with these students, some of whom were con men like him. I had originally planned to do only a portion of the novel, but they could not wait to read all of it. The sixty years that had elapsed between its writing and their reading made little difference to them, and speaking as experts, they saw the depiction of the criminal psychology as not dated. Particularly telling for them were the two side-by-side doors to the Norris flat, one labeled ARTHUR NORRIS-IMPORT/ EXPORT—in effect "public"—the other PRIVATE. Inside, there was no real distinction between public and private, indicating the symbolic blurring of the bifurcated self.

After *Norris* came "Sally Bowles," who was pegged quickly by the students as a female "Norris-in-training," who might even surpass him when her tender youth had matured. Interestingly, the gay students, particularly Kevin, who'd been raised by a poor, single mother, had a more sympathetic view of her than did the rest. Kevin and the other gay students saw Sally as a character of limited options who, through little fault of her own, resorted to "womanly wiles" to get by. I sensed this minority within a minority experiencing peer identification.

We then read enough of *Lions and Shadows* to see what youthful influences had made Isherwood so rebellious. In class, we correlated his recalcitrance with patterns of behavior common to rebellious youth in general, these students included. More important, the students closely considered the sections that describe and elucidate the Truly Strong/Weak Man. The most interesting part of their analysis was that they understood the theme with little help from me. In sum: the Truly Strong/Weak mythos had metaphysical resonances that appealed to this class.

In *The Memorial, Mr Norris,* "Sally," and *Lions,* most of the "characters" were examples of the Truly Weak Man/Woman, which meant, tacitly, that they resembled the lives of the students before they were arrested, tried, transported in shackles, and locked behind the last door. We then turned to *Prater Violet* for the first look at a character who struggles to become Truly Strong. This short novel, deeply influenced by Vedantism, was the first written from Isherwood's new perspective. From 1939 until 1945, Isherwood published little, devoting himself to the study of Vedanta. He helped Swami Prabhavananda with new translations of the Bhagavad Gita and other Vedantic texts. He thought for a while he would become a monk. His "backsliding," however, convinced him he would not last long as a full-fledged monastic. He pledged to be a lay devotee instead, meaning he could slip out the back door when the temptations of *maya*—the illusion of the sense world, via that constant enemy to serenity, the ego—overtook him. In *Prater Violet* he explores metaphysical themes and intimates how one can begin to change from Weak to Strong. Many of my students were trying to make the same transition. Taking place in 1930s London, the novel presents its protagonist as "Christopher Isherwood," the screenwriter for a film by Austrian director Friedrich Bergmann, who is consumed by fears for his family in strife-torn Europe. The class poignantly identified with Bergmann's pain at being separated from his family while having no recourse to do anything about it. The collaboration between Bergmann and the "fictional" Isherwood was based on the real-life work of Isherwood with Berthold Viertel, and their relationship is similar to the guru-disciple relationship. Typical of Isherwood's best work, his life became his art, and *Prater Violet* was testimony to the influence of his new, Vedanta-inspired path.

The Gita teaches that wisdom is found in the process of work, not in its result. This is exemplified in *Prater Violet,* in which Bergmann fights his fear and despair by throwing himself into the making of a lightweight, escapist film, turning it into an entertainment with a politically relevant message. In actual life, Isherwood learned from Viertel and Prabhavananda that a man must proceed with his work despite calamity, and, in a sense, *Prater Violet* is a parable of its author's experiences during the war. He chose a whole new life in Vedanta, which gave him the structure of moral values and security he craved. He chose to be a conscientious objector, which would lead him to Pennsylvania and a Quaker-run refugee camp where he taught English. He chose these steps to make strides in his quest to be pure-in-heart and Truly Strong—a quiet hero. In the effort, he also came to realize that learning to be strong only comes after one understands the inner demons which feed the Truly Weak ego. To understand the ego as nemesis does not entirely make it go away but allows one to confront it with greater comprehension when "backsliding" threatens to stall spiritual progress. Consequently, the dichotomies of weak/strong, public/private, inner/outer, hero/anti-hero are now grounded in a more realistic context. A man seeks perfection by overcoming imperfection; from a Vedantic point of view, these imperfections are meant to be seen as lessons rather than as obstacles. When the class looked at Isherwood's life this way, every student recognized that, like Isherwood, he was making choices about taking a new direction that could help him to become truly strong by learning about why he had been weak enough to have become a criminal. Being in the college program is, in fact, a choice made in recognition of the need for such a change.

We next read sections from *The World in the Evening* and *Down There on a Visit,* followed by all of *A Single Man.* At this point I asked the class if Isherwood had directly indicated in his previous work that any major character, including the one called Christopher Isherwood, was gay. The barest allusions and intimations aside, the answer was no. It was clear that prior to 1964 Isherwood was not writing about his own sexuality. Christopher, like many of the rest of his kind, had remained in the closet because it was dangerous to do otherwise. The students clearly grasped that in the bad old days, homosexuals had little choice but to hide their true selves from public scrutiny. This situation was just another association between themselves and Isherwood.

A Single Man was Isherwood's footprint on the moon for the gay community, but the novel's ambitions are not focused solely on sexual politics. Isherwood said of the book that "homosexuals are used as a sort of metaphor for minorities in general" (Finney, 254), and while Isherwood incorporates Vedantic metaphysics, he does so tacitly, using the technique of parable which he and Auden advocated so vociferously in the 1930s. The plot's simplicity is its virtue as it recounts one day in the life of a college professor, George, who is recovering, but not too well, from the death of his lover. The restraint of narrative incidents in favor of character delineation allows for greater reader introspection. Although some reviewers thought George's being gay was a limitation, the point that Isherwood makes is that George is an Everyman who just happens to be gay and that his bereavement is no less painful for him than it would be for anyone else. It is this portrayal of a real human being, feeling as we all might feel in a similar situation over a loss, that renders George's sexuality to be no more or less important than if he happened to be straight. The sympathy of the students for George was enormous and poignant, as they were all separated from the world in a different form of "death." One student said that George's desperate sense of being no longer connected to the world was how he himself felt about being in a prison: he didn't exist anymore outside the prison walls and fences as far as anyone knew or cared.

For Kevin, *A Single Man* was a revelation, in part because his own lover's death precipitated his spiral into alcohol, drugs, and crime. After reading the novel, Kevin came to my office and told me that he had at first wept, then allowed himself to "get sucked up in a kind of black hole for a while." He explained that when he came out of it, he had a rush of release and relief because he had finally been able to accept that Chip, the love of his life, was gone and that it was okay to let him *be* gone. Thereafter, Kevin's edginess blunted, his introversion decreased, and he began his move toward activism. Kevin wrote his term paper on Isherwood's meaning for homosexuals. Whenever I think of Kevin, I think of Christopher's influence on him. In my study, I have a copy of a poem Kevin published, inscribed to me, next to my signed first edition of *Christopher and His Kind.* I think of this inscribed poem as a relic, which Vedantists believe connects the aura of a sacred past to the present. I surround myself with relics, which I display proudly, none more so than those that recall Isherwood and that very special class.

What is Christopher Isherwood's legacy? For me, his legacy is that in the summer of 1995, Christopher Isherwood was in jail with me. Any English instructor knows that he or she can gain more insight about an author from teaching him than reading him. Christopher was a *presence* that summer, helping me help unique students who, in turn, gave much more than they received. Of any author I have ever taught in any situation, none has had the impact that Isherwood had on the student-inmates at Butner Federal Corrections Complex. He brought them joy and something to look forward to that could challenge their otherwise stultifying routine. Grown men, supposedly hardened by their trying circumstances, laughed out loud or were moved to tears because they saw themselves in Christopher and his characters.

23 *John McFarland*

"Always Dance"
Sex and Salvation in Isherwood's Vedantism

Soon after Christopher Isherwood emigrated from England to the United States, he found himself in a sorry state. He was living in a New York that didn't seem to welcome him. He was disaffected with left-wing politics, the ideology that had given meaning to his life and bound him tightly to his circle of friends. He feared the outbreak of full-scale war. And, confronting the inevitability of war, he considered the possibility of being called on to kill his German lover, Heinz, in battle. The horror that he felt at such a possibility convinced him that he was at core a pacifist, yet his espousal of pacifism added to his sense of isolation and spiritual emptiness. Nothing about the existing situation justified staying in New York. In fact, the overwhelmingly negative conditions were conspiring to push him toward something new. What would that be? What in his ken attracted him?

The far west of the United States held a mysterious appeal for Isherwood. He knew that Gerald Heard and Aldous Huxley, two men he admired, were living in Los Angeles and had been investigating Eastern philosophies in their individual spiritual quests. The intriguing combination of a landscape unlike New York and the investigations of Heard and Huxley persuaded Isherwood and his companion, Vernon Old, to head west. Although it was premature to think that southern California was

236

where Isherwood would find a like-minded group to which he could belong, he was willing to take the risk.

In Los Angeles, Heard filled Isherwood's head with talk of his current enthusiasm, Vedanta. Adrift and searching, Isherwood was particularly vulnerable to Heard's influence, and soon Heard took him to meet Swami Prabhavananda, the leader of the fledging Vedanta Society in Los Angeles. Isherwood was immediately attracted to the swami. The combined force of the swami's charisma and Isherwood's desperate need at the time, however, did not blind him to the reality that central, highly pleasurable aspects of his life would probably be in conflict with what he perceived as the spiritual quest outlined by Vedanta teachings. As early as his second meeting with Swami Prabhavananda on August 4, 1939, the day he was initiated into the Vedanta meditation practices and three weeks prior to his thirty-fifth birthday, Isherwood asked the swami, "Can I lead a spiritual life as long as I'm having a sexual relationship with a young man?" The swami answered, "You must be like the lotus on the pond. The lotus leaf is never wet" (*Guru*, 24–25). That response was just ambiguous enough to allow Isherwood to begin a dance with Vedanta and Swami Prabhavananda. The question remained whether that dance would lead Isherwood to salvation.

At that time Isherwood was still living with Vernon and writing screenplays at MGM. His social circle included many of the European expatriates in the area. He chronicles all of these activities in his diaries along with candid details of hangovers, depression, and despair. His diary entries of August 1940, a year after his initiation, also indicate that he was distinctly aware of the importance of Vedanta's spiritual practices in his life. Whatever the benefits he felt from Vedanta, however, Isherwood admitted to himself that he was fighting adopting Prabhavananda's way of life, and on one level he wanted to be left alone to wallow in his misery. He wanted and needed it both ways.

Despite not choosing one path over the other, Isherwood continued to be deeply troubled by what he perceived as the dichotomy between the quest for spiritual transcendence and his sexual drives. In *My Guru and His Disciple,* Isherwood quoted from his diary entry of November 13, 1940: "I also asked the Swami about sex. He said that all sex—no matter what the relationship—is a form of attachment and must ultimately be given up. This will happen naturally as you make progress in the spiritual life." The swami also told him the story of an initiate asking Brahmananda to lift the burden of carnality for him, "But Brahmananda smiled and answered, 'My son, if I did that, you would miss all the fun of the struggle'" (71). In no way do Isherwood's diary entries of the period paint that struggle as "fun," and he would have been grateful for any assistance along those lines. The promise that the surest, truest, and best way was for the devotee to achieve the state on his own was of little comfort to him.

Whereas the tension between new spiritual influences and old sensual habits was an ever-present anxiety for Isherwood, his relationship with Swami Prabhavananda was warm and provided a flexible ground for learning. Each man, however, kept his secrets from the other, as indicated by an episode in the spring of 1941. When the swami asked, "What is the matter with you, Mr. Isherwood? . . . Surely you do not want Eternal Youth?" Isherwood's reaction is telling: "I was silent and hung my head— because, of course, I did" (*Guru,* 86). The witty and frankly sexual Isherwood was not evaporating in the powerful initial exposure to Vedanta, even if he was temporarily doing everything to be as invisible as possible. Isherwood might have been indulging his sexual drives then, but he carried tremendous guilt about it.

By the spring of 1943, the intense need for spiritual sustenance that Isherwood manifested in the 1939–40 period had moderated and evolved into a more balanced form. Feeling less desperate and alienated, Isherwood could now state unambiguously that he saw it was his duty to stay in the United States and that he was committed to Vedanta. On February 6, 1943, he moved into the Vedanta Center and dedicated himself to becoming a monk. The new confidence in his choices is also reflected in diary entries that show him fighting his way toward a truce with the body and its demands. His recognition that the pursuit of worldly pleasures as ends in themselves was madness stood alongside his belief that we must not despise the body and its impulses.

During this same period of 1943, Isherwood was feeling strong enough to set down his attitude toward his recent writing. He later noted, "My desire to get back to work on *Prater Violet* was related to a general anxiety about my future as a fiction writer. I had good reason to be anxious. In the four years since I arrived in the States, I had produced nothing but two *New Yorker*–type short stories" (*Guru,* 124). On May 22, 1943, he wrote, "The fiction writer was thus being forced to go underground. But he was determined to survive, and maybe these restrictions were just what he needed to provoke him into becoming active again. He was now a subversive element, whose influence would grow steadily stronger and make itself felt before too long" (125).

Isherwood was gradually learning to put his insistent and very real sexual desires in perspective as his spiritual practice progressed. Soon after his thirty-ninth birthday, he again broached with the swami the troubling issue of sex. "When I told Swami, vaguely, that I'd had trouble with sex, he smiled and patted my head. 'It's a hard life,' he said: 'Just pray for strength. Pray to become pure.' So there we are, I've got to be pure" (*Diaries* 1:313). Despite the ironic, almost jaunty, tone Isherwood adopted here in describing the swami's latest assignment for him, the issue of "purity" weighed heavily. Isherwood continued carting around puritanical precepts that he devalued but could not entirely discard.

On August 28, 1944, however, he recorded what became an epiphany of sorts. A few days before, Chris Wood, the flamboyant and lovable homosexual who shared a house with Gerald Heard, came to visit the Center. Though he adored Chris Wood, Isherwood was apprehensive about the swami's reaction to such a character. After Wood left, the swami declared, "What a *good* man! . . . Purity is telling the truth." Isherwood was taken aback by this statement but agreed that if one defined purity as telling the truth, then Chris Wood was "pure" and therefore "good" (*Guru,* 167).

Isherwood's amazement at the swami's using the word "pure" in connection with Chris Wood, or any homosexual, stemmed from his persistent and continuing sense that the homosexual was by nature "not pure." That Swami Prabhavananda declared Chris Wood pure and good provided Isherwood with a new paradigm. Seeing new hope, he rededicated himself to the task at hand, becoming a monk and being aware of the multiple demands and urges within him. He embarked on a conscious process of reconciling his thoughts about his spiritual self and his sexual self: "To learn to be alone and at home inside myself—that's what I'm here for" (*Guru,* 175).

Isherwood's integration of spiritual quest, sexuality, and writing ambitions proceeded steadily from that point to August 23, 1945, the day on which he moved out of the Vedanta Center. He was certain then that he could never become a monk and that his relation to the Vedanta Society would have to be on another level: "When I did finally move out . . . it was for a reason which had nothing to do with the Vedanta Society. I had recently met a young man with whom I wanted to settle down and live in what I hoped could become a lasting relationship. His name was William Caskey" (*Guru,* 189). Although Isherwood remained deeply devoted to Swami Prabhavananda and Vedanta, he acknowledged that he was a sexual being who would never abandon his desires and that his vocation was to be a writer. The years from 1939 to 1945 had been Isherwood's period of spiritual learning. Now he knew that his individual path required him to honor these three central areas of his being simultaneously and not to waver from keeping them in balance.

Isherwood evinces a new clarity and confidence about the interrelationships among the elements in his diary a few years later. For example, on January 27, 1953, he noted: "Today I finished the rough draft of my novel. I am very grateful for this tremendous breakthrough. 88 pages in 18 days, which is about two and a half times my normal writing speed, maintained despite the interruptions of shrine sitting, kitchen chores, ditch digging, and planting trees. I feel as if my whole future as a writer—even my sanity—had been at stake. . . . This has been the toughest of all my literary experiences. A sheer frontal attack on a laziness block so gross and solid that it seemed sentient and malevolent" (*Guru*, 207).

The work Isherwood refers to is *The World in the Evening.* The novel began to take shape in 1949, starting out with the title *The School of Tragedy* and developing from Isherwood's wartime experience in America, both in Los Angeles and working as a conscientious objector with Quakers in Pennsylvania. It was finally published in early 1954. Although Isherwood himself eventually came to regard this book as his weakest, he would never deny its importance in proving that he could maintain his artistic drive and equilibrium in the midst of all the various demands of his life. Five years of literary struggle resulted in an engagingly hybrid work that marks a crossroads in Isherwood's writing.

Stephen Monk, the central character of *The World in the Evening,* is typical of Isherwood's protagonists up to that time: boyishly handsome, rudderless, searching and open to all varieties of experience. When we first meet Monk he is living in Los Angeles, rushing from one silly party to the next and harboring deeply ambivalent feelings toward his second wife, Jane. Dissatisfied, discontented, and in a fit of self-destructive rage, he leaves Los Angeles and races back to his childhood home in Pennsylvania. At the ancestral home he is embraced by the reassuring arms of Aunt Sarah, his old nanny and a Quaker. Despite the warm welcome in Pennsylvania, Monk continues to vibrate like an exposed nerve, and at last, desperate for yet another escape, he departs abruptly for points unknown. That escape, however, is foiled before Monk can leave the block: he is hit by an oncoming truck and seriously injured. This melodramatic turn of events at the beginning of the novel then allows Isherwood literally to immobilize Monk. In a body cast for an extended recovery period, Monk is forced to sit still and take stock of his life.

With frantic motion replaced by enforced physical and emotional focus, Monk revisits triumphs and disasters: his first marriage to the sophisticated European writer Elizabeth Rydal; the distressing but heady interlude of being pursued by the young, attractive, and persistent Michael Drummond; and his guilt-ridden romance with Jane Armstrong, who later became his wife in an ill-fated marriage. Once again, Isherwood has assembled a cast of eccentric sophisticates set loose in exotic locales where they flirt, float, and find out too late about the emotional cost behind what had looked like a free ride. On its surface, the novel is amusing fare filled with voyeuristic pleasures inherent in reading tales of glamorous globetrotting. Written in the mode of a Hollywood screenplay with flashbacks and cameos, it almost begs the reader to cast the parts with the stars of the late 1940s and early 1950s. Picture the young James Mason as Stephen Monk, Irene Dunne as Elizabeth Rydal, Rita Hayworth as Jane Armstrong, and Alan Ladd as Michael Drummond, and imagine the romantic intrigue unfolding.

In addition to the froth, serious new themes for Isherwood are bubbling up in this novel. The most prominent emerges in Isherwood's characterizations of Elizabeth Rydal, Aunt Sarah, and Gerda Mannheim, a German refugee who nurses Monk back to health after his accident. Elizabeth is an older worldly-wise presence, to whom Monk is deeply attached. He may strain for his freedom against her intimidating all-knowingness, but Elizabeth, accepting, accommodating, and forgiving, allows him that freedom and more. Isherwood shows Elizabeth's love as warmly embracing with no hint of an emotional choke-hold. Aunt Sarah is also portrayed as a warm and wise presence. Gerda Mannheim completes the trio of supportive women in the novel. Each of these three women provides Monk with approval, support, and the benefit of her wisdom at critical junctures. Strong individuals, they guide him without any appearance of judging him. What is more, they make no demands as they step in to rescue him and teach him.

In describing Monk's encounters with these women and his thoughts about them, Isherwood is able to explore the emotional landscape of a person confronting his basic vulnerability and neediness. In one scene Monk attends Quaker Meeting with Aunt Sarah. Monk uses the period of silence to summon up the spirit of his dear, departed Elizabeth, and they engage in a dialogue:

Elizabeth, tell me, was I crazy to come here? What am I getting myself into?
Don't worry, darling. Just be patient. You'll find out. . . .
Oh, Elizabeth, I'm so terribly unhappy.
You needn't be, darling. Nobody need be.
I know—that's what you used to say. And I remember all the things you told me. Only—you've got to help me. Don't let me ever forget them. Not for a moment. Promise you won't ever leave me.
I can't leave you, Stephen. Don't you realize that? Even if I wanted to, I couldn't leave you as long as you still needed me. We're not separate people, any more.
I'll always need you.
I hope not, darling. Not in the way you do now. (43–44)

In the most poignant moments of the novel, Monk has to face his complex connections to those who have responded with generosity to his need. This theme of recognizing both the need for the teacher and the discomfort at being dependent on that teacher parallels Isherwood's relationship with the swami and with life at the Vedanta Center.

If the central role of the trio of idealized female characters in Monk's reevaluation of his life has a slightly ponderous effect, it is counterpointed by the arrival on the scene of a gay male couple. Dr. Charles Kennedy, a lively and amusing caregiver, and his partner, Bob Wood, a painter, show up in Monk's sickroom for animated conversations. With these two characters, Isherwood is working with another serious new theme: the place of the gay man in the larger scheme of things.

Dr. Kennedy is more than willing to share with Monk the day-to-day details of being a part of a gay male couple. At one point, Kennedy reveals to Monk that he and Bob had had one of their most serious arguments the night before:

> "What about?"
> "Well, it started about you." Charles grinned at me painfully. He was obviously embarrassed. "In fact, I suppose it was a rather ordinary kind of domestic jealousy scene. As far as I was concerned."
> "Jealousy? You surely don't mean that Bob . . . ?"
> "No—it wasn't quite as ordinary as that. But he came home and raved about you. How wonderful and sympathetic and understanding you were. Meaning that *I* wasn't."
> "But, Charles, that's ridiculous! If Bob does feel that about me, it's only because I'm a complete stranger. Strangers always seem to understand everything—until you get to know them." (108)

Monk also hears about the possibilities in the future for Quaker Camp and Quaker High Camp and Bob Wood's fantasy of blasting the town's blindness to smithereens by marching down the street with a banner and singing, "We're queer because we're queer because we're queer because we're queer" (112).

By portraying Charles and Bob as so open with Stephen, Isherwood has his first opportunity to present gay men established in a loving relationship as they try to cope with the hypocrisies and "tolerances" of the society around them. Nowhere else in his fiction does Isherwood let himself go with ease and humor in writing about two gay male lovers. And on the central issue of societal attitudes to gay relationships, Isherwood uses Kennedy and Wood as characters to illustrate how the Quaker community at the time could accept that these two men lived in the same house while denying that they were indeed a couple.

Unlike other gay characters in Isherwood's earlier fiction, Kennedy, Wood, and Michael Drummond are not mere exotics; each is equal to any other character in the novel. The portrait of the Kennedy-Wood relationship in its dailiness and complexity contrasts with the way things worked out between Monk and Michael. When Monk first meets him, Drummond is a charming young man drawn to the sophistication of Elizabeth and Stephen. On their next encounter, Drummond is more intense, melancholy, and growing progressively more lovesick over Stephen. Drummond persists in his pursuit of Stephen until they eventually have sex. Misinterpreting Stephen's intentions, Drummond ends up being deeply hurt when he discovers that the sex has been casual for Stephen and has nowhere else to go. The bad feelings and embarrassment continue to haunt Monk, who is in fact less emotionally developed than the three gay characters.

The World in the Evening is an important transitional work, in part because the guru-disciple relationship uses the three idealized women as Stephen's teachers and because of the role played by the novel's gay male characters. The protagonist grows from being a young man who regards the world as his oyster to one who acknowledges he must be responsible for both the oyster and the world itself. Stephen Monk's path from sybarite to saint is the very same one that Isherwood had been struggling along since his first encounter with Swami Prabhavananda in 1939. In terms of what comes later, too, the novel shows how Isherwood was shifting his focus to issues he came to consider paramount.

Soon after completing the first draft of *The World in the Evening* in 1953 Isherwood met Don Bachardy, who would be his companion until Isherwood's death. He wrote: "I did feel awed by the emotional intensity of our relationship, right from its beginning; the strange sense of a fated, mutual discovery. I knew that, this time, I had really committed myself. Don might leave me, but I couldn't possibly leave him, unless he ceased to need me. This sense of a responsibility which was almost fatherly made me anxious but full of joy" (*Guru,* 209). This statement shows the extent to which Isherwood had internalized and was now living by the teachings of Swami Prabhavananda, who said that "the tie between the guru and his initiated disciple cannot be broken, either in this world or any future plane of existence, until the disciple realizes the Atman within himself and is thus set free. Meanwhile, the disciple may neglect, reject, or even betray the guru, but the guru cannot disown him. In such cases, the guru must continue to guide the disciple mentally, from a distance, and protect him through prayer" (67).

This newfound love and its intensity raised the usual issues of sexuality versus asceticism once again. Rather than questioning the rightness of this love or his entitlement to follow his heart as he had in the past, Isherwood describes a dream in which he and Swami Prabhavananda were sharing a bed in a hotel room. The swami turned to him and said, "I've got a new mantram for you, Chris. It is: 'Always dance.' 'What a strange mantram!'

I said. Swami laughed: 'Yes, it surprised me, too. But I found it in the scriptures'" (*Guru*, 211). As this dream suggests, Isherwood felt he needed and had received the swami's approval of his chosen path. He had grown by this time into both a devotee and a self-governing intelligence incorporating the fullness of his sexuality and his artistic ambition into his spiritual life. He had come a long way from the days when his need was so desperate that he would have given up his individuality if that had been the price of survival.

Over the next ten years, Isherwood wrote and published *Down There on a Visit* and *A Single Man,* the two novels that I regard as his most mature and affecting. Like *The Berlin Stories* in their originality and tart, affectionate angle of vision, they could have been written by nobody but Isherwood. Even better, they have the ineffable quality that all writers aim for in their work: upon each rereading, they remain fresh and alive.

In December 1963, Isherwood accompanied Swami Prabhavananda and others to India for the celebration of the centenary of the birth of Vivekananda. During this period Prema, one of the longtime devotees at the Los Angeles Vedanta Center, was to be ordained as a monk. Isherwood's diary entries of this trip provide a record of the intense conflicts that still existed for him. For example, he wrote: "Part of this resolve [not to give another lecture on God] is quite valid. I do honestly think that, when I give these God lectures, it is Sunday Religion in the worst sense. As long as I quite unashamedly get drunk, have promiscuous sex, and write books like *A Single Man,* I simply cannot appear before people as a sort of lay monk" (*Guru*, 271–72). His personal turmoil continued throughout the ceremonies in India. He left India later in January on a flight to Italy and afterwards joked that on that flight he first became aware that Vivekananda, perhaps in thanks, had given him an idea for a novel about Prema taking *sannyas.* That idea would evolve into the novel *A Meeting by the River.*

On May 31, 1966, Isherwood completed *A Meeting by the River* and knew that he had to show it to the swami, "But the thought of Swami reading the homosexual scenes makes me squirm inside. Why? I would never apologize for them, morally or artistically; they are an absolutely necessary part of the story. Furthermore, Swami has praised me for being myself and making no pretenses about the way I live my life. Just the same, I squirm. Am taking him the manuscript tomorrow" (*Guru*, 289–90). A few days later, "Swami rang up to say he'd finished my novel. 'As I finished the last scene there were two tears running down my cheeks.' What an angel he is!" (290). Isherwood's anxiety about the swami's reaction had been misplaced in this case, but it reflected his nagging uncertainty of people's response to what he was doing. He was so nervous about mixing carnality and spirituality that he may not have given himself credit for achieving the startlingly original balance that we find in the late work.

Although *A Meeting by the River* contains the most literal interpretation of Isherwood's life with Vedanta of all his novels, in fact everything Isherwood wrote after *Prater Violet* concerns Vedanta and its lessons. The dichotomy he saw between his spiritual practice and his worldly roles as a writer and gay man slowly resolved into a unity that animates and distinguishes *Down There on a Visit, A Single Man, A Meeting by the River,* and *My Guru and His Disciple,* all of which bring what he lived, absorbed, and observed into play. Looking back at the tension and anxiety surrounding the writing of *Prater Violet* and *The World in the Evening,* we can see that Isherwood was moving beyond his earlier themes and striving toward the forms and concerns that emerge in the later work.

A Single Man personifies the struggle Isherwood went through to get to that fluid and tenuous balance between the spiritual and the worldly at the same time that it casts a witty eye on the teacher-pupil relationship. In this novel, Isherwood has not distributed the qualities of the guru and the disciple among as many characters as he did in *The World in the Evening.* Instead, both roles are embedded in George, who is at this stage of life a fount of wisdom, a person of immense warmth and compassion, and a mass of contradictions to all around him. He is objective and subjective, above it all and mired deeply in it, in charge yet isolated and frail. He is, in short, a human being who has learned from his experience, and his awareness and insight guide him. Isherwood shows in George's inner dialogue how he is teaching himself the lessons he needs to know right up until the end.

In the astonishing last pages of *A Single Man,* Isherwood writes:

> Meanwhile, here we have this body known as George's body, asleep on this bed and snoring quite loud. The dampness of the ocean air affects its sinuses; and anyhow, it snores extra loud after drinking. Jim used to kick it awake, turn it over on its side, sometimes get out of bed in a fury and go to sleep in the front room.
>
> But *is* all of George altogether present here? . . .
>
> For a few minutes, maybe, life lingers in the tissues of some outlying regions of the body. Then, one by one, the lights go out and there is total blackness. And if some part of the nonentity we called George has indeed been absent at this moment of terminal shock, away out there on the deep waters, then it will return to find itself homeless. (183, 186)

Isherwood here evokes much of Vedanta's teachings and man's condition on Earth. His portrait of George is a profoundly spiritual one.

As exemplified by George, Isherwood's characters are vividly real and transmit ideas in what they say and do without "being the ideas" in a reductive, didactic sense. His characters live on the page because Isherwood was able to capture them in all their complexity and invest them with the love he felt for them as if they were real people. This quality emerges from the intensity of Isherwood's own personal relationships, his loyalty to the people from whom he learned. His need to personalize everything did not stop when it came to spiritual matters: "Vedanta, in its purest form, negates all cults, even cults of divine beings. . . . I personally am a devotee [of Swami] first and a Vedantist second. . . . My religion is almost entirely what I glimpse of Swami's spiritual experience. I still firmly claim that this isn't a personality cult" (*Guru,* 308–9). This is his truth, and he shares it with us.

Isherwood's work from 1962 to 1967, which includes *Down There on a Visit, A Single Man,* and *A Meeting by the River,* is the fruit of his spiritual quest as it is externalized as his art. It is personal, objective, and mindful of the larger spiritual dimension at the same time that it is wise, artful, and unapologetically carnal. The interplay of these viewpoints produces a complex texture in the work. We can see that Isherwood's conclusion about how we live and love in our mortal body emerges from his two lasting profound loves—for the swami and for Bachardy: "I remember how often, despite my love for Swami, I used to draw a breath of relief when I left his room. I was like a child escaping from the presence of an elder, simply because he needs to breathe a less rarefied atmosphere, to feel himself free to chatter and be silly. . . . Meanwhile, my life is still beautiful to me—beautiful because of Don, because of the enduring fascination of my efforts to describe my life experience in my writing, because of my interest in the various predicaments of my fellow travelers on this journey" (*Guru,* 337).

Swami Prabhavananda died on July 4, 1976. Isherwood wrote: "While the Guru was still within the body we called Prabhavananda, he gave us our mantrams. It is when I am saying my mantram that I very occasionally feel I am in communication with him. The mantram was a gift of his love, and love is communication. The mantram is all I have of him and all I need" (*Guru,* 336). Ten years later, Isherwood too would give up tenancy of his mortal body, but we still have him in his work. Neither a perfect man nor a saint, he is not one to idolize or idealize. Rather he is an example of a person working toward integration in his lifelong dance with Vedanta.

24 *Mario Faraone*

The Path That Leads to Safety
Spiritual Renewal and Autobiographical Narrative

As a young editor working for Virginia and Leonard Woolf at the Hogarth Press, John Lehmann published Christopher Isherwood's second novel, *The Memorial.* Reflecting on their long personal and professional relationship, Lehmann wrote that "for a long time I hoped that I should also be able to publish more of Christopher's books, and the possibility of a new novel from him was always at the back of my mind. . . . But as Isherwood became more deeply involved with the Yoga movement in Hollywood, that hope began to fade."[1] This statement is indicative of the British literary establishment's declining interest in Isherwood's writings after his "betrayal"—Isherwood's emigration to the United States in January 1939. His move, often considered an "escape" based on fear or cowardice, can more accurately be seen as the result of a considered, moral decision. What Lehmann did not understand is Isherwood's inner religious and political crisis. In a letter to Lehmann, Isherwood revealed his personal dilemma: "I myself am in the most Goddamawful mess. I have discovered, what I didn't realize before . . . that I am a pacifist. And now I have to find out what that means, and what duties it implies. That's one reason why I am going out to Hollywood, to talk to Gerald Heard and Huxley" (Lehmann, *Christopher Isherwood,* 51). An important aspect of that move was his need to rethink his way of reading the world and himself, and this change was motivated by the necessity "to find a *new tone of voice:* because

247

the ventriloquist has changed somehow and needs a new dummy."[2] He found his new tone of voice through his belief in Vedanta, which marks the turning point in Isherwood's life and the beginning of his American literary career.

A Glimpse of the Path

Vedanta is a nondualistic religion in which a person seeks the divine essence of the self (i.e., the *Atman*), which is part of the divine essence of the creation (the *Brahman,* or the Godhead). One of Vedanta's main attractions for Isherwood is its insistence that the universe and human action cannot be divided into good and evil: "All good and all evil is relative to the individual point of growth. For each individual, certain acts are absolutely wrong. Indeed there may well be acts which are absolutely wrong for every individual alive on earth today. But, in the highest sense, there can be neither good nor evil" (*Exhumations,* 110). As we can see from Isherwood's diaries, he was grappling in the early 1940s with his new identities as an expatriate, a pacifist, and a devotee. This confluence of issues must be considered in order to understand the pervasive influence of Vedanta on Isherwood's American output.

Prater Violet, the first novel Isherwood wrote in the United States, is an astonishing work, especially considering the strenuous effort he undertook during this period of personal uncertainty. Through the primary relationship in the novel—between Friedrich Bergmann and "Christopher Isherwood"—a true guru-disciple connection, we can understand more fully the long and meticulous reconsideration to which Isherwood subjects the key motifs of his early novels: "The Test," "The Enemy," the "Truly Weak Man" and the "Truly Strong Man." This reconsideration will shape Isherwood's work until his final novel, *A Meeting by the River.*

A late interior monologue in *Prater Violet,* which takes place when Christopher and Bergmann return from a party for their new film, is in fact a mental dialogue between two powerful characters. It is only too natural that this exchange should happen at "the hour of the night at which man's ego almost sleeps," a particular moment in the life of an individual when "the sense of identity, of possessions, of name and address and telephone number grows very faint" (153). This episode comes after a long period of training during which Christopher, with the help of his guru Bergmann, has turned from a superficial bohemian artist, interested only in "art for art's sake," to a person who shows deep insight and interest in making contact with others.

Christopher had arrived at a sense of futility and emptiness which comes from engaging in everyday activities with no sense of unity with the rest of creation and from striving to obtain material goals and fearing failure in that attempt: "You did whatever was next on the list. A meal to be eaten. Chapter eleven to be written. The telephone rings. You go off somewhere in a taxi. There is one's job. . . . There are things to be bought in shops. There is always something new. There has to be. Otherwise, the balance would be upset, the tension would break" (154). Yet he realizes that the secret of life is to achieve "a kind of balance, a complex of tensions," and this is possible only if one lives one's life, and its connection with others, without fear or desire.

Through Bergmann's teachings and Vedanta's frame of reference, Isherwood's protagonist "refocuses" the author's camera eye, changing the perspective through which he looks at the world. From now on, Isherwood's "ventriloquist dummy" represents Man's universal situation—the *Atman* who tries to realize the *Brahman* in himself—and this is possible because the author has understood that the Truly Weak Man and the Truly Strong Man are not antithetical human conditions, as the dualistic perspective of *Lions and Shadows* suggests, but rather complementary ones. In this sense, Paul Piazza is probably right when he states that "the Test is more akin to a conversion than to an ordeal" (148). Isherwood's hero must fight the terrible battle to reach integrity above all against himself, the "Great Tyrant Me" (*World,* 20), the real enemy.

Step by step in *Prater Violet,* Vedanta succeeds in penetrating Isherwood's heart and in giving him back the confidence he needs to believe first of all in himself and in his artistic capabilities, and then in his acquaintances, friends, and the rest of humankind. But, above all, Vedanta gives him the first glimpse of knowledge of the divine essence which surrounds every human being and which can be detected through a deep connection with his "fellow travelers": "I see something else: the way that leads to safety. To where there is no fear, no loneliness. . . . For a second, I glimpse it. . . . Then the clouds shut down" (158). This glimpse, and the entire treatment of the Christopher-Bergmann relationship, show us this connection. The understanding of man's complexity has been one of the main themes, if not *the* theme, of Isherwood's autobiographical narrative.

"The knowledge of what is behind action"

Prater Violet is the turning point in Isherwood's personal mythology and in his ultimate task, the "long road to self-understanding" and to universal harmony at the very heart of the author's writing and life. But how can he undertake this laborious reconsideration of his entire personality and thought? Which route must he follow to succeed? Who is going to help him in this spiritual and psychological journey? A consideration of Isher-

wood's personal uncertainty can provide us with a more complete understanding of this professional growth as a writer, and the key, I believe, to
this understanding is contained in two works that have not received the
critical attention they merit, namely "The Problem of the Religious Novel"
and his translation with Swami Prabhavananda of the Bhagavad Gita.

Isherwood's essay "The Problem of the Religious Novel" describes the
figure of the saint in terms of the transformation and overcoming of the
Test. According to Isherwood's definition, a saint should have some secular qualities, not only religious ones, but nonetheless should maintain a
high level of spirituality. The saint is a character "who will exhibit the
maximum variety of reactions to external events. . . . Because his motives
are not dictated by fear, vanity or desire—because his every action is a
genuine act of free will—you can never predict what he will do next. He
accepts life more fully, more creatively than any of his neighbours. And
therefore he is the most interesting person to write about" (*Exhumations,*
116). But dealing with this character presents several difficulties because,
unlike his neighbors and the rest of humanity, the saint is not a perfectly
identifiable type: "The saint, considered as an end product, resembles Mr
Jones as little as he resembles a giraffe. And yet Mr Jones and Mr Smith
and Mr Brown are all potentially saints. This is what the author has somehow to prove to his audience" (116–17). The writer should not present
him, as often happens, as "a creature set apart from this bad world, a
living reproach to our human weakness, in whose presence we feel ill at
ease, inferior, and embarrassed," but rather should try to represent and
describe "that decisive moment at which my hero becomes aware of his
vocation and decides to do something about it" (117).

The key here is that the Test has been transformed. The real necessity
is for the character (and for the author) to transcend his materialistic and
egoistic self and to move toward "the awareness of vocation." Thus, the
aim of Isherwood's postconversion narrative is to find the most suitable
and convincing way to show this inner growth. He must then determine
the technical and stylistic devices which, together with his skill for writing
dialogue and his ability to use cinematic techniques, will allow him to
represent the spiritual quality of such a "dynamic portrait": "I must show
that the average men and women of this world are searching, however
unconsciously, for that same fundamental reality of which X has already
had a glimpse. Certainly, they look for it in the wrong places. Certainly,
their methods are quite unpractical. Mr Jones will find nothing at the bot-
tom of the whisky bottle, except a headache. But the whisky bottle is not
to be dismissed with a puritanical sneer; it is the crude symbol of Jones's
dissatisfaction with surface consciousness, his need to look more deeply
into the meaning of life" (118). The saint is not someone altogether supe-

rior to his fellow beings, "for the evolving saint does not differ from his fellow humans in kind, but only in degree" (119).

The second work showing the key to Isherwood's postconversion narrative is one of his translations with Swami Prabhavananda: the renowned Hindu epic Bhagavad Gita, The Song of God. Isherwood's translation work gave him the daily contact with the swami that he desired. Although some critics have seen this translation activity as a demonstration of his versatility, Isherwood's role in their collaboration is better understood as editorial and stylistic: "I knew no Sanskrit at all. My job was literary, not linguistic. He told me the meaning of the text, sentence by sentence. We then considered how this meaning could best be conveyed in English. By the time we had finished translating the book, I realized that I had been studying it with an ideal teacher and in the most thorough manner imaginable" (*Exhumations,* 98).

The Bhagavad Gita consists of a dialogue between the warrior, Arjuna, and Krishna, who has volunteered to be his servant in the battle, though he will not fight. In his teaching of Arjuna, Krishna employs both relative and absolute values, and this combination of values helps Isherwood process the lesson more completely. For Isherwood sees parallels between his life and the dilemma Arjuna faces regarding his participation in war. The Hindu doctrine of "nonattachment" is expressed often in the Gita, and its aim is to make clear that what really counts is the action itself and not the result. Isherwood's preoccupation, then, passes from the absolute implications of this question of action to the more personal ones. "How, in this complex world, are we to know what our own duty is?" he asks in "The Gita and War." "There is no greater problem. Yet, somehow, we have to find our position and make our stand" (*Exhumations,* 111).

On the field of Kurukshetra, waiting for the impending slaughter, Arjuna asks Krishna a very important question, and we perceive hidden in Arjuna's words Isherwood's personal dilemma: "You speak so highly of the renunciation of action; yet you ask me to follow the yoga of action. Now tell me definitely: which of these is better?" (Gita, 56). In other words, which kind of behavior will bring my *Atman* to realize his *Brahman*? And Krishna, in one of his typically long answers, expresses what we can call "the theory of the four men," which I find most useful to unravel Isherwood's postconversion narrative project: "Among those who are purified by their good deeds, there are four kinds of men who worship me: the world-weary, the seeker for knowledge, the seeker for happiness, and the man of spiritual discrimination. The man of spiritual discrimination is the highest of these. He is continually united with me. He devotes himself to me always, and to no other. For I am very dear to that man, and he is dear to me" (Gita, 72).

These four men of the Gita constitute the "path that leads to safety" for Isherwood, his personal journey to religious and poetic belief. The four men can be seen in the protagonists of Isherwood's final four novels, and they represent his hard-won struggle to reach both spiritual and artistic integrity.

The World-Weary: The "Great Tyrant Me"

Isherwood's second American novel, *The World in the Evening,* constitutes an important step in his search for integrity along the path that leads to safety. The protagonist, Stephen Monk, is a self-centered egotist. He is not wicked, but vanity and immaturity permeate every aspect of his public and private life. He is jealous of his first wife's literary acquaintances, and he behaves shabbily toward Michael Drummond, a young man who is infatuated with him. Nonetheless, Stephen is the first Isherwood protagonist to believe in the immortality of the human soul, and the potential for redemption exists for him because he continuously subjects himself to a tormenting question: "What makes me behave like this? Am I so completely rotten?" (210).

Stephen represents the first of the four men of the Gita, "the world-weary," an immature youth who perceives his own unhappy condition but who is nevertheless naturally disposed to feel sorry for himself. In him can be seen the young Isherwood, who, from the safety of a cultural and social stronghold, had sneered at and snubbed the world of "the Others," those who in one way or another had made him feel inferior. But now, changing his perspective toward people, the author finds a sort of balance between his love and hatred of humanity. The main theme in *The World in the Evening* is the struggle against the "Great Tyrant Me," the egotistic and narcissistic self who prevents psychological and spiritual growth.

Until *Prater Violet* Isherwood's protagonist had asked himself, "Who am I?"; now he begins to wonder, "Who am I with someone else?" Using the autobiographical epistolary technique alongside cinematic flashbacks, Isherwood follows the "world-weary" Stephen throughout his life of abuse and nastiness and finds that his sin has always been one and the same: his lack of connection with his fellow beings. The protagonist even succeeds in "visualizing" this: "I had an amazing experience: I can only describe it as a hate-nightmare. I saw my hatred as something objective: it was a kind of black stinking bog. And I realized, just for a moment, that it had an existence all of its own. It had nothing to do with evidence or reasons, and nothing whatsoever to do with you. I had developed it myself. . . . I woke up scared, and I was scared all morning. . . . I knew I had to do something to be rid of it before it destroyed me" (267). At the end of the novel Stephen's maturation is complete. Isherwood communicates to us the firmness of Stephen's new belief, grimly fought for and grimly obtained during his "dark night of the soul."

The Seeker for Knowledge:
"What's really important is a word I couldn't say"

Down There on a Visit stars "Christopher Isherwood" in his final fictional performance. He is the protagonist in four episodes which take place during four different periods of Isherwood's life, from 1928 to 1952. But he is not the only Christopher Isherwood in the novel, because there is an "old Christopher" who watches with affection and amusement his younger self traversing the episodes of his life: "And now before I slip back into the convention of calling this young man 'I,' let me consider him as a separate being, a stranger almost, setting out on this adventure in a taxi to the docks. For, of course, he *is* almost a stranger to me" (13).

The young Christopher who lives again in the episodes of "Mr. Lancaster," "Ambrose," "Waldemar," and "Paul" mirrors the various Isherwoods. In "Mr. Lancaster," which is set in Germany and in England, he is similar to Philip Lindsay and Eric Vernon, protagonists of *All the Conspirators* and *The Memorial,* novels belonging to the 1928–32 period. Christopher is at this point a neurotic and weak young man whose main fault is a lack of connection with and interest in others. In "Ambrose," set on a strange Greek island in 1933, he is more similar to William Bradshaw and "Christopher Isherwood" of the Berlin novels. Involved in escaping with his beloved Waldemar from Nazi Germany, he only cares for himself and is hardly affected by the "nastiness" perpetrated on the island by the members of a homosexual anarchic commune. In "Waldemar," set in England in 1938, during the Munich Crisis, he is similar to the Christopher of *Prater Violet,* who has passed through the vivifying experience with Friedrich Bergmann, but who is still a disillusioned and frantic young intellectual. In "Paul," which takes place between 1940 and 1952 in California and ends up in Paris, he is the Christopher Isherwood who has met Swami Prabhavananda, has decided to follow the Vedantic path to safety, and has started to learn how to achieve inner spiritual growth.

"Paul" is for my purposes the most significant section of the novel. The title character represents the second man of the Gita, "the seeker for knowledge," a person who wonders if the divine reality exists, if there is a reason after all for the boredom and the apparent uselessness of this life. Seeking knowledge is the first step of what Isherwood has defined as "the long road to self-understanding." Early on in "Paul," Christopher is still partly the monster who is held by curiosity: "Do I care? Part of me already disapproves of Paul; part of me is bored by the tedious naughtiness of his legend. But, so far, I haven't reached my verdict. I'm waiting to see if he'll do anything to interest me; and I almost believe he knows this. I feel, at any rate, that he's capable of knowing it. That's what intrigues me about him" (194–95).

Paul struggles with "dynamic despair" and exhibits several of the attributes of the saint, according to Isherwood's definition. Together, Christopher and Paul try to live a life of discipline and prayer, of meditation and the search for the divine light. But "the Others" are not prepared to accept Paul's change and accuse him of sexually abusing an adolescent girl while on a spiritual retreat. Paul's world cracks; he leaves Christopher and substitutes drug-induced visions for meditation. Paul goes to Europe, becomes completely addicted and cynical, and encounters Christopher in Paris in 1952. "The seeker for knowledge" now needs drugs daily in order to have visions and to perceive what Gerald Heard called "this thing." But Paul is an outcast who sneers at Christopher, rejecting his attempt to save him from the hell of loneliness and separation. Defined by Paul as a tourist "sending postcards with 'Down here on a visit' on them. That's the story of your life" (315–16), Christopher reacts and declares his changed attitude toward the world and his fellow beings: "'What's really important is—' I paused because . . . I'd suddenly found there was a word I couldn't say to Paul . . . the word was 'love'" (301).

"Love" is the magical word which has transformed Christopher from a "heartless monster" to a human being, capable of connection with "the Others." His curiosity has now been replaced by the love which Vedanta, like other religions, clearly stresses as the universal and cosmic union of every creature with its Maker. The narrator has understood the lesson, has matured, has defeated the narcissistic self, but he cannot express this word to Paul, because Paul, the sinner-saint, searches for knowledge for its own sake, not to share it with "the Others," toward whom he feels contempt. Though Paul is "the seeker for knowledge," his search is on the wrong path altogether.

The Seeker for Happiness: "What I know is what I am"

The problem of identity gains central importance in *A Single Man,* which is not primarily a novel about homosexuality. It is rather a novel about middle age and loneliness in a world too closed to the existence of misfits and too arid to create commitment between human beings. In the first pages, the protagonist is called "it" and "the body," and only after washing, shaving, and dressing does it becomes a "he" and accede to human dignity: "It knows its name. It is called George" (11). The identity of the individual is therefore seen as a product of its existence in space and time, and it must be reestablished immediately, continuously, every time it awakes, because every return to the world of reality constitutes for Isherwood a rebirth. The first thoughts that burden George's mind are those of death: "Every *now* is labeled with its date, rendering all past *nows* obsolete, until—later or sooner—perhaps—no, not perhaps—quite certainly: it will come" (9).

George is happy to be alive, but he is basically incapable of having deep relationships with his fellow creatures: he is a person who is sheer biological mechanism, from the act of defecation in the morning to masturbation before going to sleep at night, this being a perfect symbol of the sterility and spiritual desert in which he lives, without even the slightest type of Conscience of the Absolute. Yet, paradoxically enough, George is the third man of the Gita, "the seeker for happiness," he who looks for the Absolute but does not know he is looking for it, because he acts with the wrong motives. According to Isherwood's philosophy, George has all the potential of the saint because he has a quality which makes him able to save his fellow beings. As a university professor, for example, he meets young people daily, talks with them, and can communicate his own experience and knowledge, his discoveries and beliefs, to them: "He is a representative of the hope. And the hope is not false. . . . George is like a man trying to sell a real diamond for a nickel, on the street. The diamond is protected from all but the tiniest few, because the great hurrying majority can never stop to dare to believe that it could conceivably be real" (48).

"The great hurrying majority" of the students consider George a nuisance and a bore. But there is one representative of the "tiniest few," Kenny, who feels and shows a particular interest in the professor. After a quick and superficial dialogue with Kenny on campus, George meets him by chance at a bar and has a lively exchange with him: "It's a dialogue. A dialogue between two people. . . . You can talk about anything and change the subject as often as you like. In fact, what really matters is not what you talk about, but the being together in this particular relationship. George can't imagine having a dialogue of this kind with a woman, because women can only talk in terms of the personal. . . . You and your dialogue-partner have to be somehow opposites. . . . Youth and Age" (154). One could recognize this meeting as the same which had happened between Christopher and Friedrich Bergmann in *Prater Violet*. George, however, standing in for Isherwood, plays the role of the wise old man, teaching the young, inexperienced searcher in a kind of guru-disciple relationship in which polarity plays a great part because it is difference that guarantees growth.

According to George, modern man's drama consists of the impossibility of true connection. Everything has been reduced "into a flirtation," one which leads to no true involvement at all, while true salvation *is* total involvement with entire humanity seen as a unique, inseparable creation: "All any of you ever do is flirt, and wear your blankets off one shoulder, and complain about motels. And miss the one thing that might really— and, Kenneth, I do not say this casually—*transform your entire life*" (176– 77). This "one thing" is once more that "love" which Christopher could not express to Paul and which George cannot express to Kenny. It is a tragedy: "the seeker for happiness" understands at last the importance of connection and of universal love, but he cannot achieve them.

The Man of Spiritual Discrimination: "What unites us is the only thing that really matters"

A Meeting by the River, though not generally well received by contemporary critics, is the logical completion of Isherwood's long road to self-understanding. The novel is the point-counterpoint type, the continuous parallel between pairs of opposites. Several episodes in the novel show the difficulty of connection between two such opposite cultures as the materialistic and pragmatic West and the spiritual and meditative East. Isherwood succeeds in presenting equally the two extremes and avoids any direct judgment.

The confrontation which structures the dialectic nature of the novel is that between two brothers: Oliver, full of fear and doubt, wants to distance himself from the world; Patrick, always happy and vital, despises Indian religion but appears to be tolerant and open-minded in the monastery in order to gain his brother's confidence. If we analyze Oliver and Patrick, we soon find out that their personalities and their thoughts complement each other. Oliver states that "in our case, being brothers, we're that much more closely involved. Heredity has made us part of a single circuit, our wires are all connected" (115), and this connection, for the first time in Isherwood's work, shows the nondual quality of reciprocal love.

Replete with fears and doubts, Oliver is the Truly Weak Man of Isherwood's mythology. In fact, he forces himself to write to Patrick, implicitly asking him to come to the monastery because he feels weak in his decision to become a monk: "What's the use of me, if I can't pass this test? What kind of a swami am I going to be? Enough of this now. Now write to Patrick. Tell him he can come" (37–38). But Patrick too shows his weakness through his dishonesty and self-deception. Writing to his lover Tom, a young Californian, he says, "We must never forget, when we go against the majority, that we are forced to be like guerrillas, our chief weapon is cunning. We can't ever attack openly. That's just exactly what the enemy wants us to do, so he can destroy us. . . . Defiance is a luxury we can't afford" (88). Oliver and Patrick represent two different aspects of the personality, which can coexist in the same person; in Isherwood's postconversion narrative, they are not mutually exclusive.

The defining moment in the novel is the temptation scene, which is carried out in three stages, recalling the temptation in the desert from the Gospel of Luke. After getting a false start by exposing his body to a not-too-embarrassed Oliver, Patrick goes straight to the heart of the matter and tries to arouse Oliver's vanity by suggesting that he has powers "to lead others and make them forget their own vanity and selfish interests and finally become almost noble" (154). Oliver is tempted, and he is weak; therefore, it is not surprising that he falters. The third temptation involves doubt arising from Patrick's silence in response to Oliver's request for advice: "I knew I shouldn't be able to sleep. . . . One moment, everything that Patrick said seems utterly idiotic and even laughable. The next, it seems terribly insidiously true" (159–60). His insecurity makes him consider leaving the monastery, and his soul is torn between ambition and weakness. But he has still one card to play, his best: "Swami, I'm praying to you as I've never prayed before—show me what I must do" (160).

Oliver has at least this certainty, which proves the strongest of all: "I have known a man who said *he knew* that God exists. . . . That man chose me for his disciple. . . . I have become more and more convinced during these last months . . . that when Swami left his body it was an intentional act" (51–52). This episode recalls Isherwood's statement that he became involved in Vedanta because he believed so strongly in Swami Prabhavananda's belief in God. Oliver's memory of his life with his own swami gives him the strength to remain in the monastery.

Oliver is Isherwood's first character to have a full perception of Universal Unity, of the *Brahman,* and, moreover, to have the right instruments— faith and connection with the others—to reach this unity and attain spiritual renewal. Oliver is thus the fourth man of the Gita, "the man of spiritual discrimination," he who has the potential to perceive and enjoy the mystery which rules Creation. A vision he has while dreaming after a long meditation makes Oliver sure that the step he is taking is the right one: "This wasn't a vision in the waking state [but it] was intensely vivid, far more so than an ordinary dream. Also, unlike a dream, it didn't altogether end when I woke up. It is losing strength now but it's still going on inside me at this moment. . . . I knew that Swami was 'dead,' and I knew that nevertheless he was now with me—*and that he is with me always, wherever I am.* . . . Now we are never separated. I woke up actually *knowing* that" (172–73).

The novel ends in harmony: Oliver takes his vows, becomes a swami, and is happy and finally confident in his choice. Happy for his brother, Patrick recognizes the wisdom of his choice and takes part in the feast given for him at the monastery. The Indians are just as happy, and Oliver, feeling even greater happiness for all this, experiences another epiphany: "At that moment I seemed to stand outside myself and see the two of us, and Swami, and the onlookers, all involved in this tremendous joke. . . . Everybody was smiling and murmuring, as much as to say how charming it was of Patrick to play this scene according to our local Hindu rules, and how very right and proper it was that we two brothers should love each other" (190–91).

The separation between body and spirit, thought and sense, one of the main bases for modern man's tragedy, is in Isherwood's view another example of *maya*. Body and spirit, sense and thought, are divine gifts which must coexist in man without gaps of any sort. The great sense of total and absolute unity comes to the surface in *A Meeting by the River*, in which Oliver succeeds in bridging the gap where Isherwood's other protagonists remained trapped. Oliver's success is not merely due to chance. A quotation from the Gita, as Krishna talks with Arjuna before battle, explains why:

> Certainly, all these [four men] are noble:
> But the man of discrimination
> I see as my very Self.
> For he alone loves me
> Because I am myself:
> The last and only goal
> Of his devoted heart.
> Through many a long life
> His discrimination ripens:
> He makes me his refuge,
> Knows that Brahman is all.
> How rare are such great ones! (72–73)

There has been a great meeting by the river. The Truly Weak Man has met the Truly Strong Man, and carnality has managed to live together with spirituality. Two parts of the same personality have merged as Patrick finds his brother, Oliver finds confidence in himself, and above all, at the end of his long and treacherous journey, Isherwood finds the path that leads to safety.

Notes

1. John Lehmann, *I Am My Brother: Autobiography II* (London: Longman, 1960), 180.
2. Ibid., 154.

25   *Carola M. Kaplan*

"The Wandering Stopped"
An Interview with Christopher Isherwood

The following interview took place in Christopher Isherwood's home—a modest, one-story, ranch-style dwelling in Santa Monica. The house, where he lived with Don Bachardy and where Bachardy still lives, is tucked into a hill on a quiet residential street above Santa Monica Canyon. To reach the house, which was virtually invisible from the street, I descended a steep staircase to a wooden gate, rang the bell, and proceeded down more steps, then along a stone patio to the entrance. Isherwood came to the door. His manner was cordial, relaxed, and welcoming. Small and slim, he looked tan, fit, and considerably younger than his almost seventy years. He ushered me into the large living room, whose walls were covered with paintings by contemporary artists. The most striking feature of the comfortable room was a large picture window, which looked down on the canyon and at the same time commanded a spectacular view of the ocean.

I had met Isherwood previously, after a talk he had given at one of the colleges in Claremont, a town some sixty miles to the east. I had rather shyly introduced myself and told him I was writing my dissertation on his work, focusing particularly on the novels he had written since his emigration to America. To my hesitant request for an interview, he had responded with alacrity, inviting me to call him at home, informing me that I could find his telephone number in the directory. On the day of the interview, I arrived, unsure of how to proceed, interview questions in one hand, tape recorder in the other. Isherwood was warm and reassuring. When I asked him if I could tape-record the interview, he replied, "Of course," and proceeded to help me set up the microphone for best reception, saying, "I have a lot of experience with these things." We sat opposite each other on two soft white contemporary couches, the tape recorder on a glass coffee table between. I had the flattering sensation that I had all his attention, while I was aware at the same time that his sharp eyes, startlingly blue against his deeply tanned, still-boyish face, missed nothing. He was dressed casually, his sport shirt open at the collar, revealing his body to be as tanned as his face. Throughout the interview, I was struck—and immensely touched—by his friendliness, his openness, and his apparent vulnerability that seemed to be strongly supported by an underlying surety. Listening to him, I had the feeling that he drew upon deep resources he had been long in acquiring.

Before the interview began, Isherwood told me that he had just finished writing the screenplay of *A Meeting by the River,* in collaboration with Bachardy. He was very pleased with the result, which was an adaptation of the play version, on which they had also collaborated. Both of these adaptations are based on Isherwood's 1967 novel, a religious comedy about two brothers whose lifelong rivalry leads to a final confrontation and ambiguous resolution. Their crisis erupts when the younger brother, Oliver, a former social activist, informs Patrick that he is living in a monastery in India and is about to take final vows as a Hindu monk. Patrick, a charming hedonist, currently juggling his marriage to Penny and his affair with Tom, whom he met while negotiating a movie deal in Hollywood, rushes to India to attempt to persuade Oliver to change his mind.

I was pleased to begin the interview with a discussion of this particular book and its adaptations because *A Meeting by the River* was the first book I had ever read of Isherwood's. I had picked it up in paperback, as light holiday reading—or so I mistakenly judged it to be. Since I knew nothing about Isherwood or his work, I had the rare and delightful experience of "discovering" him. I so loved the novel, which proved both profound and provocative, that I proceeded to read all of his fiction with an avidity I had not known since childhood. What made *A Meeting by the River* particularly attractive to me was the fact that it is a religious novel, and I admired immensely Isherwood's deftness and humor in handling this difficult form. Since I had then decided to write my dissertation on "The Search for Belief in the Novels of Christopher Isherwood," much of my interview with him centers on this theme.

I came to the interview feeling a strong kinship with the person who had emerged for me through autobiographical characters in Isherwood's novels. Of course, I feared I might be disappointed in speaking to the actual man, but the reverse was the case. I had a feeling of great rapport with him: there was an ease and flow in our conversation, and I was aware throughout that he was sincerely concerned to respond to my inquiries with care and honesty. At the time I was in a period of spiritual searching in my own life. I believe he picked up on that and took great pains to answer my questions, to allay my doubts, and to encourage me in my quest.

As I read over the interview, after the passage of twenty-five years, I am struck by its personal quality. Isherwood's responses seem to me wonderfully straightforward and unself-conscious—his remarks not at all delivered for effect, but simply as one side of a conversation between two people with a compelling common concern: how one may come to spiritual insight, and how this insight changes one's life and work. It seems to me extraordinary that he was willing to speak with a virtual stranger about so many intimate aspects of his life—in particular about key relationships and decisions and the ways in which these had entered his writing. Most of all, I can now see that Isherwood himself exemplified in that interview the qualities that he told me he had admired so much in E. M. Forster: his ability to care tremendously about the other person, even more perhaps than that person was able to do, and his concern to give reassurance. For me, this interview remains remarkable in its immediacy, warmth, and intensity—and in its vivid evocation of Isherwood as a singular man.

ISHERWOOD: A Meeting by the River *was really quite different from any of my other works.*

KAPLAN: *You mean because you really didn't have a narrator—because* A Meeting by the River *has a different structure?*

ISHERWOOD: Yes, because it's all written in letters, and documents, and because there's no real point of view. It's just as I always say: it's like a trial where both sides give evidence. But there's no judgment, no verdict, no summing up, nothing. You just hear all of the evidence.

KAPLAN: *Do you feel that you didn't in any way slant that evidence? You don't think that the scales are weighted at all in favor of Oliver?*

ISHERWOOD: They are only weighted in favor of Oliver in the sense that what he's pushing is much more practical than what Patrick is pushing. But I wouldn't say that they're weighted otherwise. As a matter of fact, one's sympathy and the sympathy of most readers goes strongly to Patrick, I find. . . . You see, I have now approached this material three times, and every time the two characters change very subtly in certain ways. When we made the play, Oliver luckily was played by a very good actor, Sam

Waterston, who gave it great energy and a kind of conviction and even a sort of sexiness, so that he held his end up very well. But otherwise, it's uphill work for Oliver, because onstage all that sort of skullduggery [of Patrick's] is very charming. It has a kind of eighteenth-century appeal, this villainy. Anyway, then you see more and more that one comes to something else in the material, which is that Patrick is doing this in a very sincere way, that's to say he is genuinely horrified by the monastery. This is something we bring out much more in the screenplay. For one thing, on the screen you'll be able to see the place and see the whole atmosphere of Calcutta and of India and everything and the scariness of it, the feeling of somebody actually doing these things. When you really see the room where he slept with all the other monks on the floor, it kind of brings it home to Patrick what Oliver has done to himself. And also, of course, in the play, and even much more so in the screenplay, matters are complicated by the fact that the other characters appear; the wife especially has come out very strongly in the screenplay.

KAPLAN: *She is a very interesting figure in the book as the brothers evoke her. Of course, she is seen so differently by Patrick and Oliver.*

ISHERWOOD: We have a rather amusing situation in the screenplay, which is a sort of nontriangle. That is to say, both the wife and the boyfriend come to India. They get along very well. And the wife, unlike all women who appear in dramas about monasteries, goes to the monastery and tells Oliver to stay there, not to come out. [Laughter] It's a very curious kind of anti-temptation scene—in which she comes to India to tell Oliver to, for God's sake, stay in there and not let Patrick upset him again. She makes a rousing speech telling him he absolutely should stay there. And also the conclusions that the two brothers come to about each other—that of course does appear in the play—comes out very strongly. At the end of the play, Oliver says of course the truth is that Patrick is really terribly influenced by this place and by the mahanta [the head of the monastery] and that he will in the end have an appalling religious conversion, which he will hate and think that he is having a nervous breakdown; he'll probably go to a psychiatrist about it and so forth.

KAPLAN: *Do you believe that it is possible for someone who isn't obviously or actively seeking a religious experience to have one nonetheless?*

ISHERWOOD: Well, of course if you get down into the inwardness of the story, the whole thing is sort of psychosomatic. In a way you might almost say that the monastery is a sort of psychosomatic event in Patrick's life. [Laughter] I'm not being very precise in my use of words, scientifically speaking, but you know what I mean. Quite aside from being a real place by the Ganges and being a place that Oliver lives in, it represents a problem of Patrick's.

KAPLAN: *One that existed even before he went there, you mean.*

ISHERWOOD: Yes. And therefore he doesn't go there really entirely just to see Oliver but from an awful kind of fascination to see how he would feel if he did go. And then of course both the brothers at the end are smiling and delighted because each thinks that he knows something about the other one. In the film we have this nice scene, after the bowing down, which was the end of the play. When you become a swami, a sannyasin, when you've taken sannyas [final vows], according to immemorial tradition, you have to go out for three days and beg your food. Now of course this is only a convention because in fact all kinds of pious people around you are only too delighted—they come out with enough food for a church picnic. But nevertheless you do go out in your robes and you have to go barefoot and you go to these houses. And the last scene in the film will be that Oliver and his fellow swamis, his brother monks, are all out there; and what they give you is a sort of gooey kind of soupy stuff with a lot of beans in it and so forth, which they empty into the fold of your cloth, so you have to hold it like this and then people dip in and taste it—which is extremely unappetizing if you're not used to it. All right, so here is Oliver in the dust by the side of the road, barefoot with the other monks, and they've got this stuff. And Patrick and Penelope are driving to the airport and they see Oliver there; so they tell the car to stop and they get out and they rather gingerly partake of these alms which are very holy and then say goodbye and they get back in the car. It's then that Patrick makes his final speech. He lights a cigar and he says, "Of course he will stay in the monastery. Little does he realize where his humility is leading him. In that yellow robe of his, he'll preside at international conferences, he'll march into palaces and confront dictators barefoot. Twenty years from now he'll be running Asia." [Laughter] Meanwhile, Oliver has taken Penelope aside and said, "Look, Penny, I want you to look after Patrick for the next few weeks because he may begin to act very strangely." Penny says, "What on earth do you mean?" He says, "Well, he may think he's got something wrong with his stomach, or he may feel he's having a nervous breakdown; but do try to reassure him because, as a matter of fact, the only thing that's wrong with Patrick is he's in a state of grace and he doesn't know it." [Laughter] And she's utterly bewildered by this statement. So then they go off, these two. And that's the essence of the comedy. It's meant to be quite balanced, really, because the real moral of the story, if it has a moral, is a sentence in the [Bhagavad] Gita which says, "God is eternally perfect. What does he care for our righteousness or for our wickedness?" *Sub spe-*

cie aeternitatis, it's absolutely immaterial, isn't it, because there isn't any such thing [as righteousness and wickedness]. It's all *maya* [illusion], and he's God, we're God, everybody's God, there's nothing but God anywhere; and all the rest is this strange playing on the surface of life.

KAPLAN: *Then there's nothing necessarily preferable about Oliver's choice over Patrick's?*

ISHERWOOD: It's relatively preferable, but not from an eternal viewpoint, no. I mean, it's symbolic, in other words. Yes, it's preferable, because after all not only is all this happening, but this play is being written from within *maya*, not from outside, so one can't say. You can't dare to say, for instance, that enormous massacres are good or are the same as any other kind of behavior. This attitude is only possible in the moment of complete union with the Eternal. You couldn't say it from any other point of view. It would be just completely heartless and insane. But nevertheless, in a certain sense, it's true. In a certain sense, the Eternal is either nonexistent or it's everywhere, by definition. If it's everywhere, then Hitler is God, then everybody is God. But as Ramakrishna said, everything is God, but Tiger God is to be avoided. [Laughter] In other words, I mean, sometimes from a distance you can say, "Yes it's God, all right, but. . . ."

KAPLAN: *And isn't there a distinction between that part within an individual which is God and that part which is* maya, *that is, the working of his illusion in terms of his ego, of his own distortions?*

ISHERWOOD: Yes, from the relative standpoint, but the absolute standpoint of Vedanta is that there is no difference, that this multiplicity is all contained in oneness. In other words, in the last analysis, from the highest view, all action is symbolic. But that doesn't mean that you shouldn't do your best. [Laughter]

KAPLAN: *One has the distinct feeling in the book that Patrick isn't doing his best, especially for his brother.*

ISHERWOOD: In the original book, I was very far from understanding exactly what I was writing about. There is so much in this theme as you get more and more into it. I was interested on a much more superficial level. Do you know that novel *Les Liaisons Dangereuses* or *Dangerous Liaisons*? Well, this kind of mischief for mischief's sake interested me. But I never thought of Patrick as being really bad exactly; he's just sort of a tease. I mean, he wouldn't do anything really fiendishly bad like Madame de Merteuil or whatever her name is, the woman who was really evil.

KAPLAN: *Just gratuitously evil.*

ISHERWOOD: Gratuitous evil is obviously the worst kind. People who are sincere who are evil because of some sort of drives are not as bad as people who just do it for no reason. When you get the late Roman emperors who were just bored and had some slaves killed in front of them—besides people like that, somebody who sincerely had drives, like Hitler, is not nearly as bad, obviously. The worst thing of all is this kind of passionless evil-doing. Where it's just utter lack of feeling.

KAPLAN: *I was thinking as you were talking that not only have Patrick's actions not been gratuitously evil, but from Oliver's point of view, Patrick has really done him a favor by the end.*

ISHERWOOD: Oh, yes, really a great point is made out of that. Very much more in the play, I think, than in the novel. But it's funny—it is all in the novel, in a sort of way.

KAPLAN: *I was thinking in terms of the novel. Of course, Oliver invites Patrick—that first letter is clearly an invitation.*

ISHERWOOD: He wants Patrick to come, of course, because he wants Patrick to approve of him.

KAPLAN: *Do you think he has some doubts that he wants allayed by having Patrick there?*

ISHERWOOD: Of course he has doubts. It's terribly, terribly hard to do anything that is against the usual concepts of your culture. It is very, very painful and embarrassing, and doubts come—always.

KAPLAN: *I am remembering the essay you wrote on "The Problem of the Religious Novel," in which you said something about wanting to show that, although ultimately a saint is so very different from the average man, in the beginning that saint was simply Mr Jones. And I have a sense that that's what you have done with Oliver. Because if Oliver were somehow certain, I don't think we could deal with him at all. His doubts and the vestiges of all the earlier feelings for his brother make him understandable to us, but not fully, because he's advanced beyond that too.*

ISHERWOOD: I don't think of Oliver as being by any means a saint, yet he might become one. The Hindus have a very different way of using the word: they don't use the word "saint" really in the sort of Western convention. What they mean when they say "saint" is quite specifically somebody who has received some degree of spiritual illumination, in other words, who has actually seen the Eternal in one way or another, cognized it, been aware of its presence. Whereas here we tend very much to dwell on the moral aspects. We say, "he's so good," "he's so charitable," he's this and that. The Hindus would reply, yes, it's quite true that having seen the Eternal, this brings you to the conclusion that the Eternal is everywhere in everybody. And therefore naturally it makes you much less antisocial than most of us are because we see they're all my brothers—whether you like it or not, they are. [Laughter] Let's face it, that's my sister and that's my brother and that goes for the cobra and for the dove and all creatures and everything and human beings of all sorts. Now, that's the Hindu idea, as I say—the idea that some degree of enlightenment has been reached. I really tried to make a saint, to describe my idea of a saint much more in the not very satisfactory novel of mine called *The World in the Evening*. Aunt Sarah. I tried to describe what I think of as a saint a little bit more with her.

KAPLAN: *Did you have a particular person in mind as the basis for Sarah?*

ISHERWOOD: It's very composite. I met a lot of Quakers when I was working with them, and many of them were, I think, very advanced. But you see, one doesn't know really. There's a wonderful story about when Claire Booth Luce became a Catholic and she immediately was very gung-ho, really going after being a Catholic in the biggest way; and she went down to see a very remarkable priest who lived downtown—I think he's dead now—who everybody said was quite extraordinary. And so she gets down there and she begins talking to him and she says, "Father, it's so sad that nowadays there are no saints at all." And he said, "Oh, I wouldn't say that." He said, "That old lady out there (he was pointing to a Mexican lady who was sweeping the floor outside), Mrs. Martinez, she's a saint." Of course, Mrs. Luce was all shattered because that wasn't at all what she meant by a saint. But probably he was right. I met people like that, yes.

KAPLAN: *I know that for me the scene in which Stephen looks at Sarah and sees her not as this old, fuss-budget aunt, but really sees what's there—well, that really came alive for me. So I felt that you had to have seen that in someone or through someone.*

ISHERWOOD: Yes, I felt that in a few people. [The English mystic writer] Alan Watts always liked that scene so much. He told me about it one time, how he often read it to people.

KAPLAN: *I found that scene very powerful—and the scene at the Quaker meeting too. The silence was extremely evocative.*

ISHERWOOD: That's all based on experience, of course. I lived with them for quite the better part of a year.

KAPLAN: *One of the things that the book implies through Stephen is that there is a reality greater than yourself, even if you are not actively seeking that or actively wanting to know that. It really is there, everywhere all around you; and there are people who embody it or know it, and so you can find it in all kinds of experiences—and you seem to suggest that throughout the book.*

ISHERWOOD: I do—I believe that.

KAPLAN: *It seemed to me that you were suggesting this possibility in certain daily states, such as, for example, when Stephen just wakes up in the morning and doesn't really feel that he is himself.*

ISHERWOOD: It's why I don't like the book. I made a terrible mistake in telling the story through Stephen, and I don't think I should have. I think I should have done it in some other way. I don't exactly know, but . . . it gave me more trouble than all the rest of the books put together, and I was working on it and messing with it for years and years, and it never came out right. Finally, I think, I should have sat down and taken it all apart and done it once more. But he's wrong. Stephen is sort of fakey in some way.

KAPLAN: *Do you feel that at that point you were trying to describe some sort of new and exciting discovery? It seems that there is much more overt statement in* The World in the Evening *than there is in the following books, in which religious experience seems to be a possibility for the characters, but it's more subtly hinted at. And when they do arrive at it, they do so in a way that's understandable in terms of their character.*

ISHERWOOD: It's very glib, I think. I don't like it. As a matter of fact, while I was staying at the Vedanta Center in Hollywood, I was writing *Prater Violet* and this thing [*The World in the Evening*] I wrote later. But I think there's something deeply wrong with it. It's fakey. I like it the least of my books. You'd be surprised at the number of people who like it, though. To this day I get letters about it.

KAPLAN: *I think it is a very interesting book because it has tremendous energy and so many new ideas. You begin to explore them in that novel but do so with more ease in the later books. For example, in* Down There on a Visit *there are three episodes in which Chris is not involved with any kind of religious experience, but in the fourth he is. The character of Paul puzzles me in that novel. He's played off against Chris in that last episode, and Paul seems so much more of an absolutist than Chris, especially at the end.*

ISHERWOOD: I don't think Paul altogether works. What I was trying to do was to write about somebody who is a kind of touchstone. Everybody he

comes in contact with, he almost unconsciously reveals any kind of false-
ness in them. There are people like that; and it's not that they're very
nice themselves at all, but they just have that kind of truth. Some kind of
truthfulness, a rather sinister kind that sort of unmasks people. I'm actually engaged at the moment in just starting a book which is, as you might
say, an autobiography, that is to say it's absolutely true, not fiction at all.
And I'm covering a good deal of the same ground. It's a sort of book of
the period of my life which Germans call *Wanderjahren*. It's about going
to Berlin and covers the time until I'd been in this country about four or
five years and it became kind of my home. I don't mean that there is a
great big thing about that, but it's that the wandering stopped.

KAPLAN: *Do you think that had to do with your adoption of Vedanta
philosophy?*

ISHERWOOD: It had a great deal to do with it and various kinds of roots
that I put down and various relationships that I had formed and one thing
and another. But it involves going over some of this material from a
different angle. It's very interesting to me, at least, doing it, because quite
different things come out. Now, the Paul character will probably hardly
appear in this book at all, but there will be a great deal about Gerald
Heard and Aldous Huxley. Gerald Heard is of course Augustus Parr. But
then again he's caricatured very much [in *Down There on a Visit*]. What
I'm really much more concerned to do in this new book [*Christopher and
His Kind*] is to write almost entirely about people who really turned me
on, as remarkable inspiring people in one way or another. That doesn't
mean they weren't absurd, ridiculous, bad, or anything, but really very
positive sort of types, all the way from hustlers in Berlin bars to the swami
or anybody, Ingrid Bergman.

KAPLAN: *Do you see them as having certain things in common?*

ISHERWOOD: People around whom one can form a myth are the people
who actually turned me on personally. I was tremendously struck reading
Jung's autobiography; and he starts by saying, I'm going to tell the story
of my myth. I'm not going to go into a lot of detail or gossip or stuff, but
I'm going to say what the themes were that sort of turned me on and
excited me, not the facts so much as the tale, the way the whole thing
unfolded.

KAPLAN: *And this is what you're trying to do?*

ISHERWOOD: Yes, but not about my extreme youth, and not about my later
life either. It's just this period, it's roughly speaking from 1929 to, let's
say, 1943.

KAPLAN: *You have gone back to periods that you dealt with earlier to deal with them again. It reminds me of what you talked about in* The Memorial— *the idea of the dynamic portrait that you go back to again and see more and more in it. The most dynamic portrait is Chris.*

ISHERWOOD: What else does one know? One doesn't have much but oneself, certainly. The last book I wrote was *Kathleen and Frank,* which of course was the facts behind *The Memorial* and the characters. Only there they did the work themselves because of all the diaries and letters.

KAPLAN: *When you created this persona, "Chris," did you see him and yourself as essentially the same person, or did you separate yourself from him?*

ISHERWOOD: I have really no idea of what I'm like totally. I mean, I have no sense of myself as a person exactly, just as a lot of reactions to things. I know from experience that as one gets older one can produce certain kinds of effects. And one knows things that one can do and things one can't do. One knows certain weaknesses, obviously, very well. But it's very hard to know—and if you start watching this thing, trying to watch it as you do in art, you're quite at a loss really. The trouble is to make fun of it too much, to make it absurd. That's the temptation one has to resist. Which is really a kind of inverted vanity, this clowning about.

KAPLAN: *I see you've gotten very interested in nonfiction and particularly in depicting yourself in a nonfictional way. Is that because you feel that fiction oversimplifies life too much?*

ISHERWOOD: I'm more interested, you see, in the comment, as it were, and the comment you can have just as well in nonfiction, as long as the thing very closely concerns you.

KAPLAN: *Don't you have less room for comment in fiction in that it has to be implicit in what's dramatically happening?*

ISHERWOOD: Yes, because you have to keep getting on with all the invention of the business, the interplay. And sometimes that's fun: I enjoy, of course, writing movies and that sort of thing. And I've enjoyed it in the past in books. I really enjoyed writing *A Meeting by the River* more than anything—I really wished it would never end. And I kept writing it and rewriting it and rewriting it. But when you really come down to it, what fascinates me is thinking about the given material and trying to see what it meant, making it into a sort of poetical shape, trying to find the inwardness of it, the myth, in fact, what it expresses. And that's difficult.

KAPLAN: *I'm sure it must be. Especially if the myth changes, as it did for you with* A Meeting by the River—*and as, in each medium, you said the characters did change.*

ISHERWOOD: Yes, they change, of course, all the time.

KAPLAN: *Does that have to do with the fact that people have illusions about themselves, so that even when you come to look at a literary character, you must see that character in terms of his illusions? But also as you change and your illusions about yourself change, that character too must change?*

ISHERWOOD: Yes, I'm trying to do that. I'm trying to contrast, for instance, the Christopher who entered that period in 1929, the Berlin period, with the Christopher who came to the United States ten years later—as far as I can judge, a considerably different person.

KAPLAN: *In what ways?*

ISHERWOOD: More hard-boiled, more cynical, more careerist, I think. But then, on the other hand, luckily that didn't work out very well—so all was well. [Laughter] That was the story of it. But then, you see, the element that goes very, very deep in the material, which is never satisfactorily expressed in any of these books and which now I am expressing, is the homosexuality, not so much from the point of view of the question of sexual preference as the whole thing of belonging to a rather small minority, a tribe, which is sometimes overtly persecuted but always sort of subtly slighted. And what this means, the boiling rage underneath the nicey-nice exterior.

KAPLAN: *You do a marvelous job of bringing that out in* A Single Man.

ISHERWOOD: It was so funny, you know, S. N. Behrman wrote about that. He found it so shocking, this feeling of oppression. But really I was speaking to every minority. How could he as a Jew say that one never feels mad at people who are non-Jewish? I mean there's a certain moment when you think, well, fuck them, you know. . . . That was absolutely said on behalf of every single minority, those passages. In fact I wrote it much more about being a minority than about being homosexual, really. It was deeply involved in the psychology of minorities in general.

KAPLAN: *One of the most moving things in* A Single Man *is George's rage. He says that it's the energy of middle age—but on the other hand it's a thing that wraps you up in your own ego, so it's hard for him to break out.*

ISHERWOOD: Oh, it's very bad, yes. And of course, that was where you might say, in a way, I was sort of, not cheating . . . but being alone has not been my life experience, I'm happy to say. Therefore I was perhaps loading the dice a bit, but I just didn't feel up to juggling a domestic homosexual relationship on top of all the other factors in the book. Just to sort of clear the decks a bit, I wanted to have George by himself.

KAPLAN: *But at the same time you have suggested very well George's relationship with Jim throughout the book.*

ISHERWOOD: Yes, I tried to. I think perhaps it might have been strengthened a bit, perhaps that would have helped. But the very last thing I wanted was to create a kind of pathos around this man, and yet of course there is some. Another thing that was depriving for him was that he had no real kind of philosophical support.

KAPLAN: *In some ways it seems to be waiting for him at points in the book, for example, in the classroom scene where he's teaching* After Many a Summer Dies the Swan. *One has no sense that it really means anything to George.*

ISHERWOOD: Well, that's why one comes back to wanting to write nonfiction. Take George—I was always juggling a little bit. There was George on the one hand, and there was me on the other. When I start clowning like that in the classroom and carrying on, this is much more me than it would have been George. My whole experience academically, of course, has been as a guest lecturer, and it's a very different thing if you're a known writer and you go to one of these places. Not that I didn't teach, really. I gave regular courses and did lots of homework, and my colleagues said, you know, you do it all right. Nevertheless I was a privileged person, and I was expected to amuse primarily, rather than instruct. . . . In the classroom, kids expect you to. I mean they have no use for somebody who doesn't. In fact, I am really more at my ease with the college generation, the succeeding college generation, than I am with any other age group of Americans. I feel so very relaxed with them all that I never feel any problem. Partly because I don't try to be young or any of that stuff, but I just go right ahead and talk to them. You can talk to them, and I see a great many of them. They come here, and we talk. But, anyway, that is the trouble—that George and I didn't quite make one person there. There are times when it begins to slip out of gear.

KAPLAN: *If George's life were happier, or fuller, you wouldn't have the sense of his need for philosophical support—which is present no matter how happy one's life is.*

ISHERWOOD: Oh, of course. The more intense the happiness, the more poignancy one feels in the fact that it can only be for a certain while, that things change, and that one is separated from people by death and circumstances. All that is very true.

KAPLAN: *Did you see George as avoiding understanding himself when such an understanding might have been possible? For instance, when Kenny asks him if he's ever taken mescaline and speaks about his friend seeing God after having taken mescaline, he does not consider the possibility of seeing God under any circumstances. It almost seems like an evasion, that it was possible for him to consider it and yet he wouldn't.*

ISHERWOOD: I think there is an evasion there. I agree with you. I was trying to write a poem, you know; I mean, it could be one of those days, like Virginia Woolf's *Mrs. Dalloway.*

KAPLAN: *I was wondering if you had* Mrs. Dalloway *in mind as you wrote the book.*

ISHERWOOD: That, and a thing you'd never imagine that there could be any connection with, but which made a tremendous impression on me: I was obsessed by Antonioni's *La Notte* at that time. I didn't take anything from it, but there was something about the feeling of *La Notte.* Those things are very individual, why one's turned on by something. But that picture meant a great deal to me.

KAPLAN: *I also thought there were certain things in* A Single Man *that were reminiscent of* Ulysses *as well.*

ISHERWOOD: Everybody has been influenced by *Ulysses.* But it's a little dry emotionally for my taste. It's too mental, it's not my scene. But as an overall thing it's obviously a masterpiece. There are amazing things in it, and the ending is tremendous.

KAPLAN: *I have the feeling that in* A Single Man *there is an ongoing theme that has to do with the metaphor of life in the Upanishads, that life is a chariot race. Did you have that in mind?*

ISHERWOOD: Possibly, yes. Somebody said that the image of the road ran all through the book.

KAPLAN: *I saw the freeway scenes and the details throughout of Los Angeles as being used to emphasize the isolation of life here.*

ISHERWOOD: You know, the funny thing is I didn't mean to write that book at all. I meant to write a book which is called *An Englishwoman.*

KAPLAN: *You wanted to focus on Charlotte?*

ISHERWOOD: The whole book was about Charlotte, but I couldn't get at her properly somehow. I had all sorts of devices, but they didn't work. It was Don Bachardy who suggested the title for the book.

KAPLAN: *It's a good title because it seems to mean so many different things.*

ISHERWOOD: He's a very good critic of things; and we just got to work on *A Meeting by the River.* In the play there were a tremendous lot of his suggestions, of all kinds.

KAPLAN: *What are we to make of Oliver's religious experience at the end— when he sees the swami? It isn't as if his experience were unmediated, but he does have an experience through the swami. Can we take that as disingenuous, something he desires and therefore sees?*

ISHERWOOD: I don't regard that as an evasion. It's absolutely necessary if you're playing a fifty-fifty game. Everything must be susceptible to two explanations. In other words, Oliver was in a jam psychologically. He was terribly bothered by his situation. He found a way out, which nobody else could find—having a vision which explained to him that, as a matter of fact, Patrick had just as much right in the monastery as he did. Now, this is very sound from every point of view, but at the same time it can all be explained away, as they say, by any San Fernando Valley psychiatrist, who just says, "Oh well, what else could he do? He had to resolve this." As a matter of fact, we've gone much further in the existing draft of the screenplay. In the existing draft, Oliver has the vision, and he sees the swami sitting on the seat, and then two absolutely identical poodles jump onto the seat, one on one side and one on the other. And he pets them and laughs. Then they turn into Patrick and Oliver, meaning that in the sight of the swami—we don't belabor the point. [Laughter] So the scene is kind of farcical. I always think that one of the best ways of conveying these sorts of states is through something on the very edge of farce because it so often is in these descriptions that people give of visions.

KAPLAN: *I remember your saying something about that in "The Problem of the Religious Novel."*

ISHERWOOD: A funny thing happened when I was with the Quakers in Haverford. Somebody produced an apparently authentic picture of George Fox in ecstasy—he was the founder of the Quakers. So everybody said, how nice to have a picture of George Fox having a religious experience. And what you actually saw in this little painting was—he was going like this [Isherwood crossed his eyes]—the eyes, you see, were centering, and his tongue was out. Somebody had really dared to paint exactly what he saw happening to this man. I believe it's in the Haverford College Museum, but I don't think it is displayed. There's an aspect of all this which is embarrassing to people who imagine things in a kind of sweetness.

KAPLAN: *People who are not believers are very demanding in what they expect from people who do believe.*

ISHERWOOD: Very demanding. Some saints are particularly farcical. Saint Philip Neri, the founder of the Oratorium, was just full of practical jokes. He used to sit in the pope's lap and pull his beard. He took the injunction of Christ, "Suffer the little children," quite literally, and so he allowed them to play all over the altar, and they were always knocking over the blessed sacrament and absolutely outraging everybody. And of course the great scene of Ramakrishna, when he was conducting a worship—and there were these very devout people, including this woman who paid for the temple, who believed in him. And this cat came in, and Ramakrishna suddenly realized that the cat was also the mother of the universe, and he bowed down in front of it and gave it the food. . . . They nearly threw him out of the place, but he was simply being the most orthodox Vedantist of all. [Laughter]

KAPLAN: *One of the things that fascinated me in your biography of Ramakrishna is not only that he himself seems to have had a great sense of humor, but that he could see that even really religious people were funny a lot of the time.*

ISHERWOOD: Because you still retain what's called your character. Ramakrishna was an extremely volatile, lively, amusing, charming person. Other people become great saints who are by nature quiet and meditative. The Bengalis are fantastically animated. When I went there, I went to the theater, and of course I couldn't understand a word, but I never wanted to leave. They were so funny on the stage. The clowning and the brilliance of the sort of mockery that they convey was fascinating. You could go on watching them for hours.

KAPLAN: *When we read or watch* A Meeting by the River, *maybe we needn't take sides at all. Perhaps each is right in all the things he sees in the other. For example, perhaps Patrick is really right in seeing this desire for power in Oliver. It may very well be a strong part of Oliver's personality.*

ISHERWOOD: I certainly intended that it should be something that was there. I really don't apologize at all for not having a kind of solution. I think it would spoil the whole effect.

KAPLAN: *And is the open ending perhaps a commentary on the either/or Western tradition? That one must be right, one must be wrong.*

ISHERWOOD: Yes. One time we were at a religious service and a very sacred moment had occurred right at the end when Swami got out some Ganges water and he was sprinkling it—and suddenly he roared with laughter and said, "You all look so funny." And everybody in the place just laughed and laughed, quite spontaneously. That happens sometimes—it's just beautiful. Of course young people now, they understand all that much better. All those things they understand so well, instinctively. You don't have to spell it out. That's marvelous.

KAPLAN: *There's always been this pull for Western writers toward Eastern traditions. You see this from the beginning of the twentieth century. Did you have any interest in this, for example, when* The Waste Land *came out?*

ISHERWOOD: No, I felt that Eliot had sort of sold out. I didn't like this religion thing. It bothered me. But I thought it was kind of a camp, you know. I didn't really take it very seriously, in some curious way. I thought it was a kind of poetic attitude. But I see more and more that so much of all this dissension is a question of semantics.

KAPLAN: *So you didn't really feel, at least until you came here, much of an interest in, say, Forster's interest in Eastern religion?*

ISHERWOOD: No, I didn't. It didn't really mean anything to him, I don't think, in the same way.

KAPLAN: *No, he doesn't ultimately come to believe.*

ISHERWOOD: No, no.

KAPLAN: *In other words, your interest really dates from . . .*

ISHERWOOD: From meeting this man, this individual.

KAPLAN: *Gerald Heard or Swami Prabhavananda?*

ISHERWOOD: Well, Heard very much prepared this thing from a kind of intellectual point of view. He got me very much straightened out semantically. I mean, a lot of my categories were simply based on being frightened of certain words; and by rephrasing things he got me into a receptive mood. But it was really basically meeting Prabhavananda. Of course, once you get into that sort of area you in fact meet other people rather easily who are equally impressive in a somewhat similar way. But my whole approach was entirely existential in that way. It was just a question of meeting this person and observing him over a long period.

KAPLAN: *Do you feel that that is really the only way that you can get on the track of this kind of thing, that you must meet a person who somehow strikes you in this way—that he has found something? Or could one come to it in a somewhat more spontaneous way?*

ISHERWOOD: I talked to a young swami in India whose parents were strongly atheistic. He had done it entirely by reading the works of Vivekananda. He became absolutely convinced and took off and joined the monastery. But that's not my idea. I must say Vivekananda was a remarkable person.

KAPLAN: *Do you think that personal religious discovery is a possibility, or do you think that really it has to be through direct knowledge of the religion?*

ISHERWOOD: Oh no, of course it doesn't! It could be in any manner or way. And I think that you could even be an atheist, you see, and you could have something. There again you come to this thing of what words you use. It's quite clear that a lot of people who are under the impression they don't have any religious belief have got some kind of insight. I felt that about Forster very much. He never would say that he was anything more than a kind of agnostic. He was interested but that was all. He was so marvelously open. When he became quite old, I really used to think sometimes he had that baby-like quality which Ramakrishna had. He was like a child, you know. Not that he was the least bit gaga or anything, but he was just very joyful. I was with him about a month before he died, the last time I saw him, when I happened to be in England. Everything he said to me was trying to reassure me. He said, "I realize I can't write anymore, I can't invent things." And he said, "It doesn't matter, it's all right, it doesn't matter." And he was very gay, very cheerful inside somehow.

KAPLAN: *He was trying to reassure you, on his behalf, so that you wouldn't worry about him?*

ISHERWOOD: Also to give reassurance, which is very important, of course, toward the end. To keep telling people, "Look, don't worry; it's not as bad as they tell you; it's nothing like they say."

KAPLAN: *He knew he was going to die soon?*

ISHERWOOD: Yes. But he was quite extraordinary, because while he was surrounded by people who were fond of him, he in some ways led a rather solitary life. He lived at King's College. And people went to see him all the time. But he spent a good deal of time alone and had a couple of strokes and fell down. One time he was unconscious the whole night, lying on the floor, and nobody found him till the morning. He was very lucky his head didn't go in the fireplace. He fell right by the fire. Things like that happened, but he kept going, and he was cheerful again and amusing. He wasn't just being stoical either; he had a real resource.

KAPLAN: *You felt that he had some kind of insight.*

ISHERWOOD: Yes, I'm sure. He was wonderful. It was tremendous, his capacity for caring about other people and minding what happened to them. His empathy was extraordinary. How he felt things, felt things terribly, felt things that happened to one more than one might oneself. You know, he'd really mind, you'd see the pain in his face. That's very advanced, all that stuff.

KAPLAN: *That reminds me of the your thirties novels and the concern with finding some political commitment. In* Goodbye to Berlin, *I recall Chris's conversation with Bernhard Landauer, in which he says to him, "You know, you really have to be committed to something." Did you feel that way yourself at the time? Did you feel the necessity for some sort of commitment, to Communism, for example?*

ISHERWOOD: I think it was very superficial. I mean, it seemed so; but, on the other hand, I was always stubbing my toe over this business of the way Soviet Russia really let Marx and Engels down completely, with regard to the private life. When they started persecuting homosexuals, I realized that I could never possibly be a Party member. It just seemed to be a kind of self-immolation that was being asked of you, that you should just sort of give up everything. I didn't really think about it enough, but deep down I'm sure I felt that, after all, politics exist for man, not vice versa. I mean, one cannot just sacrifice oneself to the state.

KAPLAN: *So you did not really see Communism as a viable alternative to Nazism? There is such a sense of despair in* The Berlin Stories—*do you think it's because you saw no political alternative, no real solutions?*

ISHERWOOD: Oh, I think I was dumb, you know, and didn't really think very much. I didn't think nearly deeply enough about it. I've never been very intellectual in that way—I didn't analyze things in that sort of manner. I repeated, I went along with people. And Auden, of course, really didn't agree with them, I don't think. And then by degrees he began to say so. But it was unthinkable for me. And then I became also increasingly a pacifist, which had some relation to going to this war in China, where one saw this thing that happens in all wars, that a most awful lot of people who couldn't give a damn get killed. When you actually see a whole lot of civilians who've been bombed, it occurs to you very vividly that it's all a lot of shit. [Laughter] All this stuff is sort of monolithic patriotism. Most people want out when the going gets rough.

KAPLAN: *But then the individuals really don't have the ability to get themselves out.*

ISHERWOOD: Exactly. In all wars you find out later, when it's too late, the most appalling economic forces that have been at work, which brought the whole thing about. Somehow or other, goddamn it, you find the same people are in charge at the end of it all—way back of the front men, the people who own the factories. They get them rebuilt and things go on and people manage; they survive.

KAPLAN: *In your recent novels, do you ever feel that you are proselytizing?*

ISHERWOOD: I never do consciously. You mean about Vedanta? No, because I really am just enchanted whenever people have any kind of belief, anything which supports them.

KAPLAN: *I didn't necessarily mean for Vedanta, but for belief, for at least testing out the possibilities of experience beyond just what we can see in our daily life.*

ISHERWOOD: I do think that's important. For that I would proselytize, certainly—to ask people to ask themselves what's it all about. Every artist does that—they have to, in one way or another. But I just meant that I didn't think that this particular brand of things is important at all. I mean, you have to swallow such a lot with anything that you do. There's all the trappings. Hinduism is exceedingly off-putting to a lot of people; it's very alien and odd. But then again the Quakers are simply marvelous. But then again there are things about them that bother some people terribly, their sort of plainness and kind of wholesomeness. What's great about the Hindu thing is that it's very lively and kind of campy and fun.

KAPLAN: *Do you think one must accept the trappings?*

ISHERWOOD: No. No. No. No. I mean, I don't tend, for instance, to take part much in their general religious doings. I've made it a more personal and more private thing, as far as I'm concerned. A lot of people get immense support out of going to pujas and sitting for hours and ringing bells and chanting and so on. Sometimes it's very exciting and really marvelous—and then again, you know. . . . The great thing is just to remember that the thing exists—that's what it's all about, and you must keep reminding yourself of that.

November 1, 1973

When Isherwood asserted that "the thing exists," I understood him to mean "God." What he seemed to be saying was that the most important understanding to come to is that God exists, but it really does not matter by what path or through what words one comes to this understanding. Thus, while Isherwood had not been at all reticent in discussing his religious beliefs, he remained somewhat reticent in the language he used to explain them. This restraint, it seems to me, is very much in keeping with his emphasis on the varieties of religious experience and the different paths to spiritual insight. He knew, from his own experience, that semantics often gets in the way of understanding, especially of religious understanding. Throughout our talk, he took pains to suggest or open up possibilities; and he seemed carefully to avoid conventional religious language, either because he himself found such terminology constricting, or because he felt such language might prove an obstacle to spiritual insight or personal discovery.

Bibliography

Works by Christopher Isherwood

All the Conspirators. 1928. Norfolk, Connecticut: New Directions, 1958, 1979.

The Memorial: Portrait of a Family. 1932. Norfolk, Connecticut: New Directions, 1946.

Mr Norris Changes Trains. 1935. London: Jonathan Cape, 1977.

Lions and Shadows: An Education in the Twenties. 1938. Norfolk, Connecticut: New Directions, 1947.

Plays and Other Dramatic Writings, 1928–1938. With W. H. Auden. Ed. Edward Mendelson. Princeton: Princeton University Press, 1988.

Goodbye to Berlin. 1939. London: Jonathan Cape, 1977.

Journey to a War. With W. H. Auden. London: Faber, 1939.

The Song of God: Bhagavad Gita. With Swami Prabhavananda, trans. 1944. New York: Mentor, 1951.

Vedanta for the Western World (editor). Hollywood: Marcel Rodd, 1945.

Prater Violet. 1945. New York: Avon, 1978.

The Condor and the Cows: A South American Travel Diary. New York: Random House, 1949.

Vedanta for Modern Man (editor). New York: Harper, 1951.

How to Know God: The Yoga Aphorisms of Patanjali. With Swami Prabhavananda, trans. 1953. Hollywood: Vedanta Press, 1981.

The Berlin Stories. New York: New Directions, 1954.

The World in the Evening. New York: Random House, 1954.

Great English Short Stories (editor). New York: Dell, 1957.
Down There on a Visit. New York: Simon and Schuster, 1962.
A Single Man. New York: Simon and Schuster, 1964.
Ramakrishna and His Disciples. New York: Simon and Schuster, 1965; 2d ed., Hollywood: Vedanta Press, 1980.
Exhumations: Stories, Articles, Verses. New York: Simon and Schuster, 1966.
A Meeting by the River. New York: Simon and Schuster, 1967.
Kathleen and Frank. New York: Simon and Schuster, 1971.
Frankenstein: The True Story. With Don Bachardy. New York: Avon, 1973.
Christopher and His Kind, 1929–1939. New York: Farrar, Straus & Giroux, 1976.
My Guru and His Disciple. New York: Farrar, Straus & Giroux, 1980.
People One Ought to Know. London: Macmillan, 1982.
October. Drawings by Don Bachardy. London: Methuen, 1983.
The Wishing Tree. Ed. Robert Adjemian. San Francisco: Harper & Row, 1986.
Where Joy Resides: A Christopher Isherwood Reader. Ed. Don Bachardy and James P. White. New York: Noonday, 1989.
The Mortmere Stories. With Edward Upward. London: Enitharmon Press, 1994.
Diaries: Volume One, 1939–1960. Ed. Katherine Bucknell. New York: Harper-Collins, 1997.
Jacob's Hands. With Aldous Huxley. New York: St. Martin's Press, 1998.

Select Bibliography

Bachardy, Don. *Christopher Isherwood: Last Drawings.* London: Faber and Faber, 1990.
Cunningham, Valentine. *British Writers of the Thirties.* Oxford: Oxford University Press, 1989.
Finney, Brian. *Christopher Isherwood: A Critical Biography.* London: Faber and Faber, 1979.
Fryer, Jonathan. *Isherwood: A Biography of Christopher Isherwood.* London: New English Library, 1977. Reissued as *Eye of the Camera.* London: Allison & Busby, 1993.
Heilbrun, Carolyn G. *Christopher Isherwood.* New York: Columbia University Press, 1970.
Heilbrun, Carolyn G., ed. *Twentieth Century Literature* 22, October 1976. Special Issue on Christopher Isherwood.
Hynes, Samuel. *The Auden Generation: Literature and Politics in England in the 1930s.* Princeton: Princeton University Press, 1976.
King, Francis. *Christopher Isherwood.* Harlow, Essex: Longman, 1976.
Lehmann, John. *Christopher Isherwood: A Personal Memoir.* Henry Holt: New York, 1987.
Lilly, Mark. *Gay Men's Literature in the Twentieth Century.* New York: New York University Press, 1993.
Mizejewski, Linda. *Divine Decadence: Fascism, Female Spectacle, and the Makings of Sally Bowles.* Princeton: Princeton University Press, 1992.

Page, Norman. *Auden and Isherwood: The Berlin Years.* New York: St. Martin's Press, 1998.

Piazza, Paul. *Christopher Isherwood: Myth and Anti-Myth.* New York: Columbia University Press, 1978.

Robinson, Paul. *Gay Lives.* Chicago: University of Chicago Press, 1999.

Schwerdt, Lisa M. *Isherwood's Fiction: The Self and Technique.* New York: St. Martin's, 1989.

Spender, Stephen. *Letters to Christopher.* Ed. Lee Bartlett. Santa Barbara: Black Sparrow Press, 1980.

Spender, Stephen. *World within World.* New York: Harcourt, Brace, 1951.

Summers, Claude J. *Christopher Isherwood.* New York: Ungar, 1980.

Wade, Stephen. *Christopher Isherwood.* New York: St. Martin's Press, 1991.

White, James P., and William H. White, eds. *Christopher Isherwood: A Bibliography of His Personal Papers.* Montrose, Alabama: Texas Center for Writers Press, 1987.

Wilde, Alan. *Christopher Isherwood.* New York: Twayne, 1971.

Woodhouse, Reed. *Unlimited Embrace: A Canon of Gay Fiction, 1945–1995.* Amherst: University of Massachusetts Press, 1998.

Contributors

DON BACHARDY is an artist and native of Los Angeles. He lived with Christopher Isherwood in Santa Monica from 1953 until Isherwood's death in 1986. He studied art at the Chouinard Institute and also at the Slade School of Art in London. A prolific artist, Bachardy has painted and drawn portraits of the famous as well as his close friends, including Jerry Brown, Bette Davis, Marlene Dietrich, Tennesee Williams, and E. M. Forster. His books include *October* and *Christopher Isherwood: Last Drawings,* as well as illustrations for Robert Altman's screenplay *Short Cuts.* His most recent book is *Stars in My Eyes,* forthcoming from the University of Wisconsin Press.

JAMES J. BERG earned a Ph.D. from the University of Minnesota. He has published essays and presented papers on E. M. Forster, W. H. Auden, and Christopher Isherwood. He is former Senior Editor for *The Evergreen Chronicles.* He is cooperating assistant professor of English and director of the Center for Teaching at the University of Maine.

DAVID BERGMAN is professor of English at Towson University in Maryland. He is the author of *Gaiety Transfigured: Gay Self-Representation in American Literature* and editor of *Camp Grounds, The Violet Quill Reader, The Burning Library: Essays by Edmund White,* and several volumes of the *Men on Men* series of gay male fiction. He is also the author of several volumes of poetry, including *Cracking the Code,* winner of the George Elliston Poetry Prize, and *Heroic Measures.*

MARSHA BRYANT is associate professor of English at the University of Florida, where she has received three teaching awards. She is the author of *Auden and Documentary in the 1930s* and editor of *Photo-Textualities: Reading Photographs and Literature.*

KATHERINE BUCKNELL is the editor of Christopher Isherwood's *Diaries: Volume One, 1939–1960.* She earned her Ph.D. at Columbia University and was a Junior Research Fellow at Worcester College, Oxford. She edited and introduced W. H. Auden's *Juvenilia: Poems, 1922–1928* and also introduced *The Mortmere Stories* by Isherwood and Edward Upward.

NILADRI R. CHATTERJEE earned his master's degree in English from Jadavpur University, Calcutta. He received a Fulbright Pre-Doctoral Fellowship in 1996 and represented the Eastern Region of India at the annual Cambridge Seminar in July 1998. His published writings include "'Siamese Twinship': 'Sally Bowles' and *Breakfast at Tiffany's*" in *Essays and Studies* and the entry on Mulk Raj Anand in *The Reader's Companion to Twentieth-Century Writers.* He is Lecturer in English at the University of Kalyani, Nadia, West Bengal.

STEPHEN DA SILVA has a Ph.D. in English literature from Rice University. He has published essays on Eve Kosofsky Sedgwick, Lytton Strachey, and E. M. Forster. He is currently working on a book that examines how late Victorian and modernist British homosexual writers used the idioms of Hellenism and primitivism to challenge the association of homosexuality with arrested development.

MARIO FARAONE is a doctoral candidate at the University of Rome "La Sapienza." He recently published a major critical appreciation of Isherwood's narrative, *Un uomo solo: Autobiografia e romanzo nell'opera di Christopher Isherwood.* He has also worked on Hindu and Buddhist influences on T. S. Eliot's works and on Giorgio Manganelli's *Cassio Governa a Cipro* as a rewriting and critical interpretation of Shakespeare's *Othello.* His Ph.D. project deals with Edward Upward's narrative and political production as a new novel form.

CHRIS FREEMAN has a Ph.D. in English from Vanderbilt University and is assistant professor at St. John's University in Collegeville, Minnesota. He is a contributing writer for *Harvard Gay and Lesbian Review.* He is currently working on a biography of Paul Monette and is editing Monette's journals for publication.

DAVID GARNES, a former English teacher, is a senior reference librarian at the University of Connecticut, Storrs. He is a frequent contributor to a variety of reference and anthology publications. His writing has most recently appeared in *Gay Histories and Cultures; Gay & Lesbian Literature,* volume 2; *Connecticut Poets on AIDS: A Cross-Culture Collection; Gay & Lesbian Biography;* and *Liberating Minds: The Stories and Professional Lives of Gay, Lesbian, and Bisexual Librarians and Their Advocates.*

MICHAEL S. HARPER is University Professor and professor of English at Brown University, where he has taught since 1970. He was the first Poet Laureate of the State of Rhode Island (1988–93). In 1990 he received the Robert Hayden Poetry Award from the United Negro College Fund. He has published ten books of poetry, two of which were nominated for the National Book Award: *Dear John, Dear Coltrane* and *Images of Kin: New and Selected Poems.* He is co-editor of the collection *Every Shut Eye Ain't Asleep,* poems by African American Poets, 1945 to the present.

CAROLYN G. HEILBRUN is professor emerita at Columbia University, where she taught for thirty-three years. A recipient of grants from the Rockefeller and Guggenheim foundations and the National Endowment for the Humanities, she is the author of numerous books, including *Writing a Woman's Life, Hamlet's Mother and Other Women,* and *The Education of a Woman: A Life of Gloria Steinem.* She was the recipient of the 1999 Modern Language Association Award for Lifetime Achievement. She has also published a dozen detective novels under the name of Amanda Cross.

DAVID GARRETT IZZO is a former New York City writer/journalist turned teacher/scholar. His book, *Christopher Isherwood: His Era, His Gang, and the Legacy of the Truly Strong Man,* is forthcoming from the University of South Carolina Press. He is the author of *Aldous Huxley & W. H. Auden: On Language* and the co-editor of *Thornton Wilder: New Essays.* From 1993 to 1998, Izzo was the coordinator and developer of College Transfer and Adult Continuing Education at Butner, North Carolina Federal Corrections.

CAROLA M. KAPLAN is professor of English at California State University, Pomona. Her paper "Moving Among Cultures: Isherwood's Multiple Subjectivities" was part of the session "Christopher Isherwood: Ten Years Gone" at the Modern Language Association Convention in 1996, where this project was begun. She is the editor of *Seeing Double: Revisioning Edwardian and Modernist Literature* (with Anne B. Simpson) and has published many articles on modernist writers, including Joseph Conrad, Henry James, E. M. Forster, D. H. Lawrence, and T. E. Lawrence. She is currently completing a book, *Silence, Exile, and Cunning: Moving across Cultures in Joseph Conrad, T. E. Lawrence, Christopher Isherwood, and Salman Rushdie.*

JAMES KELLEY has a Ph.D. in English from the University of Tulsa. He has published on poetics and male homosexuality in the Harlem Renaissance.

DAN LUCKENBILL is a senior manuscripts processor at the Department of Special Collections, UCLA Library, where he has worked for more than twenty-five years. He has curated numerous exhibits and has written catalogs on lesbian and gay studies at UCLA and the work of Stathis Orphanos and Ralph Sylvester. He has published essays and short gay fiction, and his work appeared in the early anthology *On the Line: New Gay Fiction.*

DONALD N. MAGER is the Mott University Professor of English and Director of the Liberal Arts Program at Johnson C. Smith University in Charlotte, North Carolina. He has published four books of poetry. His work in queer theory includes essays in *SubStance, Queering the Renaissance,* and *Overcoming Heterosexism and Homophobia: Strategies That Work.*

ARMISTEAD MAUPIN is the author of the six-volume *Tales of the City* series and the novel *Maybe the Moon.* Television adaptations of his *Tales* novels have so far received a Peabody and seven Emmy nominations. Maupin's latest novel will be published in 2000. He lives in San Francisco.

JOHN MCFARLAND is a freelance writer who lives in Seattle. His short fiction has appeared in such publications as *Cricket Magazine* and *Caliban.* He is the author of *The Exploding Frog and Other Fables from Aesop,* which was selected as one of the best illustrated books of 1981 by *Parents Choice Magazine.* He has also contributed essays to the anthologies *Letters to Our Children: Lesbian and Gay Adults Speak to the New Generation, A Loving Testimony: Remembering Loved Ones Lost to AIDS,* and *The Book Club Book, Second Edition.* New fiction and essays can be found in *CONTRA/DICTION* and *When Love Lasts Forever: Male Couples Celebrate Commitment.*

KATHARINE M. MORSBERGER has a Ph.D. in eighteenth-century British literature from the University of California, Riverside, and has taught film studies and science fiction. She has published numerous articles and reviews and has collaborated with her husband, Robert Morsberger, on a biography, *Lew Wallace: Militant Romantic,* and on an article on film adaptations of the Robin Hood story in *Performing Robin Hood.*

ROBERT E. MORSBERGER has a Ph.D. in American literature from the University of Iowa and is professor of English at California State University, Pomona. He has published numerous articles, short stories, and books. He is co-editor of two volumes on American screenwriters in the *Dictionary of Literary Biography.*

STATHIS ORPHANOS is a photographer living in Los Angeles. He has photographed many of today's top cultural and entertainment figures, including Julie Harris, Norman Mailer, Gore Vidal, David Hockney, and Yannis Tsarouchis. Along with his partner, Ralph Sylvester, he has published twenty-five limited-edition signed books by such authors as Paul Bowles, Philip Roth, and John Updike.

WILLIAM OSTREM has a Ph.D. from Princeton University, where he wrote his dissertation on W. H. Auden's representation of England. He has taught English literature at Princeton and at the University of Minnesota.

ROBERT PETERS has taught at the University of California at Riverside and Irvine. He is the author of over thirty volumes of poetry and a dozen volumes of criticism.

A native of Wisconsin, he is a contributor to the collection *Farm Boys*. The University of Wisconsin Press has published four of his memoirs.

P. SHNEIDRE is a poet whose work appears in *Paris Review, Exquisite Corpse,* and other journals. After an initial meeting arranged by Isherwood in the late 1960s, he studied mysticism with Swami Prabhavananda for a number of years. His English version of the Bengali poems of Swami Vivekananda, *All of Love,* was published in 1995. He is working on a book called *The Way of Isherwood.* He lives in Hollywood and works for the Vedanta Press.

ANTONY SHUTTLEWORTH is assistant professor of English at the University of Georgia, where he specializes in twentieth-century British literature and literary theory. He is currently completing a study of Louis MacNeice in the 1930s and is editing a collection of critical essays on the writing of that period.

EDMUND WHITE is the author of numerous novels, including *A Boy's Own Story, The Beautiful Room Is Empty,* and *The Farewell Symphony.* His biography *Genet* was awarded the National Book Critics Circle Award and the Lambda Literary Award. He teaches at Princeton University.

JAMES P. WHITE is a writer and teacher at the University of South Alabama in Mobile. A recipient of a Guggenheim Fellowship, his publications include the novel *Birdsong* and a bibliography of Isherwood's papers. He is the editor, with Don Bachardy, of *Where Joy Resides: A Christopher Isherwood Reader,* and is editing Isherwood's Commonplace Book. He is currently writing a book on ten California writers.

Index

Ackerley, J. R., 33, 73
AIDS, xiii, 69, 128–29, 200, 210–11, 212
Auden, W. H., xi, 4, 5–6, 17–18, 41, 55, 59, 61, 65, 67, 72, 80, 83, 89, 100, 101, 123, 139–40, 162–71, 172–86, 221, 222, 228–31, 234

Bachardy, Don, xi, xiv, 5, 7, 23–24, 25, 26, 32, 33, 35–36, 40, 43, 46, 47, 48, 52–53, 59, 72, 73, 76, 79, 89–136, 192, 205, 220, 222, 229, 246, 259, 260, 273
Baldwin, James, 58, 196–97
Beauvoir, Simone de, 122
Benjamin, Walter, 152
Bernhardt, Sarah, 101, 104
Bhagavad Gita, 81, 85, 86, 123, 220, 223, 250–58, 263
Bowles, Paul, 43
Burroughs, William, 66, 204, 207

Capa, Robert, 172
Capote, Truman, xiii, 4, 17, 203
Caskey, William, 21, 239
Cather, Willa, 33

Colton, James, 199
communism, 164, 165, 170, 171, 277
Cox, Christopher, 204

Day Lewis, Cecil, 5

Eliot, T. S., 58, 222, 275

Faulkner, William, 32, 92–93, 129
Ferro, Robert, 140, 204, 205–6, 208
Fleming, Peter, 172, 176, 179, 182–85
Forster, E. M., xiii, 5, 15, 58, 72, 83, 140, 141, 188–94, 220, 221, 261, 275, 276–77

Genet, Jean, 204, 206, 207, 209
Ginsberg, Allen, 66
Golding, William, 55, 56–57, 64
Greene, Graham, 43, 45, 49, 94, 199
Grumley, Michael, 204

Heard, Gerald, 18, 55, 61, 95, 164, 222–23, 225, 236–37, 239, 247, 254, 268, 275
Hemingway, Ernest, 92, 172

291